Johann Gerhard

Doctor of Theology and formerly a public Professor of the same at the illustrious Salana

ANNOTATIONS ON THE FIRST SIX CHAPTERS OF ST. PAUL'S EPISTLE TO THE ROMANS

in which the text is stated, troublesome questions are answered, observations are made, and passages that appear to be in conflict are reconciled as concisely as possible

with Preface and General Prolegomena on the Pauline Epistles

by the same author

With grace and privilege

Jena
Steinmann Publishers
At the expense of Christian von Saher / Erfurt Bookseller
1645

Translated by Paul A. Rydecki
2014

edited by Rachel Melvin

Repristination Press
Malone, Texas

Published in 2014

REPRISTINATION PRESS
P.O. BOX 173
BYNUM, TEXAS 76631

www.repristinationpress.com

ISBN 1-891469-67-3

Table of Contents

Translator's Preface

What follows in this book is the complete commentary of Johann Gerhard on the Book of Romans, published posthumously by his son, Johann Ernst. We are informed in the Preface and concluding remarks by Johann Ernst that only the first six chapters of Romans are treated because his father died even as he finished commenting on chapter six, making this, presumably, the final work of Dr. Johann Gerhard.

The reader will quickly discover that Gerhard's insight was heavily influenced by the Church Fathers who preceded him, although he was not blindly enslaved to their interpretations. His command of Syriac, Hebrew, Greek, German and Latin, combined with his knowledge of the history of ecclesiastical interpretation by the Fathers who spoke these various languages, make his annotations a unique exegetical compendium on the Epistle to the Romans.

Gerhard provides, verse by verse, the entire Greek text of Romans 1-6, using a source manuscript that is virtually identical to the Majority Text, including even the parentheses found in Romans 4:17. He does not, however, provide his own Latin translation of the Scripture verses, assuming that the reader of his commentary has at least a working knowledge of Greek. For the sake of the non-Greek reader, I have included an English translation (King James Version) under each verse.

As Gerhard treats each verse of Romans, he frequently discusses Greek vocables and phrases within the verse, occasionally giving the meaning of the vocable in Latin, but frequently leaving the Greek words untranslated. For the sake of the non-Greek reader, I have included my own simple English translation for most of these occurrences, given in brackets. I have done the same with the German phrases.

I consider it a distinct privilege and honor to offer this translation of Gerhard's final work to the English-reading world. Some would understandably wish that Gerhard had lived long enough to finish commenting on the entire book of Romans for the benefit of the Church, and all the more since this seems to have been his intention. But the Lord of the Church wished differently, and for that, may His name be forever praised. What He has allowed to be handed down to us is a rare, authentically Lutheran commentary on the principal chapters in Holy Scripture that fueled the Reformation of the Church, because they systematically and clearly lay out the chief article of the Christian faith as defended by Luther and his theological heirs, namely, that sinners are justified only by the imputation of the righteousness of Christ—an imputation that takes place only as Christ is apprehended by faith.

Rev. Paul A. Rydecki +
Sixth Sunday after Trinity, AD 2013
Soli Deo Gloria

Johann Gerhard

Doctor of Theology and formerly a public Professor of the same at
the illustrious Salana

ANNOTATIONS ON THE FIRST SIX CHAPTERS OF ST. PAUL'S EPISTLE TO THE ROMANS

in which the text is stated, troublesome questions are answered,
observations are made, and passages that appear to be in conflict
are reconciled as concisely as possible

with Preface and General Prolegomena on the Pauline Epistles

by the same author

With grace and privilege

Jena
Steinmann Publishers
At the expense of Christian von Saher / Erfurt Bookseller
1645

Translated by Paul A. Rydecki
2014

Dedicatory Epistle

To the celebrated and mighty citizens of Hamburg,

To the venerable Church Order,

To the men of renown, most excellent in reverend dignity, singular piety, exceptional learning and nobility of name,

To our lord elder, to the pastors and

the rest of the heralds of the divine Word,

Most vigilant,

Most worthy,

Most deserving,

Most highly honored lords and defenders,

I send many greetings.

Most reverend, noble and excellent men of renown, lords and defenders, most worthy to be honored, you have graced me with many great and lofty benefits. For two years now, I have had in mind to return something to you in recognition of this, not in the form of repayment (for the adversity of my fortune does not allow for such a thing), but at least a memorial to the benevolence I have received. But for however long and however carefully I might have, indeed, silently reflected on this in my head, it still did not occur to me how I might best be able to furnish that which was gladly owed. Nor, as far as I am concerned, would this little present itself that I now offer and consecrate to you be worthy of so much, nor will it be so esteemed, except, perhaps, that your fond memory of him who is known to be the author may add some weight to it.

From the hand of Gerhard (now deceased) it first proceeded, whose memory I know to be so holy among you that, in his honor, you hold especially dear not only his children but also his books—indeed, anything that boasts the name of Gerhard. And why not? For it has not yet perished from your minds how ardently Gerhard—my father whom I so dearly miss—held you dear, how very tightly he embraced you, especially at that time, when, in the words of the poet,

the flowery season made the spring a delight.[1]

I am referring to that season in which many of you, several years ago, nobly waged the Lord's battles here in this our Salana under the banners of Gerhard and other great men who were, and still are, at Jena, when you vigorously supported the armies of Muses and Graces. There are public witnesses—most praiseworthy public disputations that have been held by you under the auspices of Gerhard, specimens of your singular erudition and excellent talent. At that time, Gerhard hosted several of you. I am well aware from your sweet words around the table (when I passed through Hamburg two years ago and visited your houses) how glad and how willing some of you were to be hosted by Gerhard, not at his home, but at his war tent and table, as it were—and not without great joy of spirit and highest exultation.

There was, to be sure, a paternal love of Gerhard toward you, and a filial love, in turn, of you toward him. Surely this exceptional relationship between you did not suffer a decrease, when, by God's governance, you were forced to leave the rooftops of Jena and to honor now this, now that ecclesiastical Sparta? Never! On the contrary, it saw daily increases, to such a degree that, as they commonly say, the more distant he grew from your bodies, just so near, and much nearer he came to your souls, and with the closest possible bond. And your most friendly recollection of Gerhard grew closer to the heart and to the inmost senses the further the sight of him was removed from your eyes—if I may borrow the most elegant

---

1 Latin: *jucundum cum aetas florida ver ageret.* Gaius Valerius Catullus, *Carmina* (68.16).

words of the most elegant writer Master Minucius Felix, from the *Octavius*. Your most elegant and cordial letters written to my father after his death are indicators to me, or even more, most undeniable proofs how your love toward my father (of blessed memory) was not only steadfast before, but that it also took on a notable increase, as I have said. I did not forfeit those letters after the departure of my blessed father, as I indeed see many people doing (the possessors and heirs are certainly unworthy of such a treasure), like mackerels that are afraid to be caught. Far be it! Far be it, I say, that I should ever permit so many beloved and noble manuscripts

—to become wrappers of frankincense and pepper.[2]

May it never be! Indeed, I guard these carefully, together with several thousand detailed letters written by great men—by princes and men of renown—to my departed father. I guard them no less carefully than Picus guards his gold, as the proverb used to say. Nor is this said in vain, for I predict—and my prediction will not fail—that that most anticipated time will one day come when the affection and fraternal love with which such great men of renown embraced my dearly missed father—to which these letters are the most infallible witnesses—will be transformed into paternal affection and love and diverted to me and mine.

Indeed, we are able to boast in God that this has certainly been done up until now by many noble men—men of the commonwealth of learning[3] who are notably worthy, who have hardly disdained to attend to us with such affection in memory of my father (who is now among the saints), and in special honor of us, as Plinius writes about his Hispula. If I were not to count you also among the first of them, O most Reverend and most excellent Theologians, Lords and Maecenates[4], worthy of eternal respect, then I, who have received such benefits from you, would surely be most unworthy of them, and still less worthy ever to receive any further benevolence from you. I do count you among them, and rightly so.

2 Latin: *thuris piperisque sint cuculli.*
3 Latin: *republica litteraria*
4 Gaius Cilinius Maecenas, patron of Horace and Vergil

And in order that this may be firmly established for you, behold! A public pledge from me to you also in that which I am about to do, that is, that I will attend to you with due respect. I will surely seem to be straying beyond the bounds of modesty if I should ask that you would regard this work with a cheerful countenance and continue your benevolence even more generously toward me and mine.

Farewell, O most reverend men of renown, lords who are perpetually to be honored. For the good of the Church and of the commonwealth of learning, may your years surpass those of Nestor. From my muse at Jena. During the Ides of September, 1644, according to the Dionysian calendar.

A most zealous supporter of your most

reverend Excellencies and Worthy Offices,

Master Johann Ernst J. F. Gerhard

Dr. Johann Gerhard's

ANNOTATIONS ON THE FIRST SIX CHAPTERS OF ST. PAUL'S EPISTLE TO THE ROMANS

General Prolegomena on the Pauline Epistles

1. The *efficient cause* or the *principal Author* of the Epistles is the Holy Spirit. For as the holy men of God (among whom the Apostle Paul was also sent by God and called from heaven) spoke as they were inspired by the Holy Spirit, so also they wrote (2 Pet. 1:21). Hence the Scripture of Paul is likewise inspired by God, besides being preached with the living voice (2 Tim. 3:16). The Apostle Paul was caught up into the third heaven and received knowledge of the divine mysteries directly from Christ Himself (2 Cor. 12:2).

The *ministerial cause* is the Apostle Paul, to whom Christ Himself attributes this word of praise, that he is a "chosen vessel, an elect instrument of God for carrying the name of Christ before the Gentiles and kings and the sons of Israel" (Acts 9:15), namely, by preaching the Gospel, just as long ago the Levites in the Old Testament would carry the Ark of the Lord from place to place. Peter, in his Second Epistle, chapter 3 verse 15, attributes to him "wisdom," that is, a divine and clearly unique wisdom, to which the rest of the epistles bear witness. The Apostle himself does not testify concerning himself with false boasting, but with a true confession that he is a "preacher and Apostle, a teacher of the Gentiles in faith and truth" (1 Tim. 2:7, 2 Tim. 1:11), "the Apostle of the Gentiles" (Rom. 11:13), a servant, "a minister of the Law among the Gentiles" (Rom. 15:16), that he had "worked in greater measure than all the Apostles," (1 Cor. 15:10) that he had been "caught up to the third heaven" and had "heard unspeakable words" (2 Cor. 12:2,4). Tertullian, Bk. 5, *Against Marcion*, near the beginning, accommodates the prophecy of the Patriarch Jacob to Paul: "Benjamin is a ravenous wolf. In the morning he devours, and in the evening he will give food."

Chrysostom lavishly pursued the praises of Paul in eight homilies, where he matches him up against all the Old and New Testament saints. He writes in Homily 8: "With which of the Old or New Testament saints, O blessed Paul, shall I dare to compare you? You have, as it were, stored up the virtue of them all as if in a sort of ark, and with truly great abundance. Finally, if anyone were to weigh individually the entire company of the righteous against you, he would discover that the scale of virtues tips in your favor. For Paul is the second Abel, slaughtered not once, but over the course of many days. Paul is another Noah, but one who, without an ark, navigates the waves of ungodliness rising up against him. Paul is another Abraham, torn away not only from country or nation, but, after his calling, torn away also from life itself. Paul is another Isaac, willingly bound as a sacrifice. Paul is another Jacob, as if he were always watching diligently, in a certain manner, over the one flock of the whole world. Paul is another Joseph, distributing the food of truth to a world wasting away in spiritual famine. Paul is another Moses, who has led all nations away from the tyranny of the devil to Christ. Paul is another Aaron, the anointed priest for the people of the whole world. Paul is another Phinehas, piercing through the impiety of Jews and Gentiles—the prostitution of the mind—with the singular sword of faith. Paul is another David, who challenges the devil to a contest as if he were a sort of Goliath. Paul is another Elijah, more strikingly caught up into the heavens. Paul is another Elisha, who cleansed the nations from the inner pollution of leprosy. Paul is another Hezekiah, who led diverse peoples to the one faith in Christ. Paul is another Josiah, who dispersed and destroyed the abominations of the Gentiles. Paul is another John, who was beheaded for Christ. Paul is another Peter, called to faith, not from the earth, but from heaven. Paul is another Gabriel, who announced the birth of Christ to all nations at once. Paul is another Michael, assigned to be the General of the Christian host. Although I should fly all the way around the companies of angels or of righteous men, I do not find any with whom Paul fails to compare with regard to the accumulation of merits."

On the praises of Paul, from Homily 4: "Paul is the archtype of the good, to whom God has granted all preaching, the affairs of the world, all mysteries, and the universal stewardship—heaven itself with its Sun of Righteousness, the sea itself most pure and profound in wisdom.″

He says this in Homily 25 on the Acts of the Apostles: ″For this reason he becomes an athlete, a general of the war, one who duels in single combat, a lion—nor do I have a name by which I should rightly call him—he becomes a hunting dog that attacks lions, a strong bull, a bright torch, a mouth that supplies the world.″

He says the same thing in Homily 3 on the saying of the Apostle: *″Having one Spirit.* The Pauline Epistles are mines, even wells of the Spirit. They are mines indeed, because they supply us with riches more precious than any amount of gold. And they are wells, because they never run dry, but the more you draw from them, just so much and even more amply do they flow back again. Indeed, all the time that has passed can clearly attest to this. Yes, since the time when Paul lived, five hundred years have already elapsed, and in all this time many men—both commentators and teachers and many interpreters—have often drawn from this well, yet they never prevailed to empty the riches stored therein, for this is an irrational treasure; it is not used up by the hands of many excavators, but rather grows and multiplies. Indeed, what am I saying about those who went before us? I am saying what many people will say after us, and what others, in turn, will say after them, nor yet will the riches that gush forth from this well be diminished in the least, nor will this kind of mine be exhausted.″

Eusebius, in Bk. 3, *History*, ch. 24, calls him ″more learned than all the Apostles, who both in words and thoughts is most powerful and contains immeasurably great matters and innumerable mysteries in a small body of epistles, inasmuch as he who also was caught up even to the third heaven where he observed the things that were conducted—as a student of the heavenly School—received his doctrine in Paradise.″

Jerome, in Epistle 61 *To Pammachius Against John of Jerusalem,* calls him ″a chosen instrument, a channel for the Gospel, our roaring lion, the thunder of the Gentiles, a river of Christian eloquence.″ Also, in the Apology of his book *Against Jovinianus:* ″Whenever I read Paul, it seems to me that I am not hearing words, but thunders." Likewise, in Vol. 4, f. 2, *Ad Paulin.*, he calls him "the cupboard of Holy Scriptures."

Augustine says in Bk. 14, *The City of God*, ch. 9: "We most gladly view Paul as a true athlete of Christ, trained by Him, anointed of Him, crucified with Him, glorying in Him, in the theater of this world to which he was made a spectacle, both to angels and to men, lawfully fighting the good fight and pursuing the prize of the heavenly calling set before the eyes of faith."

Cyril of Alexandria, in Bk. 1 on John ch. 9, calls him "a receptacle of the Savior's mysteries."

2. *Canonical authority.* This depends on the principal author, who is the Holy Spirit. For since these Epistles are inspired by God, they are also canonical. There are three witnesses to this canonical authority. First, the innate criteria; second, the external witness of the Church; and third, the internal testimony of the Holy Spirit. To the innate criteria belong the majesty of the content, the uniqueness of style, and the most precise consensus with the rest of the Old as well as the New Testament canonical writings.

Irenaeus writes in Bk. 3, *Against Heresies*, ch. 7, p.177: "Indeed, from many other examples we may discover that the Apostle frequently employs an hyperbaton due to the rapidity of his discussions and due to the impetus within him, that is, the Spirit." Chief among the testimonies of the Church is that of Peter in 2 Peter 3:15, given by immediate inspiration of the Holy Spirit. The second comes from the Teachers of the early Church. For as many canonical New Testament books as they reviewed, all of them by unanimous decision taught that the fourteen Pauline Epistles were to be received in the Canon, with the single exception of the Epistle to the Hebrews, since it was at one time in doubt whether it was written by Paul.

And finally, it is confirmed by the internal testimony of the Holy Spirit, who testifies that "the Spirit is truth" (1 John 5:6), that is, that the doctrine of the Gospel set forth in the Scriptures, and thus also in the Pauline Epistles, is the doctrine of unshakable canonical truth. For when we read and meditate on the Pauline Epistles in true fear of God and godly zeal, the Holy Spirit efficaciously consoles, exhorts, encourages and stirs us up so that we are convinced in our heart that they are inspired by God, given by direct inspiration of the Holy Spirit.

3. *The subject matter.* The Pauline Epistles deal with the mysteries of the Law and of the Gospel of faith, and with precepts for holy living. Thomas, in his Prolegomena on the Epistle to the Romans, says: "He affirms that practically the entire doctrine of theology is contained in the Davidic Psalms and in the Epistles of Paul." An opposing view is stated by Bellarmine in Bk. 4, *On the Word of God,* ch. 4: "The Apostles do not deal with doctrines in their Epistles except in passing."

4. *The form* or the genre of speech. As with other books of Scripture, so also the style of the Pauline Epistles boasts a simplicity that is combined with majesty. Irenaeus reminds us in Bk. 3, ch. 7, that "the Apostle frequently uses *hyperbaton* due to rapidity of discussions and the impetus of the Spirit."

Jerome writes in the Apology of his book *Against Jovinianus:* "Read his (Paul's) Epistles and you will see in the testimonies that he selects from the Old Testament how skilled and how wise he is, how adept at disguising what he is doing. For the words seem simple, as if they were the words of an innocent man, of a peasant, of one who knew neither how to carry out nor even how to draw up a treacherous plan. And yet wherever you look, there are thunderbolts. He hesitates for a moment, then strikes down everything that would threaten him; he retreats in order to overcome; he pretends to make an escape in order to go in for the kill."

12

5. *The purpose* of the writing.

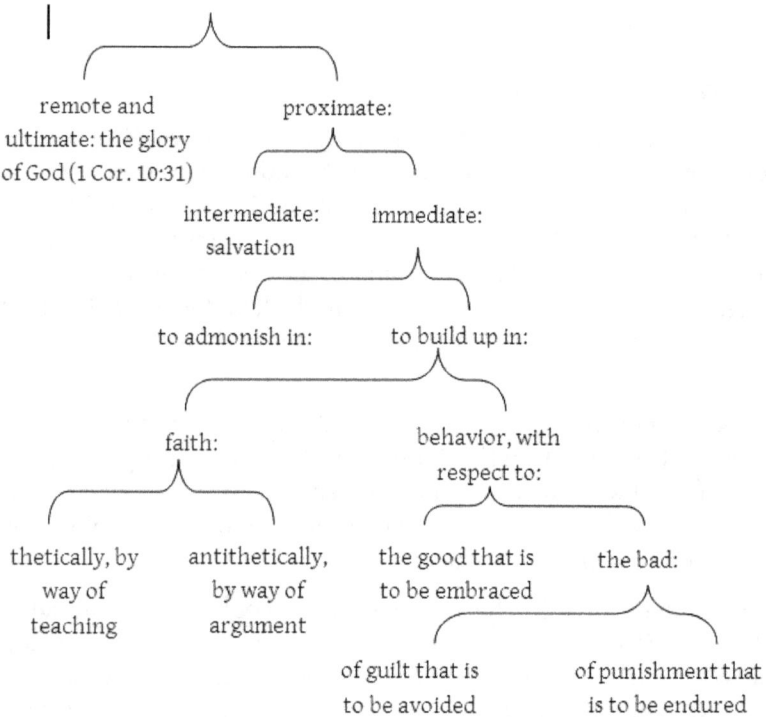

```
                    |
          ┌─────────┴─────────┐
  remote and            proximate:
  ultimate: the glory   ┌────┴────┐
  of God (1 Cor. 10:31)
              intermediate:    immediate:
              salvation        ┌────┴────┐
                        to admonish in:   to build up in:
                        ┌────────┴────────┐
                     faith:              behavior, with
                     ┌───┴───┐           respect to:
                                     ┌──────┴──────┐
            thetically, by  antithetically,  the good that is   the bad:
            way of          by way of        to be embraced     ┌───┴───┐
            teaching        argument
                                     of guilt that is    of punishment that
                                     to be avoided        is to be endured
```

The Apostle himself explains this. Rom. 15:4: "Whatever things have been written, have been written to teach us, so that by patience and the consolation of the Scriptures, we might have hope." 2 Tim. 3:16: "All Scripture is divinely inspired, useful for teaching, for rebuking, for correcting, for training in righteousness." Peter's reminder does not at all conflict with this when he states the goal of apostolic writing in 2 Peter 1:12-13. For because of diverse objects, the Apostles understood that a dual goal of writing had been set forth for them: both that they might perfectly inform and instruct the ignorant in the mysteries of the faith and prescribe for them a rule for holy living; and that they might admonish those to whom the mysteries of faith and the way of salvation had already been made known through preaching.

Nicephorus writes in Bk. 2, *History of the Church*, ch. 34: "Paul sent Epistles to the Corinthians, Ephesians, Galatians, Colossians, Philippians, Thessalonians, and also to the Jews and Romans and many others whom he was directed to address by the power and grace of the Holy Spirit, and whom he magnificently caused to be regenerated through evangelical faith in Christ. In these Epistles he gives them a summary and reminds them in his absence of the same things that he had clearly taught them in person with his preaching. In this way, then, even those things that he had previously passed by in silence—mysteries of a more secret and hidden nature—he later either declared clearly and accurately through his holy writings with words of more grandiose wisdom, or at very least (so to speak) he foreshadowed them, as it were, through riddles after the fashion and form of parables. Thus, on account of those who would be suitable for hearing the divine matters, he did not conceal them. But on account of the inept and those who were unworthy, he did not explain them entirely clearly and openly, in order to avoid contempt."

Athanasius in his Synopsis: "By means of these Epistles, he not only admonishes and corrects those whom he has seen and taught, but he also attempts to instruct and teach those whom he has not seen, as those who happen upon them can understand."

Eusebius writes in Bk. 2, *History of the Church*, ch. 34: "Paul sent Epistles to those whom he was directed to address by the power and grace of the Holy Spirit, and whom he magnificently caused to be regenerated through evangelical faith in Christ. In these Epistles he gives them a summary and reminds them in his absence of the same things that he had clearly taught them in person with his preaching."

The Apostle himself explains the intermediate purpose in 1 Cor. 9:19-22, "that I might save all."

6. *The benefit* of the Pauline Epistles proceeds from their purpose. Ambrose, in Sermon 68: "The Epistles of Paul, like breasts, nourish the peoples of the churches."

Chrysostom in Bk. 4, *On the Priesthood*: "His writings, like walls of steel, surround all the churches scattered throughout the whole world with siegeworks. He stands even now in the manner of a very brave and noble warrior as a mediator, leading captive every thought to obey Christ; and likewise demolishing strongholds and every height that exalts itself against the knowledge of God, all of which he has done through those very wonderful Epistles that he has left for us, replete as they are with divine wisdom."

From the same place: "Paul's writings are useful to us, not only that we may remove illegitimate and counterfeit dogmas from our midst and fortify ourselves with the true and genuine ones, but also because they are especially conducive to living rightly in a more blessed fashion."

In Homily 3 on the sayings of the Apostles, he says: "*Having one Spirit.* The Pauline Epistles are mines and wells of the Spirit, etc. The Pauline Epistles contain the marrow of faith and the Christian religion."

7. *The time of writing.* Chrysostom, in Homily 1 on the Epistle to the Romans, seeks to the greatest extent possible to arrive at an explanation of certain questions, if we know when the Epistles of Paul were written, and which came first and which came later. In the same place he also teaches that "they were not written in the order that we have in our Bibles today. It seems to me that the Epistle to the Galatians came before the Epistle to the Romans. Now, if there obtains a different order in our Bibles, it should not surprise us, for indeed, even the Twelve Prophets do not follow one another in order, if one takes the times into account. But while they may be quite far apart from one another with respect to time, if one were to take into consideration the sequence itself of the writings, they have been collated in order among themselves, even as Haggai, Zechariah and several others prophesied after the Prophets Ezekiel and Daniel, and many likewise after Jonah and Zephaniah and all the rest, and yet, they have been joined together with all of those from whom they are separated by such a great interval of time."

He affirms the same thing in Homily 1 on the Epistle to the Colossians, that the Epistles of Paul that were sent while he was in prison contain a more majestic doctrine. "Why did I say that the Epistles that were sent from prison contain, how shall I say, a greater measure of grace? Surely for this reason, for being in chains, he is like a man engaged in a military campaign, prevailing in the midst of the onslaught of the enemies, and then he pauses before winning the trophies and scribbles down in the Epistles the military orders he wishes to give. Thus, indeed, the blessed Apostle was doing here. He was certainly aware of how much importance this matter would convey. Wherefore, writing to Philemon, he says this: '...whom I begat in my chains.' The Epistles, then, which he wrote in prison are: *to the Ephesians, to Philemon, to Timothy, to the Philippians, to the Colossians.*"

Concerning the order of writing, Dr. Chemnitz states this in his *Examination*, p. 1, p. 25: "Paul wrote some Epistles before his captivity, and some in captivity."

Before his captivity, he wrote seven Epistles, in the following order:

(1) First Thessalonians   AD 50, 17 years after his conversion
(2) Second Thessalonians   AD 50
(3) First Timothy   AD 52, 19 years after his conversion
(4) First Corinthians   AD 53, 20 years after his conversion (2 Cor. 12:2)
(5) Titus   AD 55, 22 years after his conversion
(6) Second Corinthians
(7) Romans   AD 58 (Baronius)

He was detained in prison for two years, beginning in AD 59. During his captivity in Rome he certainly composed the rest, but there is not complete agreement about the order.

Theodoret, in the preface of his commentary on Paul, places them in this order: "(1) First Thessalonians, (2) Second Thessalonians, (3) First Corinthians, (4) Second Corinthians, (5) First Timothy, (6) Titus, (7) Romans, (8) Galatians, (9) Philippians, (10) Philemon, (11) Ephesians, (12) Colossians, (13) Hebrews, (14) Second Timothy."

Nevertheless, some place [the captivity Epistles] in this order:

(1) Philippians, (2) Colossians, (3) Philemon, (4) Ephesians, (5) Galatians, (6) Second Timothy.

Still others follow the order that is found in the Bible: (1) Galatians, (2) Ephesians, (3) Philippians, (4) Colossians, (5) Philemon, (6) Second Timothy.

8. *The number.* Everyone agrees that Paul wrote thirteen Epistles. There was, at one time, some doubt whether or not the Epistle to the Hebrews belongs to Paul.

Cyril of Jerusalem offers this reason in *Catecheses* 10, p. 134, why Paul may have written more Epistles than the other Apostles: "Lest his doctrine seem dubious, given that he was formerly an enemy and a persecutor."

Michael Medina writes in Bk. 6, *On the Right Faith in God*, ch. 6: "Neither are we to believe that all the Epistles of the Apostle Paul survived, since it is reasonable to conclude that a most holy and learned man, who was inclined to write on account of enormous zeal for the doctrine of the Gospel, and who preached the Gospel to so many cities and to so many nations, would not only have written these fourteen Epistles."

But even if some books written by holy men of God were destroyed, they were, nonetheless, not included in the number of canonical books. Augustine, in Bk. 18, *The City of God*, ch. 38, distinguishes between those things "that the Prophets wrote as men concerned about history, and between those things they wrote as Prophets by divine inspiration." And so he says that these things "were distinct in such a way that the former might finally be judged to be attributed to them, while the latter might be judged to be attributed to God, who was speaking through them. And thus the former things belong to an abundance of knowledge, whereas the latter belong to the authority of religion, by which authority the Canon is maintained."

9. *The recipient.* The Epistles were addressed either to certain regions, like the Epistle to the Galatians; or to certain cities, like the Epistles to the Romans, Corinthians, Ephesians, Philippians,

Colossians and Thessalonians; or to certain persons, such as Timothy, Titus and Philemon. The Epistle to the Hebrews was addressed to a certain people.

Because of the doctrine and the salutary benefit contained in them, they were addressed also to us, as the Apostle himself testifies in 1 Cor. 1:2: "To the Church of God that is in Corinth, to those who have been sanctified in Christ Jesus, to those who have been called as saints, together with all those who call upon the name of our Lord Jesus Christ." Augustine in Bk. 1, *Against Cresconius the Grammarian*, ch. 9: "I am mindful that the Apostolic Epistles were written not only to the hearers at the time when they were written, but also to us. For they are read aloud in the Church for no other reason."

Specific Prolegomena

1. *Occasion.* There were in Rome both Jews and Gentiles who had been converted to Christ. The Jews were claiming for themselves a certain advantage because of the divine covenant and circumcision, and thus they were urging the ceremonies of the Law still in the New Testament and were seeking to be justified partly by faith in Christ and partly by works of the Law. The Gentiles held the Jews in contempt as those who were finally rejected by God, and many of them were turning Christian liberty into carnal license. The Apostle wanted to counsel both groups by means of this Epistle.

The Jews thought of themselves more highly (1) because they had been given the Law; (2) because of circumcision; and (3) because of purity. They called the Gentiles "sinners."

The Gentiles thought of themselves more highly (1) because of philosophy; (2) because of the divine election by which they had been adopted into the people of God, while the Jews had been rejected; (3) because of the preeminence of the empire.

Augustine writes in Bk. 1, *To Simplicianus*, q.2: "Paul's intention in this Epistle is that no one may boast about the merits of works, about which the Israelites dared to boast, because they were slaves to the Law that was given to them and, for this reason, they thought that the grace of the Gospel was ultimately something that was due to their merits, since they were slaves to the Law. Therefore, they did not want this grace to be given to the Gentiles, who were, so to speak, unworthy, unless they should accept the Jewish sacraments."

Bellarmine in Bk. 4, *On the Word of God*, ch. 4: "The Apostles wrote as moved by the occasion; therefore, not by mandate."

We reply: The external occasions for writing presented by the Apostles do not eliminate the internal mandate to write. Otherwise, they would likewise eliminate the mandate to preach, since the occasion for preaching was also mentioned by them at times (Acts 17:16).

2. *Time.* Chrysostom, in his preface to the Epistle to the Romans: "It will also be necessary for those who approach this Epistle to explain the time when it was written. For it does not, as many think, precede all the other Epistles, but only those that were written from Rome. It comes later than the rest, although not all the rest."

Athanasius in his Synopsis: "It was written at a time when he had not yet seen the Romans. He had, however, heard of their faith and desired to see them (Rom. 1:11)."

Theodoret in his preface to all the Epistles of Paul: "The Epistle to the Romans was written as the last of all the Epistles that were sent from Asia and Macedonia and Achaia; it occupies the seventh place."

That this Epistle was written after both of those to the Corinthians is ascertained in this fashion: Paul wrote this Epistle to the Romans after Priscilla and Aquila became assistants of Paul in the faith of Christ and after they had already placed their lives in danger for the sake of the same Paul (Romans 16:3-4). It was also after Paul had completed his circuit from Jerusalem throughout all of Illyricum (Rom. 15:19), following which the same Aquila and Priscilla, after lingering for a time in Corinth and Ephesus, returned to the city of Rome, before Paul was led to Rome in chains. Therefore, Paul did not write that Epistle to the Romans from Corinth at that time while he was staying with Priscilla and Aquila (1 Cor. 16:19), but rather while he was staying with Gaius, since Priscilla and Aquila had already left and returned to Rome (Rom. 16:23).

Why, then, has Romans been placed first among the Pauline Epistles?

Augustine in Epistle 105, *To Sixtus:* "This Epistle is placed first because it commends the grace of faith, which is the chief and beginning of graces."

Anselm in his preface to this Epistle: "It is listed first because, since faith is the primary virtue and the foundation of other virtues, and without it is impossible to please God, it was fitting that this Epistle should be placed at the head of the others, for in it the primary virtue is treated, and in it all those who are like the Romans with regard to an imperfection of faith are corrected and called back to the perfection of faith."

Ambrosius Catharinus declares that it is "on account of the preeminence of the Roman Church" that this Epistle was placed first. But we reply with Aeneas Sylvius: "Before the Council of Nicaea there was little regard for the Roman Church."

Theodoret mentions some who declared that "in this matter of the Roman people, to whom belonged at that time the highest positions in the whole empire, there was some rationale for considering them more deserving than the other peoples." But the humility of Christ is not concerned with the arrogance of the world.

The fact that Romans occurs first in order is more properly said to be due to the sublime character of those things that are treated in this Epistle. For such a discussion is treated in this Epistle that it not only outweighs all the others—and easily so—in dignity and gravity, but it also passes on the very chief points of Christian instruction and piety, as well as the rudiments and, as it were, the very cradle thereof. For what other cradle, rudiments and principles of our religion are there than these things on which our entire religion rests—faith, grace and the merits of Christ! Indeed, Theodoret himself grants this reason a little later, that Romans comes first due to the precision of doctrine of every kind.

3. *Place.* An interlinear gloss in the last chapter of Romans states that it was written from *Athens*, where the gloss also testifies that it was Haymonis who placed Romans in its order.

Origen, in his preface on this Epistle, more properly states that it was written in Corinth: "(1) Because he commends Phoebe to the Romans, whom he calls a minister[5] of the Church that is in Cenchris (Rom. 16:1). But Cenchris is a port of Corinth. (2) Because he greets them in the name of his host, Gaius, concerning whom he writes to the Corinthians that he had baptized him there (1 Cor. 1:14). (3) He

---

5 Latin: *ministram*

greets them in the name of Erastus, the city treasurer (Rom. 16:24), who, he writes, remained in Corinth (2 Tim. 4:20). (4) The attached subscript gives the same testimony."

4. *The language* in which it was written. Salmeron states in Vol. 1, *Prolegomena.* 35, that this one Epistle of Paul was written in Latin: "(1) Because he wrote it to the Latins; (2) because his secretary was Tertius (Rom. 16:22), which is a Latin name."

Contra: (1) All the ancients state that it was written in Greek. Chrysostom and the rest of the Greek Fathers follow the Greek text as authentic. (2) This Epistle abounds in Greekisms. (3) In this Epistle, he does not contrast Jew and Roman, but Jew and Greek (ch. 1:14,16). (4) The Greek language was familiar at that time to the Romans. (5) The Latin version seems, at some point, to have been modeled after the Greek word for word. (6) Bellarmine, in Bk. 2, *On the Word of God*, ch. 7, and Cornelius a Lapide, in his argumentation on this Epistle, state the same thing.

5. *The Argument of the Epistle.* Bellarmine, in Bk. 1 *On Justification*, ch. 19, discusses it in this way: "The Apostle, in this Epistle to the Romans and in the one written to the Galatians, wanted to demonstrate that no one can be justified without faith in Christ and without the free mercy of God."

We reply: The goal of the Apostle is not only to demonstrate that no one is justified without faith in Christ and without the free mercy of God, but also that man is justified without works, by the grace alone of God, by the merit alone of Christ and by faith alone in Christ, which the clearest words of the Apostle demonstrate more clearly than the midday light. For he does not write to those who have not yet been converted to Christ and still wanted to be justified by works done without grace. Instead, he writes to those who have believed in Christ through the preaching of the Gospel (Acts 15:5,11; Gal. 2:16).

Ederus states in Bk. 4, *Oecon. Bibl.*, p. 433, that the argument of the Epistle is this: "The Apostle was eager to break up the quarrel that had arisen between those who had been converted from among the Jews and those who had been converted from among the Gentiles, in which each group wanted to be considered superior to the other, since this quarrel was vain, arrogant and useless, and he wished to encourage both groups toward concord.

"Those who were converted from among the Gentiles wanted to be considered superior (1) because of the philosophy and human wisdom that excelled to a greater degree among the Romans and the Greeks than it did among the Jews; (2) because of election, that is, the special call and grace by which Christ had turned His Word away from the Jews, who had rejected it, to the Gentiles; (3) because of the empire and the secular authority by which God had glorified the Gentiles and especially the Roman people.

"Those who had been converted from among the Jews wanted to be considered superior to the Gentiles (1) because of the authority of the divine Law, which had been given first, not to the Gentiles, but to the Jews; (2) because of the sign of circumcision and the Mosaic ceremonies; (3) because of the holiness of life in which they surpassed the Gentiles, whom the Jews called "sinners" on account of the idolatry and other filthiness of their life.

"The first reason for boasting among the Gentiles is opposed by the Gospel proclaimed by the Apostle, because he teaches that man is saved by faith and not by a philosophical knowledge (ch. 1). The preeminence of the empire is opposed by the fear of divine judgment (ch. 2). Boasting in the written Law is opposed by the transgression of the Jews and the natural law of the Gentiles (ch. 2). Boasting in circumcision is opposed by the fact that the righteousness of God does not come about by the works of the Law or by ceremonies, but by faith in the Messiah. Boasting in holy living is opposed by carnal rebellion, which no one is able to resist without the grace of Christ. Boasting in election is opposed by the fact that election is a free gift, and that the reprobation of the Jews is the cause of salvation for the Gentiles."

The goal of the Apostle is to pass on the sum of Christian doctrine, but especially to treat expressly the article of free justification. (1) He had not yet preached the Gospel to the Romans from his own mouth,[6] and so in this writing he wished to pass on to them the pattern of teaching (Rom. 6:17). (2) He knew that this Epistle would easily spread to other churches from the city of Rome, since it was the seat of the Empire. (3) Everything in this Epistle is laid out in such a way that it contains the general, necessary and common doctrine for all churches equally. Indeed, if the proper names of persons and places at the beginning and at the end were changed, it would not make much difference to which church or at what time it had been sent.

---

6 Latin: *viva voce*

General Arrangement

Some arrange the Epistle according to the three theological virtues of *faith, hope* and *love.*

Some, according to the three parts of conversion, which are *contrition, faith* and *new obedience.*

Some arrange it by analogy to the parts of medicine, for in it, (1) the malady is exposed, (2) the remedy is revealed, and (3) the course of treatment is prescribed.

There are three parts:

I.   The introduction or preface;

II. The main work, that is, the discussion itself;

III. The epilogue or conclusion.

The parts of the preface are: (1) The address; (2) Prayer.

In the main work, he first of all exposes the evil itself, that is, the malady, namely, the unrighteousness of man (chapters 1, 2 and the first part of chapter 3).

Secondly, he reveals the remedy, that is, the corresponding virtue (from the end of chapter 3 through chapter 4).

Thirdly, the origin and the simultaneous progression of evil and good into the human race (chapter 5).

Fourthly, he teaches that, although light cannot not do away with evil, nevertheless the light should increase (chapter 6).

Fifthly, how both the residual evil as well as the good that has begun remain in one and the same man in this world and are at war with one another (chapter 7).

Sixthly, he offers comfort in the face of the evil that remains, and he magnifies the corresponding remedy (chapter 8).

In the seventh place, he demonstrates to which men that good pertains—those who apprehend it, and those who have fallen out of it (Chapters 9, 10 and 11).

In the eighth place, he prescribes to them the regimen that all should observe who have been freed from such great evil and made participants in the corresponding virtue (Chapters 12, 13 and 14).

Notes on the Epistle to the Romans: Chapter 1

There are three parts to the first chapter: (1) The preface, which is composed of *the address* and *prayer*; (2) the introduction to the discussion.

In the preface and introduction, which continue through v.16, Paul renders them to whom he is writing attentive, docile and benevolent: *Attentive,* when he points out that he is dealing with them not in his own name, but as the emissary of God to the Gentiles, and that he is now dealing with a very great matter, promised long ago in the Old Testament; *docile,* when he explains the chief matter of Evangelical doctrine, namely, that Christ is, in the unity of Person, the Son of God and of David, true God and true Man, the only Mediator of the human race; *benevolent,* when he writes that their faith is being announced in the whole world. And he confirms, as one called by God to bear witness, that he pours out unceasing prayers to God and that he has been most eager up until now to address them in person.

The *address* expresses (1) *the efficient ministerial cause,* that is, the writer; (2) *the object,* that is, those to whom it was written. The first part contains the description (a) of his person; (b) of the Gospel; (c) of Christ Himself. When considering the structure, these things are connected to one another, for since he says that he was called to preach the Gospel, he then describes it from antiquity. Then, in turn, since Christ is the heart[7] of the Gospel, he therefore describes both natures of Christ. From this description he then goes back to an explanation of his office. The second part points out that the Romans were called through the preaching of the Gospel into the fellowship of the Church.

The *prayer* asks for grace and peace for them.

The pontifical institution of the Romans (in which a person's own name that he received when he was baptized is cast off, and another is chosen form him that is worthy of the papal throne), which Salmeron shamelessly cloaks with the example of Paul, has

---

7 Latin: nucleus

nothing at all to do with the change of Paul's name. (1) For "this is the reason found in Holy Scripture why the saints changed their names, not by their own will, but at God's command," as Conzenius himself admits on p.7. But no one, when he is exalted to the papal seat, has God's pontifical command to change his name. (2) The name "Paul" was given to our Apostle as an additional name; his prior name was neither despised nor cast off, but retained, as was also the case for other Apostles (Acts 13:0, Mat. 16:16, 2 Pet. 1:1, Mat. 10:2, etc.). (3) Among the ancients, no new names were imposed except when they were first converted to Christianity, as a way to show contempt for the idolatry to which they had been previously enslaved (cf. Eusebius, Bk. 8, ch. 21).

v.1   ΠΑΥΛΟΣ, δοῦλος Ἰησοῦ Χριστοῦ, κλητὸς ἀπόστολος, ἀφωρισμένος εἰς εὐαγγέλιον Θεοῦ,

v.1 Paul, a servant of Jesus Christ, called to be an apostle, separated unto the gospel of God, (KJV)

1. The first part of the address sets forth the efficient ministerial cause, or the writer of the Epistle. Both (1) his name and (2) his office are expressed.

Concerning the *name*, there is a threefold opinion rendered by the ancients:

(1) Origen thinks that "this Apostle had two names right away at the beginning, and that he was called Saul among the people of his own nation, but was called Paul among the rest, especially the Romans."

(2) Some state that he was only named Saul at the beginning, but was called Paul at the time of his conversion, or even that God Himself imposed this name on him, lest he should be seen as inferior to the other Apostles in that respect (cf. Chrysostom, Theodoret, Theophylact). Or that Paul assumed this name for himself out of the grace of modesty and humility (cf. Jerome and Ambrose on this Epistle, Augustine *On the Spirit and the Letter*, ch. 7, on Psa. 72). However, since Acts 9, where Paul is baptized, he is always called "Saul" up through chapter 13. Therefore, after his Baptism the

name "Saul" was still retained, and so the name Paul was not assumed in Baptism.

(3) Some maintain that Paul was given this name as a gift long after his conversion, based on the event of Sergius Paulus, Proconsul of Cyprus, being converted to faith in Christ (cf. Jerome, on the Epistle to Philemon; Augustine, Bk. 8. *Confessions,* ch. 4.; Bede on Acts 13).

Related to this, some want to conclude that he assumed this name in Acts 13:9 when he was set apart with Barnabas and designated an Apostle of the Gentiles, so that, by means of the name itself, he might fit in more easily with the Gentiles. Then, as Paul begins to preach to the Gentiles, he comes upon this proconsul Sergius and converts him.

Erasmus states: "The Hebrew name was borne first by Paul, for thus Christ meets him in Acts 9:4. From then on, since in Egypt, Cilicia and part of the adjoining region of Syria (due to the empire of Alexander the Great and afterwards the Roman administration) practically everyone used the Greek language by this time, the Hebrew name was changed into a Greek form and thus 'Saul' became 'Saulus,' just as 'Adam' becomes 'Adamus.' Then, since the name Paul was familiar to the Greeks and Romans, 'Saulus' was changed again to 'Paulus,' so that the word might also be more readily recognizable to them whose teacher he professed to be, and thus he should 'become all things to all men.'"

The *office* is described (1) generally, that he is a servant of Christ; (2) specifically, that he is an Apostle set apart for preaching the Gospel.

"A servant of Jesus Christ."

Origen states that "Paul calls himself a servant of Christ out of humility." Didymus, writing on James ch. 1, more properly states: "Just as men in pursuit of mortal glory place the honors they are thought to have at the beginning of their writings, so holy men esteem the title 'servant of God' above all the kingdoms of the world."

Porphyrius attributes this to "Paul's ambition." But in the eyes of the world at that time, it was not a glorious thing to call oneself a servant and Apostle of Christ.

Adamus Conzenius attacks Calvin with personal hatred for eliminating the word *minister*, since he notices that Cornelius a Lapide interprets it in that way. *"Servant,"* he says, "should be understood as an honored position, which in Hebrew is *Mescharet*, that is, *minister.*" So also in his commentary on Phil. 1:1.

The word δοῦλος [servant, slave] is more emphatic than ὑπηρέτης [minister]. For when the excellent and noble ministry in which Paul was engaged after being called was being considered, then he was always a *minister* (Rom. 15:16, 1 Cor. 4:1). But when the manner was being considered in which he was bound to this ministry and to the divine service, as one who was obliged to it on many accounts, he rightly calls himself a "servant of Christ" (1 Cor. 9:19).

Servants of Christ are (1) *de jure*, all men, with respect both to creation and to redemption, since they have been preserved by Him and freed from Satan's captivity; 2) *de facto*, all those in general who are truly godly, and specifically, the ministers themselves of the Church who serve in the preaching of the Gospel.

κλητὸς ἀπόστολος [called Apostle], "a called Apostle, an Apostle on the basis of God's calling." The Syriac version translates "called and sent." Masters who are about to commend a special office to some servant call him forth out of the mass of servants. Thus Christ called forth some men in a special way out of the company of the other servants to the apostolic office. Therefore he expresses his office in a more specific way, for he is not just any kind of servant of Christ, but one of those of highest rank who are called Apostles. Anselm's judgment that "it is out of humility that Paul calls himself, not an Apostle, but one who has been called an Apostle" is drawn from the Greek text.

In Greek, κεκλημένος [having been called] does not mean "called" as in "to be named,"[8] but κλητὸς [called] is "to be an Apostle by calling," that is, called to the Apostolate. In the Syriac translation it is the noun שְׁלִיחָא, by which it alludes to the former name,

---

8 Latin: *vocatus, appellatus*

Saul. For Saul, in Hebrew, means "called and summoned,[9]" namely, to the kingdom, just as this Saul of ours was called by God out of the same tribe to the Apostolate.

Jerome on Titus ch. 1: "What Paul says about himself, namely, that he is an Apostle of Jesus Christ, seems to me to be as much as if he had said, 'Prefect to the guard of Caesar Augustus, Master of the army of Tiberius.' For as the rulers of this world are considered more noble because of the kings whom they serve and choose titles based on the dignity with which they are endowed, so also the Apostle claims for himself a dignity that is truly grand among Christians and marks himself off immediately with the title 'Apostle of Christ,' using the very authority of that name to frighten those who would read it, indicating that all those who believe in Christ should be subject to him."

ἀφορίζειν [to set apart] is "to separate and set apart with discernment." This is why *canons* are called ἀφορισμοί (aphorisms), since they have been collected, written down and briefly conveyed with great discernment.

Some think that "Apostle" alludes to the name of a sect which he was following in Judaism. For they were called "Pharisees" from the word פרס, "he separated," because they wanted to be seen as removed and separated from the common people due to their excellent doctrine and renowned sanctimony of life. Since, then, Paul was separated by his own false opinion, and by that of others, in Pharisaism, he was truly and in a far better way made such in Christianity. But it is inferred from Gal. 1:15 that Paul was referring chiefly to the fact that God had "separated" him from his mother's womb to preach the Gospel among the nations. Secondarily, he was made to be ἀφορισμὸν [set apart] by the Church in Acts 13:2: ἀφορίσατε μοι τὸν Σαῦλον [Set apart for me Saul].

"The Gospel of God," (1) because of the eternal decree, since God, from eternity, made the decree concerning our salvation, which is announced in the Gospel; (2) because of its revelation in time.

---

9 Latin: *vocatum et postulatum*

32

v.2 ὃ προεπηγγείλατο διὰ τῶν προφητῶν αὐτοῦ ἐν Γραφαῖς Ἁγίαις,

v.2 (Which he had promised afore by his prophets in the holy scriptures,) (KJV)

He commends the Gospel's (1) antiquity and (2) veracity. For the Holy Scriptures are divine oracles that are both very ancient and entirely true. Indeed, in this way he aptly commends the dignity of the apostolic office, which was occupied with preaching the Gospel.

Compare with Acts 3:23, Rom. 3:21, and 1 Pet. 1:11. This is useful against the Photinians, who state that the Gospel was first revealed in the New Testament (Mark 1:1). With the word "Gospel," the promise of grace on account of Christ is not understood simply, but rather as the public proclamation concerning the Christ who has been provided.

διὰ τῶν προφητῶν [through the prophets]. The Syriac has "through the hand," that is, by the ministry, "of the Prophets"—a Hebraism.

v.3 περὶ τοῦ Υἱοῦ αὐτοῦ, τοῦ γενομένου ἐκ σπέρματος Δαυὶδ κατὰ σάρκα,

v.3 Concerning his Son Jesus Christ our Lord, which was made of the seed of David according to the flesh; (KJV)

The Vulgate translates, "who was made,[10]" since it is taught (1) that the Son, at a certain point in time, took on that which He was not before, since, having been born from eternity, he never *began* to exist. Therefore, the word "made" points rather to the *human nature.* (2) The origin of His arising is not by a natural[11] birth, but by the working of the Holy Spirit, in which sense He is also said to be "made of woman" (Gal. 4:4). (3) Christ is not begotten of the Holy Spirit—this is the proper work of the Father who begets an offspring from His own substance—but made. (4) He neither "was begotten" nor "is begotten" (from the verb "to beget" — γεννάω,

10 Latin: *qui factus est*
11 Latin: *communi*

gigno) as the Christ, but rather "He became" (from the verb "to become" — γίνομαι, *fio*).

Valla and Erasmus think that it should more properly be translated as "arose" or "was born," so that His eternal birth from the essence of the Father might be kept in view as distinct from that temporal birth from the seed of David. Thus the Syriac translates רָאתִילֶר, "was begotten."

"From the seed of David," that is, from the posterity and stock of David, for which reason the Syriac notably translates, "from the seed of the house of David." He mentions David in order to demonstrate that in Christ the promises made to David were fulfilled concerning the future birth of the Messiah from his posterity.

The particle κατὰ [according to] is not choristic or diameristic, separating and dividing the natures, but rather dioristic, demonstrating according to which nature Christ is said to have been made from the seed of David; and also diacritical of the natures and of the natural qualities, lest either a change or a mixture of the natures should be introduced. Syriac: בְבַסֵר, "in the flesh." Moreover, by synecdoche with the word "flesh" is understood the animated flesh, the whole human nature.

v.4 τοῦ ὁρισθέντος Υἱοῦ Θεοῦ ἐν δυνάμει κατὰ πνεῦμα ἁγιωσύνης ἐξ ἀναστάσεως νεκρῶν, Ἰησοῦ Χριστοῦ τοῦ Κυρίου ἡμῶν,

v.4 And declared to be the Son of God with power, according to the spirit of holiness, by the resurrection from the dead: (KJV)

The Vulgate translates the word ὁρισθέντος [marked off] with "predestined," and Bellarmine takes up the defense of this translation in Bk. 2, *On the Word of God*, ch. 14: "Although the word ὁρίζειν means 'to place a boundary,' and is sometimes understood by secular authors as 'to declare,' in Scripture, nevertheless, it always means 'to establish, to decide, to mark off,' but never 'to declare,' as is clear from Acts 2 verses 4 and 17, Rom. 8 and Eph. 1. Indeed, since the ordination and definition of God cannot be temporal, but are eternal, for this reason our translator, seeing that the Apostle is speaking about the eternal designation, preferred to translate it as 'predestined' rather than 'designated.[12]' Indeed, all of the most ancient Latin editions read this way."

We reply: (1) If the verb ὁρίζειν [to mark off] never means "to declare," then apparently Chrysostom did not know the force of this word, since he says that ὁρισθέντος [marked off] means the same thing as δειχθέντος [shown], ἀποφανθέντος [ruled], κριθέντος [judged], ὁμολογηθέντος [confessed]. Theophylact did not know it, since he says it means the same thing as ἀποδειχθέντος [demonstrated], βεβαιωθέντος [confirmed], κριθέντος [judged]. Oecumenius did not know it, for he says it means the same thing as ἀποδειχθέντος [demonstrated], ἀποφανθέντος [ruled]. No, we ought to believe the Greek Fathers on the proper meaning of the Greek word rather than the Latin Fathers.

(2) The Syriac translates "he was acknowledged as the Son of God," that is, He was demonstrated by clear and certain testimonies, for ὁρίζειν [to mark off] does not only mean "to decide and to define," but also "to solemnly pronounce and proclaim that which you have decreed." Suarezius demonstrates in Vol. 1 of his commentary, part. 3, Thom. Disputation 50, sect. 2, that the exposition of the Greeks is sufficiently probable. Cornelius a Lapide on this passage: "The Syriac and the Greeks aptly and clearly translate the Greek word ὁρισθέντος as, 'who was declared and recognized' as the Son of God." Toletus approves: "*Predestined* here should be explained as 'declared.' *Predestined*," he says, "or *marked off*, refers, not to the matter itself, but to what men notice, so that *predestined* is the same as 'being certified, certainly recognized by men.'" Adam Conzenius rejects that rendering, "predestined," and the reasoning behind it, as fragile and metaphysical and not at all in agreement with the text.

(3) Christ is said to be ὁρισθείς [marked off] as the Son of God by His resurrection from the dead. This cannot be understood concerning eternal predestination, but concerning the declaration and manifestation made in time.

Erasmus on this passage: "He was, to be sure, always the Son

---

12 Latin: *maluit vertere praedestinatum quam destinatum*

of God, but recognized by few, namely, the Jews—and only few of them. But after the resurrection and on the basis of the resurrection He was declared as such to the whole world, for no created force can conquer death."

(4) Cornelius a Lapide explains that predestination in this way: "The Man Christ, who was made from the seed of David, was predestined to this, that He should subsist in the Person of the Son of God. In other words, it was predestined by God that this Man should be assumed by the Son of God, and that they should be joined in hypostatic union." But Bellarmine accuses Brenz of Nestorianism when he says "man" instead of "the assumed humanity."

(5) Conrad Vorstius affirms this interpretation. "Christ was marked off according to the Spirit as the Son of God by whom He was sanctified by the Father, that is, He was truly made the Son of God in a certain definite or perfect way by His resurrection from the dead."

But the proper meaning of the word ὁρίζειν [to mark off] must oppose this Photinian corruption, because it does not mean "to make," but "to mark off, to declare," as the proper nature of the matter is declared and manifested by the Greeks in the definition they give for the word ὁρισμός (cf. Sibrantus Lubbertus, *Against the 99 Errors of Vorstius*, p. 64).

ἐν δυνάμει [in power], that is, δυνατῶς, "powerfully," according to the Hebrew usage.

κατὰ πνεῦμα ἁγιωσύνης [according to the spirit of holiness]. "Through the Spirit." (1) Some understand the divine nature of Christ, which is a spiritual, holy and sanctifying essence, due to the contrast of the flesh and the spirit, that is, of the divine and human natures in Christ (1 Tim. 3:16, Heb. 9:14, 1 Pet. 3:18).

(2) Others, however, understand the third Person of the Deity, namely, the Holy Spirit whom Christ sent to the believers after His resurrection. Both explanations are analogous to the faith, but the first is more congruent with the apostolic text. The Syriac translates "with might and with the Holy Spirit," which some join

together in this way through hendiadys, "by the powerful might of the Holy Spirit."

But he calls that Spirit "the Spirit of holiness," not only because He is essentially holy, but also because He is powerfully sanctifying.

ἐξ ἀναστάσεως νεκρῶν [by resurrection of dead]. Theodoret explains it this way: "Christ was declared the Son of God through the power conferred on the Apostles by the Holy and sanctifying Spirit, by which they confirmed the resurrection of Christ with miraculous signs and deeds."

Origen and Jerome explain it this way, "that He was declared with divine power and the Spirit of sanctification based on this, that many bodies of holy men were resurrected together with Christ (Mat. 27:52)."

But it is more properly understood concerning the resurrection of Christ Himself. For the sense is that Christ was declared, manifested and recognized as the Son of God (1) with power, that is, through the miraculous divine power that resulted; (2) through the Spirit of sanctification, that is, through the visible outpouring of the Holy Spirit; (3) through His glorious resurrection from the dead.

As for the genitive Ἰησοῦ Χριστοῦ [of Jesus Christ], Laurentius Valla refers it to the preceding περὶ τοῦ Υἱοῦ [concerning the Son], and sets up a *hyperbaton* in the Apostle's words. More properly, that genitive is said to have been added exegetically, so that it may be understood to be referring to the message of the resurrection of Christ Himself. For this reason the Syriac translates, "who rose from the dead—Yeshua Christ, our Lord," where the relative (Hebrew ד) can be taken as a redditive of cause, "since He rose from the dead."

The Hebrews often repeat the antecedent noun in place of the relative pronoun. Therefore, Paul adds the phrase "of Jesus Christ" in order to teach that this is the proper name of the Son of God.

Observe: Christ was efficaciously declared the Son of God on the basis of His resurrection from the dead and through His resurrection from the dead, since He rose by His own power, which is proof of divine and infinite power (John 2:19, 10:18; Acts 1:3).

He applies the commendation of the Person of Christ to the commendation of his apostolic office.

v.5 δι᾽ οὗ ἐλάβομεν χάριν καὶ ἀποστολὴν εἰς ὑπακοὴν πίστεως ἐν πᾶσι τοῖς ἔθνεσιν ὑπὲρ τοῦ ὀνόματος αὐτοῦ,

v.5 By whom we have received grace and apostleship, for obedience to the faith among all nations, for his name: (KJV)

In the verb ἐλάβομεν [we have received], Schmaltz says in *Contra Schopp.*, p.6, that "it is the way of glory (דֶּרֶךְ כָּבוֹד), the manner of lordship or the majestic use," on the basis of which he opposes the argument that we form for constructing the mystery of the Trinity out of the plural number used for God.

We reply: (1) The argument for the mystery of the Trinity is neither solely nor primarily sought from the plural number. (2) Paul is describing the office which was common to him together with the rest of the Apostles, which is why he speaks in the plural (1 Cor. 4:9).

By χάριν καὶ ἀποστολὴν [grace and Apostleship], most interpreters understand χάριν ἀποστολῆς, "the grace of the Apostolate," as if it were a hendiadys that meant that Paul was received by the fellowship of the Apostles out of free mercy (1 Cor. 15:10). But it is more properly said that the Apostle is here celebrating two distinct benefits: (1) That he had received "grace," that is, that although he was formerly a blasphemer and a persecutor, he received God's mercy and was converted to faith in Christ (1 Tim. 1:13 & 16). (2) That, in addition, he was divinely and immediately called to the high office of Apostle, and was equipped with the gifts necessary for it (Rom. 12:3, 15:15).

Εἰς ὑπακοὴν πίστεως [to obedience of faith], "that the nations may be obedient to faith," that is, to the Gospel, which is the doctrine of faith, so that the word "faith" is taken *objectively* as the faith which one believes,[13] as the Syriac also translates. Or: "That the nations may be obedient by faith," namely, to the word of the Gospel, so that the word "faith" is taken qualitatively, referring to the faith by which one believes.[14] In both cases, it amounts to the same thing: the purpose and the aim of apostolic preaching is denoted.

The Vulgate translates less suitably "for the obeying of faith." This phrase properly signifies that obedience which Paul himself was supposed to furnish, although it is meant [in the Vulgate translation] as the obedience which is demanded of the nations.

Ἐν πᾶσι τοῖς ἔθνεσιν [among all the nations]. Some take this specifically as referring to the Gentiles, of whom Paul was especially the Apostle, though in a practical rather than an exclusive sense (Rom. 11:13, 15:16; Gal. 2:7-9; 1 Tim. 2:7; 2 Tim. 1:11). But it is more rightly understood in general of all people, that is, of Jews and Gentiles, since a little later in verse 6 he says, "among whom you are also." He is writing, moreover, to the converted from among the Jews and the Gentiles. The Syriac transposes the words in this way: "through whom we received grace and the Apostolate among all nations, that they may be obedient to the faith of His name."

Ὑπὲρ τοῦ ὀνόματος αὐτοῦ [for the sake of His name]. Stapulensis refers this identification to the more remote phrase: "We received the Apostolate with regard to the name of Jesus, which means, with regard to preaching among the nations." Cornelius a Lapide on this passage: "We received the Apostolate by the name and in the stead of Christ and we discharge it by delegation." But the Greek scholars refer this to the nearer "to the obedience," namely, of faith, as if the sense were, that the nations should be obedient to the doctrine of faith, which is concerning the name of Christ. Luther translates, "under His name." It could also be translated "for the sake of his name," that is, that the name of Christ may become manifest among the nations.

---

13 Latin: *pro fide quae creditur*
14 Latin: *pro fide qua creditur*

v.6 ἐν οἷς ἐστε καὶ ὑμεῖς κλητοὶ Ἰησοῦ Χριστοῦ·

v.6 Among whom are ye also the called of Jesus Christ: (KJV)

He connects his calling to those to whom he is writing. For he says that they, too, are among the number of those to whom he was sent to preach.

Luther translates, "called by Christ Jesus."

It can also be translated, "called to Christ," that is, to the knowledge, faith and worship of Christ, just as he said above, that he was called an Apostle, that is, to the Apostolate (v.1).

The Syriac translates בְּיֵשׁוּעַ, "in Jesus Christ," that is, Christ being the Author, or even "to Christ," as if the בּ were substituted for לְ.

2. The latter part of the address describes the object, that is, those to whom the Epistle was written.

v.7 Πᾶσι τοῖς οὖσιν ἐν Ῥώμῃ ἀγαπητοῖς Θεοῦ, κλητοῖς ἁγίοις· Χάρις ὑμῖν καὶ εἰρήνη ἀπὸ Θεοῦ Πατρὸς ἡμῶν καὶ Κυρίου Ἰησοῦ Χριστοῦ.

v.7 To all that be in Rome, beloved of God, called to be saints: Grace to you and peace from God our Father, and the Lord Jesus Christ. (KJV)

Concerning the note of universality in πᾶσι [to all], some are careful to observe that it should be understood as "to the confessors of Christ and the members of the Church." But the Apostle himself adds the limitation when he submits "to the beloved of God, to the called saints."

Theodoret on this passage: "'To all, etc.': To the rich, to the fine craftsmen, to the servants, to the lords and to the vassals. He does not, however, claim to be writing to 'all' indiscriminately, but to the beloved of God, to the called saints."

Ἀγαπητοὶ Θεοῦ [Beloved of God], in the passive meaning, are "those who are loved by God". Luther translates it with a superlative, "*den liebsten GOttes* [the most beloved of God]." He thus expresses the cause of the calling, which is the love of God.

They are called κλητοὶ ἁγίοι [called holy] (1) who have been called with a holy calling (2 Tim. 1:9); (2) who have been called to holiness, or, that they may be holy. Just as he had called himself a "called Apostle," that is, an Apostle on the basis of God's calling, so he called them "called saints," that is, those who have been sanctified by the same calling and through the Word of God. The Syriac inserts a copulative, "called and holy." This particle has an exegetical force, "called that they may be holy." The calling is joined together with the love of God, because God called them with a holy calling, not according to works, but according to grace, etc. (2 Tim. 1:9). Sanctification is joined together with the calling, because the final cause of the calling is sanctification.

Observe: If Christians wish to answer their calling, they should strive for holiness.

Χάρις ὑμῖν καὶ εἰρήνη [grace to you and peace]. With *grace*, some understand "spiritual good things;" with *peace*, "bodily good things and pleasant success." Lyranus on 1 Pet. 1: "Grace refers to the present life, peace to the future life."

Ambrose on this passage: "*Grace*, because we have been absolved from sins; *peace*, because from among the ungodly we have been reconciled."

In the same way Augustine, in his exposition on the Epistle to the Galatians, ch. 1: "It is the grace of God by which sins are forgiven to us, so that we may be reconciled to God; but it is peace by which we are reconciled to God."

Therefore, with *grace*, they understand the acquisition of the benefits of Christ; with *peace*, they understand the application of these benefits.

Estius and Cornelius a Lapide understand *grace* by metonymy as "the benefits that are conveyed by grace that lead to man's eternal salvation, which are faith, hope, love and the remaining virtues." But it is more correctly understood as the source of all those benefits, namely, the free favor of God by which He embraces us in Christ, remits sins to us and justifies and saves us by grace, since, in Jude 2, *grace* is explained as ἔλεος [mercy], and *peace* in this greeting is distinguished from *grace*.

With the noun *peace*, the Hebrews customarily embrace all happiness and prosperity (Gen. 43:27; Psa. 119:165, etc.). Based on this, some state that peace here is understood as every kind of benefit, whether physical or spiritual, temporal or eternal. Some, with the noun *peace*, understand the concord of those upon whom that grace comes. But in the greeting of Christ in Luke 24:36 and John 20:19 and of the Apostles, that special and unique benefit of divine grace conferred on us in Christ is understood with the noun *peace*, for we who have been justified by faith have peace with God (Rom. 5:1), which is peace in God and with God. On the basis of God's grace furnished for us in Christ and received by faith, there arises reconciliation with God and peace of conscience in the Holy Spirit.

Jerome says this in his Epistle *To Cyprian the Presbyter* in explanation of Psalm 99: "All the Epistles of Paul, in the initial greeting, have, not peace first and then grace, but first grace and then peace, so that, once our sins have been forgiven us, we may receive the peace of the Lord."

Tertullian, in Bk. 5, *Against Marcion,* ch. 5, admonishes "that this was the greeting of the Jews: 'Peace to you.' But the greeting of the Apostles is: 'Grace and peace to you,' because they were heralds of the grace conveyed through Christ."

Bede, on 1 Peter 1: "Without the grace of Christ, no one ever comes to the peace of reconciliation. Therefore, grace and peace are joined together in the Apostolic greeting in such a way that grace is sent ahead of peace."

The Syriac less properly inverts the word order and places peace ahead of grace, undoubtedly considering the usual custom of the Hebrew greeting.

Ἀπὸ Θεοῦ Πατρὸς ἡμῶν [from God our Father]. He wishes for those spiritual gifts to be granted to them from God as our author and Father, since He adopted us as sons, and from Christ as the Mediator, since He merited them for us by His suffering and death.

Καὶ κυρίου [and the Lord], etc. Another participle ἀπὸ must be repeated here based on the preceding, or it must be deduced from it, because otherwise the order would be preposterous, since God is first and foremost, that is, by nature, on account of the eternal generation, the Father of Christ; and secondly He is also our Father because of Christ through the grace of adoption. This is why the Syriac participle מן is notably repeated twice. "Peace to you from God our Father and from our Lord Jesus Christ."

Observe: The greetings of the saints are efficacious prayers and benedictions that procure the good things that they long for with their greetings (Mat. 10:13).

v.8 Πρῶτον μὲν εὐχαριστῶ τῷ Θεῷ μου διὰ Ἰησοῦ Χριστοῦ ὑπὲρ πάντων ὑμῶν ὅτι ἡ πίστις ὑμῶν καταγγέλλεται ἐν ὅλῳ τῷ κόσμῳ.

v.8 First, I thank my God through Jesus Christ for you all, that your faith is spoken of throughout the whole world. (KJV)

In the introduction he aims at securing their benevolence and their attention by congratulating them on their knowledge of the Gospel and by expressing his desire that he might have the opportunity to teach them.

The first part of the introduction in which he congratulates them on their knowledge of the Gospel both bears witness to his benevolence toward them, and, in turn, provokes their benevolence toward him.

Πρῶτον [first] in this passage is not an adverb of order, but of intention, meaning the same thing as "above all," unless we wanted to understand it as connected to what follows. "I point out the same thing, that I have often desired to come."

The pronoun μοῦ [my] is the voice of faith: "I give thanks to my God, whom I know to be propitious toward me, who has called me to the Gospel, and whom I serve in the Gospel." See John 20:28, Gal. 2:20.

I give thanks to God "through Christ as Mediator, from whom faith, grace and all good things for which we give thanks to God come to us" (Ambrose). "...as High Priest, by whose offering everything that belongs to us is pleasing to God the Father" (Origen).

ὑπὲρ πάντων ὑμῶν [for all of you], "over all of you." The Syriac translates, "on account of the faces of all of you." But the פֿאַ is redundant, just as it is frequently in Hebrew, פֿנֵי.

Your faith καταγγέλλεται [is announced thoroughly], "is announced and preached," or even "is commended and praised." The Syriac has the verb אֶשְׁתַּמֲעַת, "is heard."

Origen states that "there is hyperbole in his words, that the faith of the Romans is being announced in the whole world." But since Rome was the capital of the empire, it could easily have been that, due to the flow of travelers, their conversion to faith in Christ was broadcast far and wide.

He understands the preceding based on what follows. For he does not properly give thanks to God for the reason that their faith is announced in the whole world, since at times the subject matter itself does not correspond to this announcement concerning the virtues of a certain person, but that their faith was actually of such a kind that it was deservedly celebrated in the whole world.

The papists seek a certain advantage for the Roman Church in this, that its faith is said to be announced in the whole world. But we reply: (1) The Apostle adorns the Thessalonian Church with the same word of praise (1 The. 1:8): "your faith which is in God has descended into every place." (2) The Apostle seriously—and almost presciently—stifles the haughtiness of the Roman clerics in Rom. 11:21-22.

Baronius, in *A.D. 58*, par. 50: "Cyprian, writing to Pope Cornelius in Epistle 57, maintains that what Paul says, 'your faith is being announced in the whole world,' was spoken prophetically."

We reply: (1) It was not the intention either of Paul or of Cyprian to predict anything prophetically, nor to promise that anything would happen in the future, but rather to describe historically the present state of the Roman Church; (2) and at the same time, to encourage the Romans toward a perpetual and invariable profession of the true faith. (3) The very same papists admit "that Rome would, at some time, be the nest of the Antichrist" (cf. Anglo Remens. on Revelation ch. 17). "Before the end of the world, Rome will be the seat of the Antichrist" (cf. Ribera on Rev. 14, n. 39). John speaks about Rome, that just as it once was under Gentile emperors, and so it would also be at the end of the world after it fell away from the Roman Pontiff.

Blasius de Viegas, in his commentary on Revelation 17, sect. 3: "The name Babylon must be transferred to that Rome which had served idols before it received the faith of Christ, and to that Rome which will be at the time of the Antichrist, which John predicts will fall away from the high Pontiff and from the faith."

Cornelius a Lapide urges: (1) The saying of Jerome in Bk. 3, *Against Rufinus*, ch. 4: "Treachery has no place for the Romans who are praised by the mouth of the Apostle."

But we reply: The status of the Roman Church at the time of Jerome was different than it was in the times that followed.

(2) The saying of Cyprian in Epistle 57[15]. "As with you there is one spirit and one voice, the entire Roman Church has confessed. Dearest brothers, the faith which the blessed Apostle predicted about you has become evident, and as he attests your merits by a proclamation of things to come, in praising the parents he was inspiring the children."

We reply: He praises them because they remained constant in faith at the time of the persecution of Decius. He does not predict that they will always remain such. Rather, in the controversy concerning the rebaptizing of those who had been baptized by heretics, Cyprian does not concur with the Roman Church.

(3) The saying of Chrysostom on this passage: "Paul did not say 'is being manifested,' but that your faith 'is being announced,'

---

15 Actually found in Epistle 56.

making it clear that nothing was being added to or subtracted from his sayings."

We reply: He affirms that nothing was being added to or subtracted from that doctrine which Paul and Peter had passed on to the Romans. But he does not at all predict, nor was he even able to predict, that the Romans would always do this.

(4) The saying of Irenaeus in Bk. 3, *Against Heresies*, ch. 3: "He teaches that the truth of the faith and of the apostolic tradition was to be sought from the Roman Church, as from a womb."

We reply: Irenaeus is not referring to the Roman Church alone, but to the Churches founded by the Apostles in general. "The Church in Ephesus," he says, "a Church that was indeed founded by Paul, is a witness to the true tradition of the Apostles."

v.9 Μάρτυς γάρ μού ἐστιν ὁ Θεός, ᾧ λατρεύω ἐν τῷ πνεύματί μου ἐν τῷ εὐαγγελίῳ τοῦ Υἱοῦ αὐτοῦ, ὡς ἀδιαλείπτως μνείαν ὑμῶν ποιοῦμαι,

v.9 For God is my witness, whom I serve with my spirit in the gospel of his Son, that without ceasing I make mention of you always in my prayers; (KJV)

The second part of the introduction, in which he explains his most fervent desire to visit them. This affection was the motivating cause that moved Paul to give thanks to God for the faith of the Romans.

The ministers of the Church ought to serve God *in spirit*, that is, with serious zeal and with their whole effort, without hypocrisy or deceit, with sincere eagerness and cheerfulness of spirit.

We observe: There is a twofold worship of God—the inner worship that takes place in Spirit and truth, and the external worship that takes place by external work, which is the only kind that the hypocrites pursue, having overlooked the inner kind. But Paul served God, both with inner worship—by true faith and invocation—and with external worship, namely, by preaching the Gospel.

I serve God ἐν πνεύματί [in spirit]. This is in contrast to (1) Jewish ceremonies, and (2) hypocrites. Thus we are enjoined to call upon God in spirit and in truth (John 4:23).

Ἀδιαλείπτως [unceasingly]. The Apostle uses the same word in 1 The. 5:16, where he exhorts the godly to pour out prayers without ceasing. But an absolute continuation of uninterrupted time is not understood by this, nor is a perpetual act of prayer intended, but rather a constant attention and devotion of the believing and persevering mind is called for—a mind that does not murmur out of a lack of faith in God, but follows Him patiently and commends its whole self to Him and expects help from Him. For thus Christ explains in Luke 18:1 that "it is necessary to pray at all times and not give up." The Syriac on this passage translates "without resting."

v.10 πάντοτε ἐπὶ τῶν προσευχῶν μου δεόμενος εἴ πως ἤδη ποτὲ εὐοδωθήσομαι ἐν τῷ θελήματι τοῦ Θεοῦ ἐλθεῖν πρὸς ὑμᾶς.

v.10 *Making request, if by any means now at length I might have a prosperous journey by the will of God to come unto you. (KJV)*

There are some who make the following distinction between δέησις [entreaty] and προσευχή [prayer], that δέησις is a prayer in which we ask for the things that we need or that we lack; προσευχή is a direct prayer to God in which we wish for something. The Syriac has the emphatic verb מֶתְחַנַּן, which means "to plead for the mercy of God."

Some claim that δέησις is a prayer to ward off evil, while προσευχαί are prayers in which good things that are necessary for salvation are also solicited from God. But it is clear that this distinction cannot always be made, nor does it hold true in this passage.

Εἴ πως ἤδη ποτὲ εὐοδωθήσομαι [if somehow, at some time, I will be granted a pleasant journey], "that a prosperous journey may befall me at length, that I may be successful, etc." The Syriac: "If a way may be opened to me at length, by God's will, that I may come to you."

Observe that the godly depend on God alone, even in all outward actions, and keep His providence in view.

v.11 Ἐπιποθῶ γὰρ ἰδεῖν ὑμᾶς ἵνα τι μεταδῶ χάρισμα ὑμῖν πνευματικὸν εἰς τὸ στηριχθῆναι ὑμᾶς,

v.11 For I long to see you, that I may impart unto you some spiritual gift, to the end ye may be established; (KJV)

The third part of the introduction, in which he explains the final cause of his desire.

Ἐπιποθεῖν means to have a singular desire. The Syriac translates, "I well desire," that is, intensely.

With χάρισμα πνευματικὸν [spiritual gift] he understands the doctrine, the consolation, the exhortation, as he explains in the following verse. Syriac: "The gift of the Spirit." Likewise, with an increase in faith and in the knowledge of the mysteries of God. Thus it says in Rom. 15:29 that he would come "with the full blessing of the Gospel."

Εἰς τὸ στηριχθῆναι ὑμᾶς [in order to establish you]. The Syriac translates, הֲבָ, "through which gift," or "through which Spirit you may be confirmed." The relative can have both meanings.

v.12 τοῦτο δέ ἐστι, συμπαρακληθῆναι ἐν ὑμῖν διὰ τῆς ἐν ἀλλήλοις πίστεως ὑμῶν τε καὶ ἐμοῦ.

v.12 That is, that I may be comforted together with you by the mutual faith both of you and me. (KJV)

He softens what he had said, that he wants to confirm the Romans with some spiritual gift, lest he should arrogate to himself the whole power of the Holy Spirit, or lest he should seem to hold in contempt those who had instructed the Romans. He therefore says that he wants to receive some spiritual gift from them no less than he wants to confer it on them. Chrysostom maintains that "he is tacitly suppressing the haughtiness of the Romans as he insinuates that they lack his instruction and admonitions."

When the Apostle speaks about the Romans alone in the preceding verses, he uses the word στηριχθῆναι [to establish]. But when he includes himself also, he uses the word συμπαρακληθῆναι [to be encouraged together]. In the former case, he points to "confirmation," and in the latter, "mutual consolation." The sense, therefore, is that the Romans were to be confirmed in faith by the arrival of Paul, whereas Paul would receive mutual comfort from their confirmed faith, for he denies that he had received the faith from man. But even though the Apostle had received the faith through direct revelation with regard to both knowledge and assent, nothing prevents him from being able to increase his faith from the mutual conversation with the godly with regard to confidence.

It consoles the minister most if he sees that his hearers are constant in the faith and growing in it daily. In turn, it also consoles the hearers if they see and hear their teacher in person.

v.13 Οὐ θέλω δὲ ὑμᾶς ἀγνοεῖν, ἀδελφοί, ὅτι πολλάκις προεθέμην ἐλθεῖν πρὸς ὑμᾶς (καὶ ἐκωλύθην ἄχρι τοῦ δεῦρο), ἵνα καρπὸν τινὰ σχῶ καὶ ἐν ὑμῖν, καθὼς καὶ ἐν τοῖς λοιποῖς ἔθνεσιν.

v.13 Now I would not have you ignorant, brethren, that oftentimes I purposed to come unto you, (but was let hitherto,) that I might have some fruit among you also, even as among other Gentiles. (KJV)

He responds to the tacit objection as to why he had not yet come, if indeed he had such a burning desire to visit the Romans, namely, that he has been impeded. Then he repeats the first reason given above why he wants to come to them, namely, that he may convert some of them, or that he may confirm the converted.

The Syriac: "I want you to know, my brothers, that at times," that is, on many occasions, "I wanted to come to you."

There are some who want this impediment in his journey to be imposed by God, who preferred to use his service in some other way (Acts 16:6, Rom. 15:20). But others want it to be imposed by Satan, who begrudges the Romans the presence of Paul (1 The. 2:18). But the certainty of this can hardly be determined, since it is not revealed.

"That I may have some fruit," by confirming the believers in the faith and by leading the unbelievers to faith. For this is the fruit of evangelical preaching.

v.14 Ἕλλησί τε καὶ βαρβάροις, σοφοῖς τε καὶ ἀνοήτοις ὀφειλέτης εἰμί.

v.14 I am debtor both to the Greeks, and to the Barbarians; both to the wise, and to the unwise. (KJV)

He expresses the motivating cause of his desire, and actually, the second reason why he aspires to come to them, that he may educate them also. Inasmuch as he was an Apostle, he was obligated by divine mandate to teach Jews and Gentiles.

The Syriac changes the distinction made in the Greek, for it combines the words that appear prior to this verse with verse 13, and inserts a sort of paraphrase: "For I am a debtor to every man, that I may preach."

He is called a βάρβαρος [Barbarian] who speaks with a vicious or harsh tongue, that is, stammering or stuttering or uncivilized. The Greeks judged all to be such who are outside of Greece, as is clear from Strabo, who says as much in these words from Bk. 14: "Since the Greeks observed this defect in foreign tongues, they took to calling them βαρβάρους [Barbarians] as an insult, as if they were thick-tongued or harsh-tongued. But eventually they called by this name everyone who used a different speech than they."

Indeed, they wrote: "When foreigners come to Athens and learn the Greek language, and then attempt to say something in Greek, they usually stumble over this word βάρβαι ("barbai"), which is why, afterwards, those who were ignorant of the Greek language were called Barbarians."

Paul, who up to this point had spent time among the Greeks and was writing these things from Greece, follows the Greek custom and contrasts the Barbarians with the Greeks, in which sense even the Romans themselves were Barbarians.

Just as the Hebrews call the other nations לֹעֵז (Psa. 114:1), so the Greeks call the other peoples *Barbarians*. לֹעֵז is every language

50

that is not Hebrew. The Chaldean dictionary renders the Hebrew word לוֹעֵז with בַּרְבָּיַר (*barbarai*), which is why some think the word βάρβαρος [Barbarian] was formed from the Chaldean noun בַּרְבָּרִי (*barbarai*), which means "alien, foreign, unknown," from בַּר (*bar*), "outside," repeated by doubling. But in 1 Cor. 14:11, he is called a Barbarian who has a foreign and unknown language, in which sense also Ovid, when he was living in exile at sea, sings:

Here I am a Barbarian, for I understand no one.

"To the wise and to the foolish, etc." There are some who state that this latter member is explanatory of the first, since the Greeks wanted to be considered wise, while they held that the Barbarian nations should be looked down upon as foolish. But nothing prevents this from being understood in a general way, since among the Barbarians there were wise people, and among the Greeks there were foolish.

Ὀφειλέτης εἰμί [I am a debtor]. He has in view the Apostolate that was divinely entrusted to him, for he was obligated by reason of his calling to preach the Gospel (1 Cor. 9:16). Because of this, the Syriac adds that very thing.

Observe: No one is so wise that he has nothing to learn from the Word of God.

v.15 Οὕτω (τὸ κατ᾽ ἐμὲ) πρόθυμον, καὶ ὑμῖν τοῖς ἐν Ῥώμῃ εὐαγγελίσασθαι.

v.15 *So, as much as in me is, I am ready to preach the gospel to you that are at Rome also. (KJV)*

Whatever is in me—that is ready and willing also to preach the Gospel to you. I have not refused to preach also to you.

The Syriac has the verb מֶתְחַפַּט, "I was solicitous, I gave care," so that, in addition to a ready will, zeal may also be included.

v.16 Οὐ γὰρ ἐπαισχύνομαι τὸ εὐαγγέλιον τοῦ Χριστοῦ, δύναμις γὰρ Θεοῦ ἐστιν εἰς σωτηρίαν παντὶ τῷ πιστεύοντι, Ἰουδαίῳ τε πρῶτον καὶ Ἕλληνι.

v.16 For I am not ashamed of the gospel of Christ: for it is the power of God unto salvation to every one that believeth; to the Jew first, and also to the Greek. (KJV)

The third reason why he wishes to come to them and teach them is the excellence of the evangelical doctrine, of which he was made an Apostle.

The Syriac: "I do not blush on account of the Gospel," that is, I am not ashamed of the Gospel. Tertullian in Bk. 5, *Against Marcion,* ch. 13: "I am not ashamed of the Gospel."

The Vulgate translation of this passage omits the name "Christ," even though it is emphatic. It is "the Gospel of Christ" (1) because of the efficient cause, since it was revealed through Christ (John 1:18); (2) because of the object, since it deals with Christ and His benefits.

The δύναμις Θεοῦ [power of God] is the divine and efficacious means which God uses to save men, (1) because in it the benefits obtained by the suffering and death of Christ are offered, among which are also life and eternal salvation; (2) because through the preaching of the Gospel, God works the faith in hearts through which they embrace the good things offered in the Gospel and apply them to themselves; (3) because through the Gospel faith is preserved and increased, so that we are thus "guarded for salvation by the power of God, through faith" (1 Pet. 1:5); (4) because, in all adversities and temptations, it furnishes a life-giving consolation, so that we may be preserved to eternal life under the weight of the cross.

Cornelius a Lapide on this passage: "Neither the spoken Word itself, nor the Scripture of the Gospel, but preaching and faith, or rather the thing preached through the Gospel, namely, the death, merits, Sacraments, precepts and promises of Christ, are the strength and power of God through which He powerfully works salvation in believers, that is, faith, righteousness and life."

We reply: (1) It is full of vice—this contrast between the spoken Word of the Gospel and preaching. For what else is the preached

Gospel than the spoken Word itself of the Gospel? What else is the written Gospel than the Scripture of the Gospel? (2) This thing that is preached is attributed to the Gospel, not with regard to the external sound or of the letters, but with regard to the inner sense. At the same time, neither should the spoken Word be separated from the preached Gospel, nor should the Scripture be separated from the written Gospel. (3) This analysis is worthless—that the Gospel, that is, faith, is the power of God through which He works faith—unless by the word *faith* the doctrine is understood, which is the Gospel itself. (4) It is one thing to speak about the Gospel; it is another thing to speak of the benefits of which the Gospel is the vehicle; and it is another thing to speak of the object which is shown to us in the Gospel, which is the death of Christ.

Schwenkfeld says that "with the word *Gospel*, Christ Himself is to be understood, the essential Word of God, since the Apostle speaks there of such a Gospel to which the essential characteristic of God, namely, power, pertains."

We reply: (1) The Gospel is the preaching about Christ, but the Gospel is not Christ Himself. (2) Never in all of Scripture is the word *Gospel* understood of Christ with regard to essence. (3) Paul had said in the preceding verse that he is eager to preach the Gospel also to the Romans; then he says of that same Gospel, "for it is the power of God, etc." (4) He notably calls it "the Gospel of Christ." Therefore, it is not Christ Himself. (5) In v.9 he says that he serves God in the Gospel of His Son, and in vv. 1 and 3, that he has been set apart for the Gospel concerning the Son of God. Therefore, that Gospel of which he says that it is "the power of God for salvation," is distinct from Christ Himself, about whom the Gospel preaches. (6) In the preached Gospel there are two things: the external sound and the inner sense. In the written Gospel there are likewise two things: the external characters and the inner sense. When the Gospel is called "the power of God for salvation," then this power of God is being proclaimed concerning the Gospel, not with regard to the external sound, or the external characters, but with regard to the inner sense. (7) Nor is it called "the power of God" in that sense in which Christ Himself is called "the strength of God" (1 Cor.

1:24), namely, because He is the essential and hypostatic strength of God; but because, with regard to the divine sense, it has divine power attached to it, which exerts itself in preaching, reading and meditation for the conversion, illumination, vivification and salvation of men.

Ambrose on this passage: "The Apostolic preaching is the power of God that invites to faith and gives salvation to every believer, even as it forgives sins and justifies, so that he cannot be detained by the second death and is marked by the mystery of the cross, for the preaching of the cross of Christ is the evidence that death has been conquered."

Cornelius a Lapide on this passage: "Faith works salvation, not by itself alone and directly, but through the hope, repentance, good works and Sacraments to which it drives a man."

We reply: Faith is not considered here as bare knowledge and assent, but as the confident grasping of the merit of Christ. And since faith alone has the power to grasp this, for that reason, also in this respect, justification and salvation are attributed to it alone.

Cornelius a Lapide on this passage: "This sentence of the Apostle can also be extended to the salvation of the body, for it is generally true. For the Gospel is a power and instrumental cause of salvation and life, not only for the future life, but also the present life—and that, not only by the spoken word, but also by the written word, etc. And from this arises the custom of the faithful in which they wear and carry about the Gospel of Saint John to ward off poisonings, hexes, illnesses and other detriments."

Salmeron in Vol. 4, *Commentaries*, p. 614: "It is customary for Christians to wear the Gospel or other sacred things or relics as a necklace. Nor is this wrong, as long as they are worn with hope, for perhaps God will be merciful."

We reply: (1) Cornelius himself submits: "But the Apostle is not properly speaking of bodily salvation here, but of spiritual." Therefore it cannot be elicited from this passage that wearing the Gospel leads to bodily salvation. (2) A little earlier Cornelius had written

54

what he afterwards repeats, that "the Apostle is not speaking about the Scripture, but about the preaching of the Gospel." Therefore it cannot be proved from this passage that wearing the written Gospel is a cause of bodily salvation. (3) The Holy Spirit never testifies in the revealed Word that He wishes to remove poisonings and illnesses by carrying about the written Gospel. It is, therefore, superstition. (4) The syllogism which Cornelius asserts from Thomas (2.2., q. 96, art. 4) begs the question when he reasons: "The Word of God does not have less efficacy than the relics of the saints. But we use relics for salvation. Therefore, in a similar fashion, it is all the more permissible to use the written Word of God or the Gospel."

(5) When Augustine says in Treatise 7 on John, that "if you have a headache, we approve it if you place the Gospel near your body rather than running immediately to the amulet," he is speaking, not absolutely, but relatively. For he immediately adds: "The infirmity of men is prone to this, and those men are to be mourned who run to amulets. We may rejoice that, when we see a man lying on his bed, tormented by fevers and pains, he places the Gospel at his head. This indicates that he has not placed his hope anywhere else. We do not rejoice that it was done for this purpose, but we do rejoice because the Gospel was preferred to amulets. Therefore, although it is placed at the head so that it may calm his headache, it is not placed at the heart that he may be healed from sins. Very well, then. What should be done? Let him place it at his heart, that his heart may be healed."

(6) Chrysostom, in Homily 43 on 1 Corinth,[16] refutes this superstition: "Isn't the Gospel read in Church daily and heard by all? To whom is there no benefit when the Gospels are placed in their ears? But how can the Gospels save when they are hung around the neck? Where, indeed, is the power of the Gospel—in the form of the letters or in the understanding of the senses? If in the form of the letters, then they should well be hung around the neck. But if in the understanding, then they are better placed in the heart than hung around the neck."

---

16 Gerhard adds a note here: *Autor imperf. oper. hom. 43*

Ἰουδαίῳ τε πρῶτον καὶ Ἕλληνι [to Jew first and to Greek]. The particle καὶ [and] in this passage means the same thing as "then" or "secondly," as is gathered from the word πρῶτον [first].

Adam Conzenius on this passage: "If the Gospel only reveals that the sins that remain are not imputed, it is not the power of God. For the power or strength in it is that sins should be conquered, an evil will should be changed, the Old Man should die, the New Man should be born."

We reply: (1) The Gospel is the strength of God, because through it God kindles faith in our hearts (John 17:20, Luke 4:32, 1 Cor. 1:21, Rom. 10:17, 1 Pet. 1:23, James 1:21), through which the righteousness of Christ revealed in the Gospel is imputed to us. (2) From hearing the Gospel we receive the Holy Spirit (Gal. 3:2), who renews our hearts. But since this renewal is imperfect in this life, it does not justify before God.

v.17 Δικαιοσύνη γὰρ Θεοῦ ἐν αὐτῷ ἀποκαλύπτεται ἐκ πίστεως εἰς πίστιν, καθὼς γέγραπται· Ὁ δὲ δίκαιος ἐκ πίστεως ζήσεται.

v.17 For therein is the righteousness of God revealed from faith to faith: as it is written, The just shall live by faith. (KJV)

This is a declaration and confirmation of the preceding assertion, explaining how the Gospel is power for salvation, namely, because through it God not only makes known, but also offers and furnishes in the thing itself free justification by faith. Yet at the same time it explains the principal proposition of the entire Epistle, as a favorable opportunity presents itself at the end of the introduction. This principal proposition is that there is no other way to be justified before God except by faith in Christ, whom the Gospel sets before us, as confirmed by the prophetic testimony.

From the particle γὰρ [for], some wish to conclude that the Gospel is called the power of God for salvation only with regard to its manifestation, namely, because it manifests to us Christ the Savior, who has been made to us righteousness from God (1 Cor. 1:30). But the inclusion of the one does not mean the exclusion of the other. The Gospel is the power of God for salvation, not only with regard to manifestation, but also with regard to operation, since it is the salutary and efficacious instrument through which God works faith in the hearts of men for their salvation (Rom. 10:17). The former is a matter of learning; the latter, a matter of doing. For this reason the Apostle himself mentions faith in this passage.

Some assert that that which comes before is understood from that which follows. Righteousness is revealed in the Gospel, that is, it is furnished and supplied by the thing itself. Thomas on this passage: "This righteousness is indeed revealed in the Gospel, inasmuch as men are justified by faith in the Gospel." Lombard on this passage: "The Gospel reveals this righteousness by the effect itself, namely in that it gives man the faith through which he is justified."

The righteousness of God that is revealed in the Gospel is not "the essential righteousness of God," as Osiander wants; nor is the word *righteousness* understood in this passage as "distributive righteousness," as Origen wants; nor as "promise," as Ambrose wants; nor as "mercy," as Chrysostom wants; nor as "satisfaction," as Theodoret wants; nor as "the habitual or actual righteousness of works," as the Papists want. But rather, as the Apostle himself explains in this very verse and in chapter 3:22, it is understood as "the righteousness of faith."

Augustine in *On the Spirit and the Letter,* ch. 9: "The righteousness of God is divine righteousness, not Jewish righteousness, not philosophical righteousness. In other words, it is that righteousness by which God justifies us through Christ, and that actually makes us righteous in the eyes of God."

Luther in the preface to his works, near the end: "I have been seized with a surprising ardor to understand the word "righteousness" in the writings of Paul and others. There I have begun to understand righteousness as that by which the righteous lives by the gift of God, namely, by faith; and I understand this to be the sense, namely, that through the Gospel the righteousness of God is revealed—that is, a passive righteousness, in that the merciful God justifies us by faith. In this I have felt myself to be entirely reborn."

It is called "the righteousness of God": (1) Because God decreed in His eternal counsel to justify men in no other way but by faith in Christ. (2) Because He has revealed it in the Word of the Gospel, as the Apostle testifies concerning it in this passage. (3) Because Christ, true God, obtained it by His suffering and death, whence the Syriac notably calls it the righteousness רֵאלָהָא "of God Himself." (4) Because God gives it to man for free, by imputing the righteousness of Christ, whence it is called in chapter 5:15 "the gift of God." (5) Because it stands firm in the judgment of God, and God considers it to be fixed, as Luther translates in this passage: "*die für GOtt gilt* [that avails before God]." Thus John 6:29 has "the work of God," that is, the work that is acceptable to Him. (6) Because it is contrasted with human and Pharisaical righteousness.

Ἀποκαλύπτεται [is revealed]. With respect to (1) human reason, from which this righteousness and this manner of being justified is plainly hidden; (2) the Old Testament figures of speech, for it is set forth clearly and perspicuously in the New Testament without types and figures of speech (Is. 56:1, Rom. 3:21).

Ἐκ πίστεως εἰς πίστιν [from faith unto faith]. Augustine in *On the Spirit and the Letter,* ch. 11: "From the faith of the preachers to the faith of the hearers." Theodoret and Oecum.: "From faith in the past things in Christ to faith in the future things in us." Anselm explains this passage in three ways: "(1) From faith in the one God to faith in the Trinity. (2) From faith in the first advent of Christ to save, to faith in His second advent to judge. (3) From faith in the humanity of Christ to faith in His divinity."

But none of these explanations agrees sufficiently with the text. The same judgment is made with regard to the explanation of Bede: "From faith that is here obscure, to faith—that is, to clear vision—in heaven."

(1) There are, in addition, some who think that it has in view the consonance of both Testaments in testifying about this righteousness. Clement of Alexandria, Bk. 2, *Stromata*: "*From faith to faith.* The one faith brought to completion, from the prophecies to the Gospel, through one and the same Lord." The sense, then,

would be this: The Gospel saves for this reason, because even long ago in Old Testament times, it taught people to believe that Christ would come, and now it teaches people to believe that the Christ has already been provided. Origen, Chrysostom, Theodoret: "From the obscure faith of the Old Testament to the clear faith of the New Testament, to which the former leads us."

Augustine: "From the faith of the Prophets to the faith of the Apostles; from the faith that was obscure and latent in the Old Testament to the faith that has been manifested and revealed in the New Testament; from faith in things past to faith in things to come." Bede in *Collectanea*: "From a faith of words, in that we now believe what we do not see, to a faith of things, in that, in eternity, we will obtain what we now believe."

Yet (1) when it is said that "a man is justified by faith," that faith is to be understood as the faith that someone has, not that he does not have. Therefore, it is not understood as the faith of the things that are announced, the faith of the Prophets, etc. (2) A true faith is understood, therefore not an unformed or dead faith. (3) Therefore, both perseverance and an increase of faith are meant.

(2) Some maintain that it means that the Old Testament Fathers had the same righteousness by which they were justified before God as we have in the New Testament, namely, the righteousness of faith (Acts 15:11).

(3) Some want to insinuate "that the Gospel, in which the righteousness of faith is revealed, teaches that our faith increases little by little, and that it goes from a lesser faith to a greater faith" (cf. Clement of Alexandria, Bk. 5. *Stromata*, 2 Cor. 3, the last verse; Rom. 6:20). Cornelius a Lapide on this passage gives the most suitable explanation: "From an incipient and imperfect faith to a proficient faith, perfected and formed by love." But the Scriptures know nothing about a faith that is formed by love or perfected gradually.

(4) Some think that this is said because of the relationship between the faith (or the truth) of the God who promises, and the faith of the man who receives the good things offered in the Gospel.

Ambrose on this passage: "Righteousness is revealed from the faith of the God who promises to the faith of the one who believes, since, to the believer, God appears righteous, while to the unbeliever who denies that God is speaking the truth, He appears unjust."

(5) Some want to understand it with regard to a continuous act of faith, so that the sense should be this: In the matter of justification, only faith rules, and the righteousness of God is revealed from faith to faith, that is, from faith alone, just as we are said (2 Cor. 3:18) to be transformed from glory into glory, where that anadiplosis signifies perpetuity and continuity. In this way also the phrases "from power to power, from age to age" are used in the Scriptures. Nothing in these explanations is at odds with the analogy of faith, although the last one seems to agree most closely with the text.

Cornelius a Lapide gathers the following from the prophetic text in which liberation is promised to the Israelites through Cyrus: "The Prophet is speaking about the faith whereby we believe God in any matter. The Prophet's assertion is applied to faith in Christ, because true faith is that which God has confirmed and instituted. But God has already confirmed that true faith is faith in Christ the Redeemer. It is also applied to Christ because the faith concerning Cyrus was an allegorical representation of faith concerning Christ."

"The righteous shall live by faith." This statement is taken from Hab. 2:4, where it is predicted that, in the devastation that was to be inflicted on the people of Israel by the Chaldeans, there would be a disparity in the condition of the godly (that is, believers) and the ungodly (that is, unbelievers). The ungodly would vanish like a bubble because of their distrust toward God and the vain confidence they placed in human protection; the godly, on the other hand, would live by faith, by which they know that they have a propitious God. That is to say, they would thoroughly delight in a true and life-giving consolation.

The Apostle accommodates this as a general statement belonging to the doctrine of the Gospel, which is the doctrine of faith, because the faith that sustains us in affliction first requires the gracious remission of sins and reconciliation with God before this statement can be apprehended by that faith.

The occasion and purpose of this statement can be specific, while the statement itself may be general. The Prophet demonstrates how they are able to sustain themselves in any temptations and calamities and how they can be at peace in the midst of the waves, namely, by a true and singular faith in the Messiah. They know that they are justified and placed in a state of grace with God by this faith, and so they endure and, indeed, look down with scorn at all adversities with great courage. Consequently, he admonishes the Israelites, specifically with regard to the terrible things that were to be inflicted by the Chaldeans, to sustain themselves by faith. Most properly, therefore, what was stated in general by the Prophet, the Apostle applies specifically to the special office of faith. He demonstrates that, just as in physical tribulations, so also—and much more so—in spiritual tribulations and temptations of eternal death which a man feels that he has deserved because of his sins, "no one is able to live." That is, no one is able to be sustained, to endure and to delight thoroughly in life-giving consolation, unless he has been justified by faith in the Messiah. In addition, liberation had been promised through Cyrus as a type of the liberation to be expected from Christ.

Therefore, Cornelius a Lapide properly writes on this passage: "The Holy Spirit means to use Cyrus and the liberation of Cyrus as a representation of Christ and the redemption of Christ, in that Christ bestows on His faithful life, righteousness, grace and glory, to the point that, in Christ, this sentence is absolutely true: 'The righteous lives by faith in Christ.'"

And afterwards: "Although Habakkuk applies this sentence literally to the Jews who were held captive in Babylon, with God promising the believers that Cyrus would free them, nevertheless he offers it as a general statement and as a sort of common axiom or proverb, which is then rightly applied by Paul also to Christians."

The Greeks very properly render the particle ב on some occasions with ἐκ or ἐξ [from] (Deu. 6:5, Mark 12:30, Luke 10:27), which is how the Apostle also translates it in citing this prophetic saying, both in this passage and in Gal. 3:11 and Heb. 10:38. At times he uses διὰ with the genitive, that is, "through," Deu. 32:21, Psa. 78:2, John 1:4, Acts 17:27, Phil. 4:13. At times, when he denotes an instrument, he simply uses the ablative case. Therefore, we may conclude that, in this article, it has the same force in Paul's writings whether he says ἐκ πίστεως, διὰ πίστεως, or πίστει, Rom. 3:18,22,26, etc. (cf. Buxtorf, Bk. 2, *Thesaurus Grammaticus.*, ch. 13, p. 444, and ch. 20, p. 514.)

The future ζήσεται [he will live] does not exclude the present. For based on the Hebrew idiom, he uses a future in a general statement as a continuous present, and means not only what is to come, but what always was, is and will be, and what should perpetually occur. Psa. 1:1-2, "he shall meditate," that is, he meditates continually. Hosea 1:2, "it shall commit fornication," that is, it shall remain in continual prostitution.

Ribera makes the following comment on this passage: "It is often the custom of Scripture to make use of a difference of tense, by which it signifies a certain permanence and duration of the matter under discussion, Is. 24:22."

Buxtorf, Bk. 1, *Thesaurus Grammaticus*, ch. 12: "The Hebrews technically do not have a present tense, and so, at times, they indicate a present meaning through the use of the participle. At other times, in general statements, they indicate a present meaning using the preterit and the future, when the meaning is not what was or will be, but what should perpetually be or happen."

Aben Ezra on Psalm 1:1: "When they want to speak of a static time, that is, a present tense, they use a preterit or a future."

On this basis it is easy to respond to the corruptions of this statement. Bellarmine, in Bk. 1, *On Justification*, ch. 16, argues: "The Prophet is not speaking of a life of righteousness, but of a life of hope which causes the righteous to wait patiently, or a hope that is commended, from which the life of the righteous makes a beginning."

However, (1) the Apostle in this passage expressly accommodates the prophetic saying to the life of righteousness by faith.

(2) From justifying faith, hope also arises through which we live in the midst of dangers. In other words, we patiently wait, certain of the presence and aid of God. But it should not be inferred from that that spiritual life does not happen to us through faith.

(3) The opposite, rather, must be inferred from this. For unless we are certain by faith that we have been reconciled to God and have obtained the remission of sins for Christ's sake, we cannot have a quiet spirit in the midst of dangers and adversities.

(4) The matter itself demonstrates that through faith we become partakers of spiritual life. Christ is life (John 11:25, 14:6.) Therefore, he who believes in Christ has life (John 3:16 and 36, 1 John 5:11 and 12.) "I live by faith in the Son of God," says the Apostle in Gal. 2:20. "To me, to live is Christ" (Phil 1:21). "Christ is our life," (Col. 3:3). Therefore, spiritual life not only makes a beginning from faith, being afterwards perfected with love, but "the righteous lives by faith." That is, by believing in Christ, he has eternal life.

(5) Augustine speaks to this on Psalm 93: "There is no other righteousness of man in this life except to live by faith." Luther on Genesis 48, Vol. 4, f. 192: "The power of faith is so great that it makes us alive from the dead. And right at that very hour in which we begin to believe and grasp the Word, we also begin to live with eternal life, since the Word of the Lord remains for eternity, etc."

(6) Thomas himself writes thus in 2.2, q.12, art. 1: "Faith is the life of the soul. Just as, when bodily life is taken away, all the members and parts of a man withdraw from their due order, so when the life of righteousness is taken away, which is through faith, disorder appears in all acts."

Ribera, writing on on Hab. 2:16, recognizes that "the Apostle here is dealing with the life of grace, which happens to no one except by faith in Christ."

Cornelius a Lapide on this passage: "Habakkuk is speaking not of the life of the body, but of the soul; not of natural life, but of supernatural, namely, of grace and righteousness, by which the righteous, insofar as he is righteous, lives. For he contrasts these two things, namely, to live, which he attributes to the righteous and faithful, and not to have a right soul, or to displease God, which he attributes to the unbelieving and unrighteous."

Adam Conzenius on this passage: "The righteous will live by faith. In other words, faith is the gift of God by which we assent to all the mysteries revealed by God. Our life proceeds from this faith as from a beginning, a root, and a pattern. From the same faith already formed and working through love, the life of the righteous remains and is perfected."

Cornelius a Lapide on this passage: "The life of grace by which the righteous lives begins from faith alone; it grows and is perfected by faith, yet not alone, but growing into a living faith of grace and love, by observing the commandments, so that you do those things that faith demands. Just as Prov. 4:23 says, 'life proceeds from the heart,' that is, man lives from the heart and draws life out of it, namely, because the heart is the root of life. Yet in saying this, the rest are not excluded—brain, lungs, liver, stomach, etc., as if man did not also live and draw his life from them. So likewise it is said that the righteous lives by faith, since faith is the beginning, root, and, in a sense, the heart of the spiritual life of grace. Yet in saying this, neither hope nor the other virtues are excluded, as if the righteous did not also live by them."

We reply: (1) The cause and the effects of spiritual life are being confused. Faith is the cause of spiritual life, because it grasps Christ as the efficient and meritorious cause of spiritual life; or, to say the same thing in another way, Christ is grasped by faith, and the righteousness of Christ that is grasped by faith is our spiritual life. Good works are the effects and signs of spiritual life.

(2) Therefore, as in a man, the brain, lungs and liver are naturally alive, yet nevertheless, life does not proceed from them, but rather from the heart as the source of life, so also the whole man becomes a partaker of spiritual life. And there are many new and

spiritual motives in the regenerated man, while the spiritual life actually proceeds from faith alone as the source and origin.

(3) Spiritual life does not only arise from faith, but also continues through the same, which is why the Prophet here uses the verb in the future tense, "The righteous will live by faith."

(4) Love neither effects nor perfects that spiritual life, but arises from it and bears witness to it externally. 1 John 3:14: "We know that we have been transferred from death to life, because we love the brothers." The Apostle does not say, "We have been transferred from death to life because we love," but, "We know that we have been transferred." Therefore, love is not the cause of spiritual life, but the effect and sign of it.

(5) Cornelius himself admits: "Habakkuk and the Apostle are speaking both about the beginning of spiritual life and about the increase of righteousness and spiritual life, since this statement, 'the righteous lives by faith,' is general and universal, pertaining both to Jews and to Christians, both to sinners when they are first justified, and to those who have already been justified. For the spiritual life of each of them begins, is preserved, and grows by faith."

And afterward: "When in Hebrew it is said that 'the righteous will live in his faith,' the 'his' signifies both the initial cause and the life that is preserved. For the sense is that 'the righteous goes on living in his faith, even as he begins to live in it.'"

Costerus in *Enchiridion*, p. 197: "'The righteous lives by faith' seems to mean nothing other than that the righteous conforms his entire life to the rule of faith, and is guided by it. As we are wont to say, 'a person lives medicinally,' that is, by the prescription of medicine."

We reply: (1) The Apostle proves from this prophetic testimony that a man lives by faith, that is, that he is justified before God by faith, without works, as he later explains in chapter 3:28. The explanation of Costerus is opposed to this purpose.

(2) One must distinguish between the faith of the Scriptures

which one believes, and the faith of the heart by which one believes. And the doctrine of faith revealed in the Gospel must not be confused with the rule of good works prescribed in the Decalogue.

(3) The alleged comparison does not fit, for the manner of speaking is different. The Prophet does not say, "The righteous lives faithfully," but "lives by faith." It is one thing to live medicinally and another thing to live by medicine.

(4) Not only the manner of speaking is different, but also the manner of living. We live a "medicinal life" by doing, when, through certain works properly performed according to a prescription of medicine, we acquire and maintain a soundness of body. We live with a life of righteousness by believing, yet we neither prepare nor maintain for ourselves the salvation of the soul through works. Faith does not prescribe the works through which we acquire eternal life. Instead, faith sets forth Christ the Mediator, and by believing in Him we have eternal life (John 20:31).

v.18 Ἀποκαλύπτεται γὰρ ὀργὴ Θεοῦ ἀπ᾽ οὐρανοῦ ἐπὶ πᾶσαν ἀσέβειαν καὶ ἀδικίαν ἀνθρώπων τῶν τὴν ἀλήθειαν ἐν ἀδικίᾳ κατεχόντων.

v.18 For the wrath of God is revealed from heaven against all ungodliness and unrighteousness of men, who hold the truth in unrighteousness; (KJV)

Here begins the first part of the Epistle, which convicts all men of sin on the basis of the Law, from which it readily follows that no one can be justified before God by works of the Law.

He beautifully connects this preaching of the Law with the preceding proposition concerning the gracious justification through faith. It was necessary for the righteousness of faith to be revealed in the Gospel, because the wrath of God, who damns all men on account of sin, is revealed in the Law. He demonstrates this connection with the causal particle γὰρ [for].

The aim of the Apostle is to demonstrate that both Gentiles and Jews are accused and damned as sinners by the divine law. He demonstrates this concerning the Gentiles, beginning in this verse and continuing to the end of the chapter. He demonstrates the same thing concerning the Jews in chapter 2.

The principal syllogism of the Apostle is this: It behooves those who want to be justified through the Law and the works of the Law to obey the Law fully and continually, and to have such a heart and all the powers of the soul as the Law requires. But no one fulfills the Law perfectly. On the contrary, everyone transgresses it, if not with an external work, then certainly with the inner uncleanness of the heart. Therefore.

The Apostle proves the minor premise by sufficient enumeration: All men are included in the scope of Gentiles and Jews. But neither the Gentiles nor the Jews obey the law perfectly. Therefore.

He proves the minor premise concerning the Gentiles, whom he accuses in this chapter. First, because they neither inquired further after the true God to the extent that He is known by the light of nature, nor did they honor Him as they ought. Instead, they became idolaters.

Ἀποκαλύπτεται [is revealed], not only through the voice of the law written and engraved on the hearts of all, but also through divinely imposed penalties (Jeremiah 24:10). But he chiefly has in view that preaching of the law which first was broadcast throughout the whole world at the time of the Apostles—something that had not previously been done among the Gentiles (Acts 14:16, 17:30).

Ἀσέβεια [ungodliness] is with respect to the First Table of the Decalogue and is considered to be against God; ἀδικία [unrighteousness] is with respect to the Second Table of the Decalogue, and is considered to be against the neighbor.

Ἀσέβεια denotes idolatry; ἀδικία, the remaining sins. Abstract things are used in place of concrete. God is angry both with ungodliness and with the ungodly.

Ἀλήθεια [truth] means things that are known naturally, or true concepts of the mind that are known by nature and deduced from principles of nature concerning the worship of God and love for the neighbor, which is elsewhere called "the light of nature."

What it means to κατέχειν [hold] the truth in unrighteousness, as if to hold it captive, the Apostle himself explains in the following verses.

Ἐν ἀδικίᾳ [in unrighteousness], some explain as ἀδίκως, "violently or forcefully," but it is more properly understood concerning the ungodliness of the Gentiles by which they extinguish the truth, that is, those true things that are known about God by observing His work. Nor do they suffer those things to shine forth in their life and behavior. The Syriac has the verb אחר, from the Hebrew אחז, which has the meaning of "a violent holding back."

He does not say what he could have said—that they held back the truth in error. He says they held it back "in unrighteousness." For he is speaking about those who knew that God exists and that He is the Creator and Preserver of all things, and still they devoted the right worship that was due to God instead to creatures and idols. In this way, then, they imprisoned the truth, so to speak, and detained it with the unjust bars of the will, lest it should go out and also perform the works that conform to the acknowledged truth (cf. Augustine, Sermon 55, *On the Word of the Lord According to John*).

v.19 Διότι τὸ γνωστὸν τοῦ Θεοῦ φανερόν ἐστιν ἐν αὐτοῖς, ὁ γὰρ Θεὸς αὐτοῖς ἐφανέρωσε.

v.19 Because that which may be known of God is manifest in them; for God hath shewed it unto them. (KJV)

(1) Since someone could have objected to the Apostolic assertion that the Gentiles are accused by the law as sinners, observing that the Gentiles did not receive the law from God and were therefore incapable of being accused by the law, the Apostle teaches that the Gentiles had the law inscribed on their hearts. Nor were they lacking all means of knowing God, but were able to attain some degree of knowledge of God by contemplating His creation.

(2) Since he had said that the Gentiles held back the truth in

unrighteousness, he therefore explains, first, what he understands with the word *truth,* and second, what it means "to hold it back in unrighteousness."

Τὸ γνωστὸν τοῦ Θεοῦ [The knowledge of God]. The Vulgate less desirably translates, "what is known of God." The Syriac renders it as "the knowledge of God." But the Greek is more emphatic, "what can be known about God." For there are many divine mysteries that belong to sheer revelation and pure faith—things that cannot be deduced from the natural light and acumen of the mind.

Some explain it in this way: "What is lawful and expedient to know about God, what pertains to elucidating the glory of God." But since not all the things that are expedient to know about God, or the knowledge of the things that pertain to elucidating the glory of God, can be known from the light of nature, Luther translates: "*daß man weiß / daß ein Gott sei / ist ihnen offenbar* [It is clear to them that one knows that there is a God]."

The Photinians understand τὸ γνωστὸν τοῦ Θεοῦ [the knowledge of God] as whatever is known about God or also can be known, in order that they may maintain that Paul is here dealing, not with natural knowledge, through which not everything becomes known that can and must be known about God, but with salvific knowledge, revealed in the Gospel. But the Apostle himself states sufficiently in v.21 that "although they knew God," namely, that He exists, "they did not glorify Him as God." Therefore He is speaking only of that knowledge by which it can be known that God exists. The Apostle is not speaking universally, but indefinitely, and declares in the immediate context what he understands with τὸ γνωστὸν τοῦ Θεοῦ [the knowledge of God], namely, "the power and divinity of God."

Ἐν αὐτοῖς [in them]. The Apostle signifies that those naturally known things have been written on the hearts of men, for which reason the Syriac repeats that בְּהוֹן a second time at the end of the verse. "God has manifested it," the knowledge, "in them." The knowledge of God has been revealed in them, that is, in their mind, intellect and conscience.

Some (such as Augustine, Jerome, Ambrose, Chrysostom, Theophylact) understand the passage concerning acquired knowledge only, because of the etiological particle γὰρ [for] in the following verse, which demonstrates that, in both places, it is dealing with the same knowledge.

Others understand it concerning innate knowledge. (1) Because of the universality of the subject, since the Apostle speaks, not about those who have greater understanding among the Gentiles, but about all the Gentiles, and explains the reason why the wrath of God comes upon all—because all hold back the truth in unrighteousness. But acquired knowledge applies only to those who have greater understanding. (2) Because of the word κατέχειν [to hold back], which demonstrates that the things that are known innately are detained by the Gentiles like captives in a sort of prison of injustice. But those known things pertain to innate knowledge. (3) Because of the manifestation of τὸ γνωστὸν [the knowledge] in the Gentiles, for it is said that that thing that is revealed in them is made known without laborious discourse, not among them, but in their hearts. (4) Because of the explanation of that thing that is known (v.32) where it is called δικαίωμα [righteousness] (v.18) and αλήθεια θεοῦ [truth of God] (v.20), which properly applies to the true things known about God that are innate by nature. (5) Because of the qualifying clause[17], "that they may be without excuse." But that distinction cannot be deduced directly, manifestly and *per se* from a consideration of the created things.

This illustrious passage concerns the innate natural knowledge of God, contrary to the Photinians who deny it.

The heathen, according to Justin in q.1, *To the Greeks*: πάντες ὅτι ἔστιν θεὸς, ὁμολογοῦσι κοινῇ ἐννοία. "All confess by common knowledge that God exists." Damasc. in Bk. 1, *On the Orthodox Faith.*, ch. 3: πᾶσιν ἡ γνῶσις τοῦ εἶναι θεὸν ὑπὸ αὐτοῦ φυσικῶς ἐγκατέσπαρται. "That knowledge—that God exists—has been naturally ingrained in all people by God."

Chrysostom in Homily 95, *To the People*: "Not through angels,

---

17 *prosdiorismos*

not through Prophets, not through Evangelists has it been manifested to the Gentiles that God exists. But they know this because
they observe the invisible attributes of God the Creator that are
understood by the creation."

v.20 Τὰ γὰρ ἀόρατα αὐτοῦ ἀπὸ κτίσεως κόσμου τοῖς ποιήμασι
νοούμενα καθορᾶται, ἥ τε ἀΐδιος αὐτοῦ δύναμις καὶ θειότης, εἰς τὸ
εἶναι αὐτοὺς ἀναπολογήτους.

v.20 *For the invisible things of him from the creation of the world are
clearly seen, being understood by the things that are made, even his eternal power and Godhead; so that they are without excuse: (KJV)*

He states more fully what that truth of God is that the Gentiles held back in captivity in unrighteousness, and in what way the
Gentiles knew God or certainly could have known Him if they had
opened their eyes.

With τὰ ἀόρατα [the invisible things], some understand the invisible essence of God, which is how Luther also translates it. The
Apostle himself explains it as ἥ τε ἀΐδιος αὐτοῦ δύναμις καὶ θειότης
[His invisible power and divinity]. It can, therefore, also be translated thus: "That which is in the invisible God, namely, His eternal
power and divinity."

Origen understands it concerning angels. But the Apostle is not
speaking about them here, but about God, as the context shows.
Thomas: "The invisible thing of God is the invisible divine essence,
which is known by way of activity; the might of God is the power
of God which is known by way of causality. Divinity is to be the
ultimate goal and the noble end to which all things aim, which is
known by way of excellence." But divinity is nothing other than
the divine essence.

Ἀπὸ κτίσεως κόσμου [from the creation of the world]. Socinus,
in *Praelectiones*, p. 5, understands it with regard to time, not the
means of knowing, and connects this qualifying clause, not with
the verb καθορᾶται [are clearly seen], but with the noun τὰ ἀόρατα
[the invisible things]. "It must be understood that the words 'from
the creation of the world' should be connected with the word 'in-

visible,' and that the sense is the same as in Mat. 13:35, 'hidden since the foundation of the world.'"

Similar statements are found with Ostorodus, as in *Instit.*, ch. 1, p. 11. Piscator, following Olevianus, here supports the Photinians. They confirm this explanation (1) from the preposition ἀπὸ [from]. The Apostle does not say ἐκ κτίσεως [on the basis of the creation], but ἀπὸ κτίσεως [from the creation]; (2) from the Syriac version מֶן תַּרְמָיתֵה דְעָלְמָע, "from the foundation of the world;" (3) from the elegance of the style, "since an uncomfortable tautology arises from the diverse exposition."

We reply: (1) That ἀπὸ κτίσεως κόσμου [from the creation of the world] does not pertain to ἀόρατα [unseen things], but to the following verb καθορᾶται [they are clearly seen], as the insertion of the particle γὰρ [for] teaches, as well as confidence in those who approve the manuscripts, as Arias Montanus testifies. (2) Mat. 13:35 does not have ἀπὸ κτίσεως [from the creation], but ἀπὸ καταβολῆς κόσμου [from the foundation of the world]. Therefore, that passage is not parallel to ours. (3) ἀπὸ means, not only "from"[18] but also "on the basis of,"[19] which is generally the proper meaning for it when it is being used of acquiring knowledge (Mat. 7:16, 24:32; Mark 13:28; Wisdom 13:3). Henry Stephan in his *Thesaurus*, Vol. 1, p. 490, on the vocable ἀπὸ, proves with many examples that ἀπὸ and ἐξ or ἐκ are often used without any distinction. In this way, then, ἀπὸ κτίσεως κόσμου is the same as "on the basis of the created world,"[20] so that it signifies the means by which we are led to the knowledge of the invisible God. (4) The word κτίσεως [creation] is almost always used in the New Testament, not of the action itself of creating, but of the created works; not of the act, but of the effect, namely, of the very substance of the creation. (5) When the continuation and carrying on of something from the beginning of the world is indicated, it does not say ἀπὸ κτίσεως, but ἀπ' ἀρχῆς κτίσεως [from the beginning of the creation] (Mark 10:6, 13:19; 2 Pet. 3:4); ἀπὸ καταβολῆς κόσμου [from the foundation of the world] (Mat. 25:34; Heb. 9:26;

---

18 Latin: *a*
19 Latin: *ex*
20 Latin: *ex creato mundo*

Rev. 13:8, 17:8). (6) There is no need to fear a tautology here, since the word ποιημάτων [the things made] is exegetical and explains more clearly what is to be understood in this passage with κτίσιν κόσμου [creation of the world].

With κτίσιν [creation], Anselm understands "man, who is lord and participant, the band and the bond of all creation, Mark 16:15. For man, by himself and by his members, by the powers of his soul, etc., is certainly able to know the Creator." But it is more properly said that, with κτίσιν, all creation in general is understood, that is, the world, which is the creation of God.

With τὰ ποιήματα [the things made] the Photinians understand the works of the Gospel, the miracles of Christ and the Apostles. However, (1) the word ποιήματα is never used this way in the New Testament. It is rather used of the work of creation (Eph. 2:10). (2) The miracles of Christ did not yet exist from the beginning of the world, as noted, (3) nor were the heathen idolaters, whom the Apostle mentions unfavorably in this passage, aware of them.

With τὰ ποιήματα [the things made], the works of God produced in creation are understood, but especially the visible works, which is why the Syriac translates לִבְרָיְתֵה, "in His creatures."

Some distinguish between κτίσιν [creation] and ποίημα [what is made] in this way: They say that κτίσις has in view a situation in which, when nothing existed beforehand, God gave the order and suddenly the things arose and came into existence; ποίημα, on the other hand, has order in view, "a connecting of joints as if done by workmen," as Lactantius calls it.

To others, κτίσις [creation] signifies "the primeval creation," while ποίημα [what is made] signifies "sustenance, preservation, administration, governance." It is most simply said to be exegetical of what was said before, so that τὰ κτίσματα [the created things] is to be understood with κτίσιν.

Νοούμενα καθορᾶται [being understood are clearly seen]. Some connect that νοούμενα [being understood] with the words ἀπὸ κτίσεως κόσμος [from the creation of the world], in this way: While the invisible things of God are understood by the hidden things, they are perceived by the creation of the world. But there is no need either for any transposition or distribution, especially when it does not agree with the subject matter.

The word νοούμενα [being understood] signifies that some discourse and deduction are necessary for us to ascend to a knowledge of the creation by means of the created things. There is a beautiful paronomasia here in the Greek. Τὰ ἀόρατα καθορᾶται [the unseen things are clearly seen], namely, through the creation, as if through a κάτοπτρον, that is, through a "mirror."

The Syriac translates בְּסוּכָלָא, "with the intellect," or, "they are observed with the intellect," since that acquired knowledge is certainly acquired with the benefit of the senses, yet only through the intellect and discourse. Therefore, the works of God are, indeed, first perceived in the creation, or the κτίσματα [created things], with the eyes, and are then considered more deeply. Afterwards, they become νοούμενα [being understood]—they come under the intellect, so that it is concluded from them that God exists and that He is good, wise and powerful.

Those words, ἥ τε ἀΐδιος αὐτοῦ δύναμις καὶ θειότης [His invisible power and divinity], should be referred to τὰ ἀόρατα αὐτοῦ [the unseen things of Him], and are inserted here almost as a parenthesis.

The Syriac connects the adjective ἀΐδιος [invisible] with the word θειότης [divinity], but the Greek text connects it with the word δύναμις [power].

Some make a distinction between θειότητα [divinity] and θεότητα [Godhead], so that the former, since it is from the adjective θεῖος [divine], has the formal and primary meaning of "divine attributes," but has the connotation, due to the actual identity, of "essence;" while the latter, since it comes from the noun θεὸς [God], has the formal and primary meaning of "essence," but has the connotation, due to the actual identity, of "attributes." This observation has some merit[21], since the Gentiles were able to know

21 Latin: *non est de nihilo*

74

τὸ ὅτι—*that* God exists and what some of the attributes of God are: power, wisdom, goodness, etc.; but τὸ τί ἐστι—*what God is*, they were not able to know from the light of nature.

Ambrose, Bk. 3, *On the Holy Spirit*, ch. 2, Cyril, Bk. 1, *Thesaurus*, ch. 5, and Anselm on this passage: "'The invisible things' signify the invisible Father; 'the power' is the Son; 'the divinity' is divine goodness, which is attributed to the Holy Spirit."

But the philosophers did not know the Trinity from the creation. "The invisible things" are the spiritual attributes of God— that He is eternal, immense, omniscient, the highest good, the greatest. "The power of God" is the power by which he governs and rules all things. "Divinity" is the essence and majesty of God, namely, that God is the prime, most perfect Being on whom all things depend, and that He is the ultimate end of all things, and especially of human works. The power of God is included among those ἀόρατα [unseen things], but the Apostle names it specifically because it shines forth especially in the created things.

Εἰς τὸ εἶναι αὐτοὺς ἀναπολογήτους [In order that they may be without excuse]. Piscat. & Tossan.: "That God granted to them this knowledge of Himself, in order that, afterwards, they might have no excuse to offer." But Theophylact properly admonishes that "these things must be understood not as expressing purpose[22], but as expressing result[23], for they depend on the verb καθορᾶται [are clearly seen]." Therefore, εἰς τὸ εἶναι [in order that they may be] in this passage means ὥστε εἶναι [so that they are]. Luther: "*Also daß sie keine Entschuldigung haben* [In such a way that they have no excuse]."

The true purpose of natural knowledge is that it may be a sort of guide to the greater and more fruitful knowledge of God set forth in the Word and revealed to the Church. It is a more accidental effect that, through it, men are rendered without excuse.

The sense is that they are unable to escape or offer any defense

---

22 Greek: τελικῶς
23 Greek: ἐκβατικῶς

in the judgment of God to avoid being legally damnable. (1) Either because, through the knowledge of God that is both drawn from the creation and innate, they have been led to understand that they cannot feign ignorance when they sin. Nor, indeed, did they rightly use the natural light when it showed them the difference between noble and shameful deeds, but acted against it through idolatry and the most heinous crimes. (2) Or because they should have used the natural knowledge of God as a sort of guide to a more fruitful and salvific knowledge of God that was to be sought in the Church (Acts 17:27). The Syriac translates it literally: "That they may be without an exit into a spacious place." In other words, that, constricted and convicted, they may be held for a proper damnation.

This is a wonderful passage on which to base the acquired natural knowledge of God. Ambrose, in his commentary on this passage, p. 14: "The manifest knowledge of God comes from the fashioning of the world. For in order that God, who is, by nature, invisible, may also be known by visible things, a work was made by Him that manifested the architect by means of its visibility."

Augustine, in Sermon 55, *On the Word of the Lord*: "We see the Creator through the creation, the Doer through the deed, the Maker of the world through the world (Psalm 34). There are two things that lead to a knowledge of God: The Scripture and the creation." Bk. 1, *Confessions*, ch. 1: "Heaven and earth cry out, O Lord, that we should be joined to You. You made us for Yourself, O Lord, and our heart is restless until it rests in You."

Prosper, in Bk. 2, *On the Call of All Nations*, ch. 1: "What is the witness that has always served the Lord and has never been silent about His goodness and power, but the unspeakable beauty of the whole world and the riches and ordered largesse of His unspeakable benefits? Through these the tablets, as it were, of the eternal law were afforded to human hearts, in order that the common and public doctrine of divine institution might be read on the pages of the elements and in the chapters of time. The heavens, therefore, the sea, the earth, and all things that are in them, bear witness to the glory of God with their consonant splendor and harmonious order, and speak of the majesty of their Author with unceasing proclamation. Nevertheless, the greater number of men did not understand their voice."

Basil, in Homily 11, in *Hexaemeron*: ὁ κόσμος οὗτος ὅλος ὥσπερ τὶ βιβλίον ἔγγραφον ἔστιν ὑπαγορευόμενον τὴν τοῦ θεοῦ δόξαν. [This whole world is like a kind of inscribed book, dictating the glory of God.] Likewise: ὁ κόσμος τῶν ψυχῶν λογικῶν διδασκαλεῖον καὶ τῆς θεογνωσίας παιδευτήριον. [The world is the teacher of rational souls and the schoolroom of the knowledge of God.]

Meanwhile, the natural knowledge of God is not salvific. The things that are naturally known make men inexcusable, but not blessed. For they are rudimentary principles, not saving principles.

v.21 Διότι γνόντες τὸν Θεόν, οὐχ ὡς Θεὸν ἐδόξασαν, ἢ εὐχαρίστησαν, ἀλλ᾽ ἐματαιώθησαν ἐν τοῖς διαλογισμοῖς αὐτῶν, καὶ ἐσκοτίσθη ἡ ἀσύνετος αὐτῶν καρδία.

v.21 *Because that, when they knew God, they glorified him not as God, neither were thankful; but became vain in their imaginations, and their foolish heart was darkened.* (KJV)

Up to this point, the Apostle has explained what he wanted understood with the word "truth." Now he joins it together with an explanation of why the Gentiles held that truth captive in unrighteousness. The truth showed them one God, but they, by indulging their reasoning, collapsed into horrible idolatries.

Some simply translate the phrase γνόντες τὸν Θεόν as "they knew God," but Luther renders it more properly and more significantly, "although they knew that God exists." In this way, then, that phrase γνωστὸν τοῦ θεοῦ [the knowledge of God] in v.19 is limited to investigating ὅτι [that].[24]

"They neither glorified Him with deeds, nor did they give thanks to Him with words." The Syriac has "and they gave thanks," without repeating the negating particle. For it is common in He-

---

24 I.e., that God exists.

brew for the negative placed at the beginning of the verse to negate the whole verse (Psa. 9:10).

Ἐματαιώθησαν [They were made vain]. The word μάθην means "in vain." Some, therefore, claim that the sense is that it turned out far differently than those Gentiles had thought. But since the phrase τοῖς διαλογισμοῖς αὐτῶν [in their thoughts] is added, it is more properly understood in this way, that they were made vain in their reasoning and thoroughly confused.

"They have been made vain in their thoughts," since their thoughts were vain. (1) Because, in place of the true God, they worshiped idols, and the Scripture calls idols and idolatry "vanity." (2) Beyond—no, contrary to—divine revelation, they invented various ways of worshiping God out of their own clever devices. (3) They were occupied with vain and ludicrous things. (4) They did not achieve their goal while they were consulting their oracles. (5) Because they did not aim at the goal and purpose of the knowledge of God, which is honest deeds and the worship of God. (cf. Bernard, Sermon 36 on Song of Solomon).

The Syriac translates אֶסְתָּרַקוּ, "they became devoid of the light of heaven," of the true knowledge of God and of all godliness.

Διαλογισμὸς [thought] is not simple "thought," but the thought of reasoning and judgment, which is not related to faith.

Their foolish heart was darkened, because they rejected the true wisdom that consists in godliness and the true worship of God, and out of pure stupidity worshiped idols made by hand as gods.

He attributes to the Gentiles a καρδίαν ἀσύνετον [a senseless heart], because they were devoid of the true and spiritual συνέσει [understanding], which consists in the knowledge of Christ and the revealed Word, and which is combined with the glorification of God and the true worship. A parallel passage is Eph. 4:17: "The Gentiles walk in the vanity of their sense"; v.18 "having an intellect that is obscured with darkness" ἐσκοτισμένοι τῇ διανοίᾳ [darkened in their thinking].

Observe: Man, by nature, lacks the understanding of God and of His salvific will.

v.22 Φάσκοντες εἶναι σοφοὶ, ἐμωράνθησαν,

v.22 Professing themselves to be wise, they became fools, (KJV)

Φάσκω [I say] is the same as φημὶ [I say], "although they profess themselves to be wise." The Syriac translates, "although they think in their souls," that is, in themselves.

The Apostle alludes to the fact that, before the time of Pythagoras, the Gentile philosophers used to call themselves "Sophos (wise)."

v.23 καὶ ἤλλαξαν τὴν δόξαν τοῦ ἀφθάρτου Θεοῦ, ἐν ὁμοιώματι εἰκόνος φθαρτοῦ ἀνθρώπου, καὶ πετεινῶν καὶ τετραπόδων καὶ ἑρπετῶν.

v.23 And changed the glory of the uncorruptible God into an image made like to corruptible man, and to birds, and fourfooted beasts, and creeping things. (KJV)

Some understand *the glory of God* to be "the true religion," but it is more properly understood as God Himself, whom the Gentiles changed in their opinion. The Hebrew phrase, then, *the glory of God* means "the glorious God."

Augustine, in Bk. 3, *The City of God*, ch. 12; Bk. 4, ch. 10; Bk. 18, ch. 15; and in many places teaches that "the Gentiles worshiped birds, serpents, cats, crocodiles, not to mention pestilence, fever and other things more absurd than these, as gods."

The glory of God is (1) absolute, in that God is glorious in and of Himself. In other words, the majesty of God, in that He is the greatest and the Most High, is essential (Is. 42:8, John 2:11). (2) The glory of God is relative, in that it is the acknowledgement and celebration of God, that is, the praise and worship that is due to God, which is not in God, but in rational creatures (John 11:4, Phil. 1:11). In this passage, the glory of God is understood in the latter sense. For the Gentile idolaters are said to have "changed the glory of the incorruptible God into the image of corruptible man," not by changing or diminishing the essential and absolute glory of God, but by transferring to the creation the glory of adoration and worship that is due to God alone. They changed the glory of God, not with regard to God, but with regard to themselves; not in the truth of the object, but in the falsehood of the subject, namely, by their false opinion.

Parallel passages with regard to this phrase include Psalm 106:20: "They changed their glory into the likeness of a calf chewing on hay." ἐν ὁμοιώματι εἰκόνος [in the likeness of an image], "into a similar image." Ἐν [in] is used for εἰς [into], and a noun is used in place of an adjective in the Hebrew. Also Jer. 2:11: "My people have changed their glory into something that profits nothing."

v.24 Διὸ καὶ παρέδωκεν αὐτοὺς ὁ Θεὸς ἐν ταῖς ἐπιθυμίαις τῶν καρδιῶν αὐτῶν εἰς ἀκαθαρσίαν, τοῦ ἀτιμάζεσθαι τὰ σώματα αὐτῶν ἐν ἑαυτοῖς,

v.24 Wherefore God also gave them up to uncleanness through the lusts of their own hearts, to dishonour their own bodies between themselves: (KJV)

The second main point of accusation against the Gentiles is that they had contaminated themselves with the foulest desires. This sin, he says, is punishment for the preceding sin.

The particle διὸ [wherefore] signifies that idolatry is the source of all wickedness, and the shameful acts of idolaters committed against themselves and others are the penalties for the idolatry that comes before. For just as he who turns away from the light cannot but thrash about in the dark, so idolaters, who have turned away from the light of the supreme light and divinity, cannot but fall into a variety of dark sins.

"God handed them over" by His righteous judgment ἐν ταῖς ἐπιθυμίαις [in the desires], that is, εἰς τὰς ἐπιθυμίας [into the desires], just as afterwards it is explained in v.26, "He handed them over to disgraceful passions."

Where God is said to have handed them over to carnal desires, some argue that this is to be understood as a result clause, not as a purpose clause, since God handed them over, not as the efficient cause of their shameful acts, but as the righteous Judge punishing sins with sins. But this righteous judgment of God involves more than a mere result. For it is neither bare permission that is being asserted here, nor is God declared to be no more than an idle spectator. Rather, God, as the righteous Judge, hands the men who have turned away from Him over to the devil as the executor of divine justice, by whom they are driven to various shameful acts (1 Kings 22:20ff). Cornelius a Lapide on this passage: "In one sense, man permits sins; in another sense, it is God who permits it—man in a negative way, God in a positive way. For God holds the wills of men tightly in the grip of His omnipotent hand like a fierce animal. The more He positively slackens His grip, the more he is able to do evil. This is why such slack and permission is called an action and a handing over, especially when it comes from God as Avenger for the purpose of punishing the preceding sin."

Yet nothing in this explanation approximates a defense for the Calvinists. For Ambrose rightly argues in his commentary on this passage: "To hand over is to permit, but not to incite or to provoke, so that, with the devil's help, they fulfill in deed those things that they had conceived in their desires." And when the Apostle says in this passage that "God gave the Gentiles over to carnal desires," it is explained in this way in Acts 14:16: "He permitted them to walk in their ways." Psalm 81:13: "I have let them go according to the desires of their heart." Euthymius on ch. 15 of John, and Damasc., Bk. 4, *The Orthodox Faith*, ch. 10: "It is worth noting that it is the custom of divine Scripture to call the permission of God an action. Accordingly, 'He has blinded' and 'He hardened' mean that He permitted them, as incurable men, to be blinded and hardened."

Nevertheless, the righteous judgment of God also agrees with this permission, as was just said. Augustine, Bk. 20, *The City of God*, ch. 19 near the end: "God will release the efficacy of error, for by His righteous judgment, He will permit the devil to do whatever he does by his unjust and malignant counsel."

The Syriac combines these two things, ἐν ἐπιθυμίαις τῶν καρδιῶν αὐτῶν [in desires of their hearts] and εἰς ἀκαθαρσίαν [into impurity], in this way: "He handed them over to the unclean carnal desires of their heart."

Τοῦ ἀτιμάζεσθαι [to dishonor]. This is done by the righteous judgment of God, for the ones who robbed God of His glory are the same ones who, in their own body, become full of indecency and disgrace.

Ἐν ἑαθτοῖς [in themselves]. The Syriac translates בְּהוֹן, "among themselves," which agrees best with the sin of lust in that one sins, not only against his own body, but also against the body of another.

Observe: Augustine, Bk. 5, *Against Julian*, ch. 5: "Crimes are avenged with crimes, and the punishments inflicted on sinners are not only torments, but also the increase of vice."

v.25 οἵτινες μετήλλαξαν τὴν ἀλήθειαν τοῦ Θεοῦ ἐν τῷ ψεύδει καὶ ἐσεβάσθησαν καὶ ἐλάτρευσαν τῇ κτίσει παρὰ τὸν Κτίσαντα, ὅς ἐστιν εὐλογητὸς εἰς τοὺς αἰῶνας. Ἀμήν.

v.25 Who changed the truth of God into a lie, and worshipped and served the creature more than the Creator, who is blessed for ever. Amen. (KJV)

He repeats the accusation of idolatry set forth in the first part in order to demonstrate that idolatry, which is spiritual adultery, is the source and fount of those most shameful lusts.

With τὴν ἀλήθειαν [the truth], in this passage as well as in v.18, is understood the natural knowledge that is both theoretically and practically embedded in the mind, as well as that which is drawn from the creation. The former is said to have been "changed for a lie," or "into a lie," by way of a vicious and perverse application, since in place of the true God and the true divine worship, they invented false gods and false forms of divine worship.

With *lie*, some understand "a lying and false idol".

Παρὰ τὸν κτίσαντα [alongside the Creator]. Vulgate: "They served the creation rather than the Creator." Syriac: "Much more the creation than Him who created them." Luther: "More than the Creator." It can also be rendered "in place of the Creator" or "together with the Creator" or "against the Creator." For this, too, is idolatry, when a false god is worshiped together with the true God.

Ὁ εὐλογητός [The Blessed]. When the Hebrews make mention of the true God, they usually add, הברוך לעלם, "may He be blessed forever." The Syriac translates this passage, "to whom are," that is, to whom are owed praises and blessings forever and ever.

v.26 Διὰ τοῦτο παρέδωκεν αὐτοὺς ὁ Θεὸς εἰς πάθη ἀτιμίας· αἵ τε γὰρ θήλειαι αὐτῶν μετήλλαξαν τὴν φυσικὴν χρῆσιν εἰς τὴν παρὰ φύσιν,

v.26 For this cause God gave them up unto vile affections: for even their women did change the natural use into that which is against nature: (KJV)

With τὰ πάθη ἀτιμίας [the passions of dishonor], the depraved carnal desires are understood through which, by carrying them out, they afflicted themselves and their bodies with disgrace. The Syriac translates לכאבא, which properly signifies "sorrows and afflictions." And so a general word is used for the specific, chiefly by way of synecdoche.

It is common for the Hebrews to use a noun in place of an adjective. Thus πάθη ἀτιμίας [passions of dishonor] are "disgraceful passions."

Εἰς πάθη, "to sexual and shameful lusts."

"The women changed the natural use," namely, of a man, for lying together, "to that which is beyond nature." These things are conveyed as a euphemism. For the fact that here the word ἄρσενος [of a man] is implied must be understood from the following verses, where it is said about the men that "they abandoned the natural use of a woman."

But some explain it concerning the lying together of women with animals (Lev. 18:23, 20:16).

Ambrose and Theodoret: "Just as men with men is contrary to

nature, so also women with women. All the transcendent boundaries of nature and of honor were completely erased."

Seneca, in Epistle 95, teaches that "women actively engaged with other women in the way of men." Since, he says, women reached the same level of license as the men, they also rivaled the men in the vices of the body. "They stay awake just as late, they drink just as much, they challenge the men with oil and wine, and they by no means lag behind the men in *libido*, since they were born to prostitute themselves.[25] May the gods and goddesses wickedly destroy them! They have even devised a perverse kind of sexual immorality—they enter men."

These women are called τριβάδες [Tribades] by the Greeks, that is, "those who rub." Tertullian mentions them in his book *De Pallio*. This is why that mad and nefarious lust is called τριβαδικὴ ἀσέλγεια [lesbian sensuality], the inventress of which is believed to have been Philaenis, and on account of this she wickedly listened to Sappho.

The Syriac translates: "Their women changed the use, the habit, חֲשַׁחְתָא, of their nature, and made use of רֵכָנְהֵין a thing, or a manner, that is not from nature, or that is foreign to their nature." Where it has כּינא, one should understand התולדה.

v.27 ὁμοίως τε καὶ οἱ ἄρρενες, ἀφέντες τὴν φυσικὴν χρῆσιν τῆς θηλείας, ἐξεκαύθησαν ἐν τῇ ὀρέξει αὐτῶν εἰς ἀλλήλους, ἄρσενες ἐν ἄρσεσι τὴν ἀσχημοσύνην κατεργαζόμενοι, καὶ τὴν ἀντιμισθίαν ἣν ἔδει τῆς πλάνης αὐτῶν ἐν ἑαυτοῖς ἀπολαμβάνοντες.

v.27 And likewise also the men, leaving the natural use of the woman, burned in their lust one toward another; men with men working that which is unseemly, and receiving in themselves that recompence of their error which was meet. (KJV)

Not only the common people among the lower class, but also among the Philosophers, who wanted to appear more sensible, struggled with the vice of pederasty. Philo, in Bk. 2, *On the Contemplative Life*, makes Socrates guilty of this. Likewise Laertius, Gellius

25 Latin: *pati natae*

in Bk. 18, ch. 2, Plutarch, *On the Education of Children*, attribute it to Plato. Chrysostom teaches on this passage: "Solon and other Philosophers not only practiced pederasty, but even praised it as something noble and sanctioned it in their laws and declared that free men could practice it, but not slaves."

The verb ἐξεκαύθησαν [they burned] is emphatic, expressing those horrifying and monstrous lusts of the Gentiles that arose from the fire of depraved desires, and thus were pronounced worthy of hell fire.

Ἀντιμισθίαν τῆς πλάνης [the reward of error]. He understands it as error, because they recklessly turned away from the true God and from the true worship of God to which the natural knowledge of God could have led them. Ἀντιμισθία is "a recompense, reward for merits." Since they abandoned the Creator and worshiped idols contrary to the natural order, they were permitted by the righteous judgment of God to turn the natural order upside down in the act of procreation.

Cornelius a Lapide on this passage: "Even our age has seen and advanced such monsters of lust, born of heresy." But this could more properly have been said of the papists and the popes and the papal kingdom. (See the passage *On the Church*.)

Ἐν ἑαυτοῖς [in themselves] is also emphatic, for, having engaged in errors of the mind, they received the righteous retribution in their bodies.

Observe: Physical and spiritual harlotry—that is, idolatry and shameful lusts, are very closely joined together, because the devil, "the father of lies, is an unclean spirit" (Wisdom 14:12).

v.28 Καὶ καθὼς οὐκ ἐδοκίμασαν τὸν Θεὸν ἔχειν ἐν ἐπιγνώσει, παρέδωκεν αὐτοὺς ὁ Θεὸς εἰς ἀδόκιμον νοῦν, ποιεῖν τὰ μὴ καθήκοντα,

v.28 *And even as they did not like to retain God in their knowledge, God gave them over to a reprobate mind, to do those things which are not convenient;* (KJV)

The third point of accusation against the Gentiles is that, in addition to idolatry and shameful lusts, they had also contaminated themselves with other filthy deeds, all of which, he says, is the punishment for idolatry.

There is a beautiful paronomasia here. Since they did not ἐδοκίμασαν [approve] to have God in knowledge, God handed them over εἰς νοῦν ἀδόκιμον [to a reprobate mind]. The sense is that, since they did not consider it to be fair and just—that is, it did not seem right to them to properly acknowledge and worship God, therefore God handed them over by righteous judgment to a reprobate mind.

Τὸν θεὸν ἔχειν ἐν ἐπιγνώσει, "that they should retain God in knowledge," that they should remain and grow in that knowledge of the true God, the beginning of which they had received through the light of nature. That they should retain the knowledge of the true God, advance in it and live according to it.

Νοῦς ἀδόκιμος [Reprobate mind] is a mind that is so corrupt that it cannot conclude or judge anything that is right, but is carried off as if by a blind force to those things that oppose the laws of nature. The Syriac translates: "to a mind רְסָרִיקוּתָא, to a mind of emptiness," that is, "an empty mind," with a genitive being used in place of an adjective, according to Hebrew custom.

A reprobate mind is a distorted and perverse judgment, making depraved and preposterous judgments about all things, but especially about those things that concern the worship of God and noble behavior—a mind that approves the things that ought to be disapproved and disapproves the things that ought to be approved.

Τὰ μὴ καθήκοντα [the things that are not fitting]. Τὸ καθῆκον is the office which corresponds to someone.

Observe: Gregory, in Bk. 25, *Moralia*, ch. 9: "Those who err in the knowledge of God are justly handed over so that they err equally in the things they do."

v.29 πεπληρωμένους πάσῃ ἀδικίᾳ, πορνείᾳ, πονηρίᾳ, πλεονεξίᾳ, κακίᾳ· μεστοὺς φθόνου, φόνου, ἔριδος, δόλου, κακοηθείας,

v.29 Being filled with all unrighteousness, fornication, wickedness,

86

covetousness, maliciousness; full of envy, murder, debate, deceit, malig-
nity; whisperers, (KJV)

The verb πεπληρωμένους [being filled] is dependent on the verb
παρέδωκεν [He handed over]. By the very fact that God handed
them over to a reprobate judgment, they were filled with all wickedness.

First he says in general that the Gentiles were full of all unrighteousness. Then he enumerates various specific kinds of sins
through a sort of synathroesmus.

Πονηρίαν [wickedness]. The Syriac translates with מְרִירוּתָא, "bitterness," understanding those things that are no less to be rejected
by right judgment than the palate rejects things that are bitter.

They say that πονηρίαν is "wickedness or depravity of the intellect and will," while κακίαν is only "a malice of the will."

Πλεονεξία [greed] is more than "avarice," for it embraces also
the evil tricks by which one does whatever it takes to transfer the
goods of his neighbor to himself.

There is a paronomasia in the phrase φόνου καὶ φθόνου [envy
and murder], and the asyndeton serves as an exaggeration.

The Vulgate translates κακοηθείαν with "malice," the Syriac
with "evil thoughts." But malice is when some singular perversi-
ty also has a zeal for harm and for interpreting everything in the
worst way, as Aristotle also describes it.

Some translate it with "a roughness of behavior." But this is
what the word disorderly means.

v.30 ψιθυριστάς, καταλάλους, θεοστυγεῖς, ὑβριστάς, ὑπερηφάνους,
ἀλαζόνας, ἐφευρετὰς κακῶν, γονεῦσιν ἀπειθεῖς,

v.30 Backbiters, haters of God, despiteful, proud, boasters, inventors
of evil things, disobedient to parents, (KJV)

Ψιθυριστάς is rendered by the Vulgate as "whisperers." The
Syriac, "mutterers." But ψιθυρισταί are "secret informers."

Θεοστυγεῖς [God-haters] are those who hate God, and, in turn, are hated by God. Cyprian in Epistle 68: "'Those who abhor God,' for στυγέω also means 'to abhor'—both those whom God abhors and those who detest God. Paul is speaking about the vices of unbelievers, which were clinging to them and were committed by them, and so, more properly, they were God-haters."

Ἀλάζονες [boasters] are "those who glory and boast."

After "inventors of evil" and before "not obedient to their parents," the Syriac inserts "of a destitute mind" from the following verse.

"Inventors of evil" are those who, by extreme cunning, devise the worst counsels and shameful devices.

v.31 ἀσυνέτους, ἀσυνθέτους, ἀστόργους, ἀσπόνδους, ἀνελεήμονας·

v.31 Without understanding, covenantbreakers, without natural affection, implacable, unmerciful: (KJV)

There is again a paronomasia in ἀσυνέτους, ἀσυνθέτους [not understanding, not keeping coventants]. They are called ἀσύνθετοι who do not observe συνθήκας, the covenants that have been agreed upon. The Vulgate translates "disorderly," as if it were from α + συντίθημι. The verb ἀσυνθετεῖν, "to transgress" or "to violate the agreed upon covenants," is used in Esdras 10:10.

Ἀστόργους, "without affection;" the Vulgate has "inhumane," those who love no one, who have no friend. (cf. Theoph., Oecum.)

Some translate "without piety," that is, impious toward their parents and acquaintances.

"Uncivil, behaving like Barbarians, separated from all honorable society and conversation, those who cannot get along with others in the community or in the family"—thus Suidas from Demosthenes.

Oecumenius translates "separating themselves from everyone," that is, pursuing and shunning everyone with hatred.

Ἀσπόνδους—"treacherous."

Ἀνελεήμονας—"unmerciful and cruel."

The Syriac translates, "in whom there is no mercy."

v.32 οἵτινες τὸ δικαίωμα τοῦ Θεοῦ ἐπιγνόντες, (ὅτι οἱ τὰ τοιαῦτα πράσσοντες ἄξιοι θανάτου εἰσίν) οὐ μόνον αὐτὰ ποιοῦσιν, ἀλλὰ καὶ συνευδοκοῦσι τοῖς πράσσουσι.

v.32 Who knowing the judgment of God, that they which commit such things are worthy of death, not only do the same, but have pleasure in them that do them. (KJV)

He concludes his description of the unrighteousness of the Gentiles—that they had knowingly and willingly sinned against conscience. And not only had they sinned, but they had even extolled highly those who sin.

Τὸ δικαίωμα θεοῦ [The righteousness of God], according to some, means in this passage "that judicial authority of God by which He assigns to each one according to works." The Syriac translates with דִּינָה, "judgment." Others understand it concerning the naturally ingrained distinction between the honorable and the base, namely, that good should be done and evil should be avoided, and that God is the most righteous Avenger of evil deeds.

The Vulgate translates, "who, although they were aware of the righteousness of God, did not understand that those who do such things are worthy of death—not only those who do these things, but even those who give their consent to those who do them." Laur., Valla, Erasmus and Jacob Faber acknowledge that this passage has been rendered incorrectly in the Latin version. Bellarmine attempts to prove them wrong in Bk. 2, *On the Word of God*, ch. 14, loc. 4. "The Latin version is better than the original itself. For according to the Greek, the sense is that it is worse to give one's consent to those who act wickedly than to do evil. According to the Latin, the sense is the opposite, that it is worse to do evil than to give one's consent to evildoers. But certainly it is absolutely worse to do evil than to give one's consent to an evildoer."

We reply: (1) The sense which Bellarmine attaches to the Greek text is not genuine. Rather, this is the meaning of the Apostle: They are not content to commit shameful acts themselves, but they increase this impiety of theirs with something new in that they even approve the sins of others, and they render themselves participants in them by means of their assent. (2) Chrysostom, Oecumenius, Theophylact explain it as it is in Greek. Bellarmine sets the Latin Fathers up against them. But it is certain that the Greeks preserved the purity of the Greek text more faithfully. (3) The rationale itself supports the reading of the Greek text. For if they were aware of τὸ δικαίωμα τοῦ θεοῦ [the righteousness of God], how could they not have understood that those who do perversely or who give their consent to those who do them are worthy of death? (Confer Chamierus, Vol. 1, *Panstat.*, Bk. 14, ch. 13, par. 13 ff.)

Cornelius a Lapide on this passage: "Our reading is simpler and easier to understand. For the Apostle seems to have in mind the wiser men who knew that the worship of idols and other vices already mentioned are evil, and who did not commit or perpetrate them constantly. Nevertheless, they approved of those things done by others, or ignored them, either for fear of the law, or for love of pleasing them or for fear of displeasing them."

We reply: Cornelius himself expresses sufficiently the neatly ordered sense of the Greek reading, which agrees exactly with the preceding. This giving consent, he says, is more and worse than doing. For it proceeds from malice, while doing often flows from mere weakness.

Franc. Titelm. asserts in his commentary on this passage that those words read in the ancient Greek manuscript as οὐ συνῆκαν [they did not understand]. But those ancient fathers who passed on the manuscripts make no mention of this variant.

Συνευδοκοῦσι τοῖς πράσσουσι [they have pleasure in those who do], "both by agreeing in spirit with those who do such things, and by verbally excusing those things and praising those who do them" (Chrysostom, Theophylact).

Observe: It is a matter of extreme wickedness to approve and to praise sins, whether in oneself or in others.

Notes on the Epistle to the Romans: Chapter 2

The aim of this entire chapter is to convict the Jews of sin. There is a general syllogism here:

Those whose works are just as unrighteous as the works of the Gentiles are just as unrighteous and liable to the judgment of God as the Gentiles.

The works of the Jews are just as unrighteous as those of the Gentiles, if not externally, then internally.

Therefore, the Jews are just as unrighteous and liable to the judgment of God as the Gentiles.

He proves the major premise from the fact that the judgment of God is according to the truth when He rewards each one according to works without any respect of persons. The minor premise and the conclusion of this syllogism are located in the first verse. In the second, the proof of the major premise. In vv. 3, 4, & 5, a fuller explanation of the first verse is contained, that is, of the minor premise and conclusion in the principal syllogism. In vv. 6, 7, 8, 9, 10, 11 & 12, verse 2 is expanded and, indeed, confirmed—that the judgment of God is according to truth when He rewards each one according to works. In vv. 13-26 the minor premise of the syllogism is confirmed, that the Jews are unrighteous and sinful, together with the Gentiles. From v. 26 to the end, the conclusion is treated.

v.1 Διὸ ἀναπολόγητος εἶ, ὦ ἄνθρωπε πᾶς ὁ κρίνων, ἐν ᾧ γὰρ κρίνεις τὸν ἕτερον, σεαυτὸν κατακρίνεις, τὰ γὰρ αὐτὰ πράσσεις ὁ κρίνων.

v.1 *Therefore thou art inexcusable, O man, whosoever thou art that judgest: for wherein thou judgest another, thou condemnest thyself; for thou that judgest doest the same things. (KJV)*

In the preceding chapter, the Apostle had dealt with the Gentiles whom he had convicted (on the basis of idolatry, shameful lusts and other evil deeds) as transgressors of the divine law. Now he turns to the hypocritical Jews and demonstrates that their works are even worse—if not externally, then internally.

Some think that the Apostle is still occupied with accusing the Gentiles. For after accusing the open and notorious sinners among the Gentiles in the preceding chapter, he now makes further unfavorable mention in the first part of this chapter of the hypocrites who managed their outward behavior honorably enough while complaining about those more heinous crimes in other. Meanwhile, however, they carried around the poisonous root of sin in their hearts and committed the same sins on the inside, and thus they condemned themselves with their own judgment. They think this (1) because with the illative particle διὸ καὶ [therefore also], these things are connected to the preceding; and (2) because in v. 17 he eventually accuses the Jew.

But the circumstances of the text demonstrate the opposite. (1) At the end of the first chapter the conclusion of the preceding was complete. (2) He is dealing here with the internal uncleanness of the hypocrites who condemned others, and these hypocrites were, properly speaking, Jews. (3) The Gentiles were open idolaters, impure, and sinners in public view of God and men, nor did they excuse their sins, but rather publicized them. (4) It says in v.13, "For not the hearers of the law are righteous before God, etc." This pertains to Jews. Thus, since that statement is connected to the preceding by an inseparable link, the preceding must also be determined to pertain to the Jews.

Διὸ [Therefore] looks back to v.18, in which the general purpose of this section is set forth. Since the wrath of God is now solemnly revealed against all sins, therefore even you, O Jew, are just as liable to the law and divine wrath on account of internal sins as the Gentile open sinners. Indeed, this is the general purpose of this entire chapter. Such a connection can also be made: If the Gentiles are worthy of death on account of sins, much more so are you, O Jews!

He tacitly admonishes those critics with the title "Man," implying that, since they are men, they should understand that nothing human is foreign to them. The Syriac translates: "O son of man." With τοὺς κρίνοντας [the judging ones], he does not have in mind the magistrates or the judges who are divinely positioned for judging. Rather, he has in mind the hypocrites who seek to stand before God through their own righteousness, who hardly acknowledge their inner sins and even condemn in others what they themselves do. Nor does he prohibit the judgment of discretion, but rather the rash kind of judgment.

There is emphasis in the singular number. For since he accuses the entire Jewish people of sin, it is as if he takes one man from their entire assembly and forces him to serve as a rhetorical figure; he presses him with numerous interrogations and wrenches the man's condemnation out of his own mouth.

There is a beautiful paronomasia. "Wherein you κρίνεις (judge and damn) another, you κατακρίνεις (condemn) yourself." He states the effect of κρίσεως [judgment] as κατάκρισιν [condemnation], demonstrating that one's own condemnation regularly follows upon the rash judgment he makes on the vices of others, and that, by the righteous order of divine judgment. It is an effective reproof, for he demonstrates that they are condemned by their own judgment.

But how is it that rash judges of this kind can themselves do the very things they condemn in others? Secret hypocrites do the same things that open sinners do, yet not in the same way, but with the internal motives of the soul. They do those things within, in the heart, if not outside in the open. Therefore when they are investigated more closely and on the inside, which God does, they are found to be guilty of the same crimes they condemn in others.

The words of the Apostle do not help the Anabaptists at all in their effort to tear down the magistrates and the authority of the public courts. For divine justice is also accustomed to avenging evil deeds by means of evil judges.

v.2 Οἴδαμεν δὲ ὅτι τὸ κρῖμα τοῦ Θεοῦ ἐστι κατὰ ἀλήθειαν ἐπὶ τοὺς τὰ τοιαῦτα πράσσοντας.

94

v.2 But we are sure that the judgment of God is according to truth against them which commit such things. (KJV)

He responds to the tacit objection. You hypocrite! You deny that you carry out the same sins together with the Gentiles because you refrain from external sins. But the judgment of God is not content with this external kind of righteousness. It therefore heightens the truth and severity of divine judgment, which does not judge according to external appearance, nor according to external works, but according to the truth and according to the attitudes of the heart.

The word οἴδαμεν [we know] has special emphasis and places the evidence of the thing right before the eyes, as it were.

"The judgment of God is according to truth." In other words, God does not judge according to the external appearance, but according to the internal disposition of a person's heart.

Luther: "God's judgment is just." Parallel passages are 1 Sam. 16:7, Is. 11:3, John 7:24. But in this passage the Apostle means chiefly that God, as the righteous Judge, searches the hearts and kidneys of men, and there He sees, accuses and damns original corruption and unrighteousness; nor does He pass by or ignore the internal sins of men; nor is He content with only the appearance of outward discipline, like the hypocrites dream who seek to be justified before God in their external works.

v.3 Λογίζῃ δὲ τοῦτο, ὦ ἄνθρωπε ὁ κρίνων τοὺς τὰ τοιαῦτα πράσσοντας καὶ ποιῶν αὐτά, ὅτι σὺ ἐκφεύξῃ τὸ κρῖμα τοῦ Θεοῦ;

v.3 And thinkest thou this, O man, that judgest them which do such things, and doest the same, that thou shalt escape the judgment of God? (KJV)

He intensifies what he had said in v.1, that the Jews are hypocrites ἀναπολογήτους [without excuse], and that they condemn themselves by their own judgment. He also answers another objection of the Jews. "The judgment and punishments of God do not oppress us. Therefore we are not transgressors of the law." But, says the Apostle, you bring the wrath and judgment of God on yourselves by this very security.

Λογίζη δὲ [and do you think]. The emphasis is on the rhetorical figure[26] and the interrogation. The sense is, "You deceive yourself if you say this."

v.4 Ἢ τοῦ πλούτου τῆς χρηστότητος αὐτοῦ καὶ τῆς ἀνοχῆς καὶ τῆς μακροθυμίας καταφρονεῖς, ἀγνοῶν ὅτι τὸ χρηστὸν τοῦ Θεοῦ εἰς μετάνοιάν σε ἄγει;

v.4 Or despisest thou the riches of his goodness and forbearance and longsuffering; not knowing that the goodness of God leadeth thee to repentance? (KJV)

He magnifies the sin of security and impenitence in the hypocrites by pointing out the effects—that they despise the kindness of God that invites them to repentance. Some conclude that the Apostle specifically and chiefly has in view the security of the Jews in that they imagined they had no punishment to fear for rejecting and repudiating the Messiah.

There is great force and exaggeration in all these things. He calls it πλοῦτον τῆς χρηστότητος καὶ τῆς ἀνοχῆς καὶ τῆς μακροθυμίας [the riches of his goodness and forbearance and longsuffering] in order to celebrate the abundance of divine kindness.

Πλοῦτος [riches], as elsewhere with the Apostle, means "unnatural plenty and abundance." πλοῦτος τῆς χάριτος [the riches of His grace] (Eph. 1:7). ὑπερβάλλων πλοῦτος τῆς χάριτος [the exceeding riches of His grace] (Eph. 2:7).

Χρηστότης means "kindness," which includes a facility in giving and a forbearance in waiting. The Syriac translates with בַּסִימוּת, meaning "sweetness, gentleness, indulgence."

Ἀνοχὴ, from ἀνέχειν, means "patience" and "forbearance" (so to speak).

Μακροθυμία is "longsuffering." μακρόθυμος, as in μακρύνων τὸν θυμὸν, "slowing down wrath, He does not punish immediately."

---

26 apostrophe

96

The Syriac renders periphrastically: "Indeed, you dare," namely, to despise, "the place, that is, the opportunity that He gives you," namely, to repent.

Observe: The postponement of divine punishments is an invitation to repentance.

v.5 Κατὰ δὲ τὴν σκληρότητά σου καὶ ἀμετανόητον καρδίαν, θησαυρίζεις σεαυτῷ ὀργὴν ἐν ἡμέρᾳ ὀργῆς, καὶ ἀποκαλύψεως δικαιοκρισίας τοῦ Θεοῦ.

v.5 *But after thy hardness and impenitent heart treasurest up unto thyself wrath against the day of wrath and revelation of the righteous judgment of God; (KJV)*

Τὴν σκληρότητά σου καὶ ἀμετανόητον καρδίαν [your hardness and impenitent heart]. The Syriac joins the phrases together, rendering it this way: "...on account of the malice of your heart, which does not repent."

Θησαυρίζεις σεαυτῷ ὀργὴν [you treasure up for yourself wrath]. The verb θησαυρίζειν [to treasure up] indicates that divine wrath is being stored up little by little, so that eventually it all resembles a treasure. Deu. 32:34: "Is it not hidden with me, sealed up in treasures?" V.35: "Mine is the vengeance and the retribution." Jeremiah 50:25: "God opened his treasures and produced the weapons of His wrath."

There is emphasis on the pronoun σεαυτῷ [for yourself]. For it means that an impenitent heart of this kind is the cause of so much evil for him, since the kindness of God invites and leads him in another direction.

With ὀργὴν [wrath] is understood by metonymy "the divine punishment owed for sins which is inflicted on the day of wrath," that is, both in this life and in the Last Judgment, when the wrath of God will be fully poured out on the wicked.

Observe the description of the Last Day of Judgment, that it is ἡμέρα ὀργῆς [a day of wrath] (namely, with respect to the impenitent, for God has not appointed the godly εἰς ὀργὴν [for wrath], 1

The. 5:9) καὶ ἀποκάλυψις τῆς δικαιοκρισίας τοῦ θεοῦ [and revelation of the righteous judgment of God].

In this life the wicked seem to flourish, because of which one might infer that the judgment of God is not just. But on that Last Day it will become manifest to the whole world that the judgment of God is very just.

The revelation of the righteous judgment of God is the demonstration of wrath and divine judgment through the imposition of punishments. These are carried out against the impenitent Jews, both in the destruction of Jerusalem, and in subsequent punishments, and chiefly on the Day of final judgment.

v.6 ὃς ἀποδώσει ἑκάστῳ κατὰ τὰ ἔργα αὐτοῦ.

v.6 Who will render to every man according to his deeds: (KJV)

Connection: A richer exposition of that which he had said in v.2, that God judges according to truth, that is, not only with regard to external works, but also the inner motives of the heart. In vv. 2 & 3, he threatened that the judgment of God was coming. Now he demonstrates what that judgment of God is.

The verb ἀποδώσει [he will repay] involves more than δώσει [he will give]. Since He promised that "He would give," He will, therefore, "repay." So God has made Himself a debtor, not by receiving something from us, but by promising something by grace. Parallel passages are Psa. 62:13, Mat. 16:27, Rev. 12:12. The papists abuse this passage in order to heap up the merits of works. Pererius, Disputation 5 on Rom. ch. 2, n. 39, p. 279: "He rewards according to works, for He will repay each one on account of good works—for the character and merit and dignity of works." Conzenius, question 1 on this verse: "To reward according to works is to reward the merits of works."

We reply: (1) It is one thing to reward someone *according to works*, that is, according to the testimony of works which testify concerning the inner faith or unbelief; but it is another thing to reward someone *on account of works*, that is, on account of the merit of works. Gregory, on the *Seven Penitential Psalms:* "It is one thing to reward *according to* works, and another to reward *on account of* the works themselves. For when it says 'according to works,' the character itself of works is understood, so that to him whose works appear to be good—to him also belongs the glorious reward."

(2) The relationship between evil and good works is disparate. Evil works are deserving of punishment, but good works are not deserving of reward and glory. Hence Gregory makes the connection with this passage: "On the other hand, no labor can equal—no works can be compared to that blessed life, in that it is lived with God and near God, especially since the Apostle says: 'The sufferings of this age are not worthy of the future glory, etc.' Rom. 8:18."

(3) It never says διὰ τὰ ἔργα, "on account of works," but κατὰ τὰ ἔργα, "according to works" rewards are given. The first denotes the merit, dignity and efficacy of works; the second denotes the character and testimony of them. As the works of men are to be, so also it is demonstrated that the judgment of God will be. This explanation is handed down from the Spirit Himself. Rev. 22:12: "My recompense is with me, to reward each one ὡς τὸ ἔργον αὐτοῦ ἔσται [as his work will be]." 2 Cor. 5:10: "He will repay each one τὰ διὰ τοῦ σώματος πρὸς ἃ ἔπραξεν [the things done in his body, according to the things he has done]."

(4) The Holy Spirit does not use the word ἀντιδόσεως [recompense], which could be applied to a recompense properly so called that corresponds in some specific way to merits from the other party—a recompense that repays from a debt of justice. He uses the word ἀποδώσεως [repayment], which is general. It occurs at that time when God, by grace, awards, not our merits, but His gifts.

(5) It is also never said that eternal life is given on account of the merits of works. In the matter of justification and salvation, grace and works are always contrasted with one another (Rom. 11:6).

(6) Finally, this apostolic saying is clearly legal, as is manifest from the aim of the apostolic disputation. For this is the Apostle's purpose, to remove from all men the perfect fulfillment of the law

and then to demonstrate that "no flesh," that is, absolutely no man, "can be justified before God by works."

The Gospel absolves us from this judgment and damnation of the law by revealing and applying to us the righteousness of Christ, who furnished perfect obedience to the law in our place.

v.7 τοῖς μὲν καθ᾽ ὑπομονὴν ἔργου ἀγαθοῦ, δόξαν καὶ τιμὴν καὶ ἀφθαρσίαν ζητοῦσι, ζωὴν αἰώνιον·

v.7 To them who by patient continuance in well doing seek for glory and honour and immortality, eternal life: (KJV)

Connection: He expounds the preceding general statement with distinct kinds of good and evil men and explains...

1. The rewards of doing good.

Some think that the relative οἱ [those who] should be understood, as if ζητοῦσι [living] were a verb. But there is no need to imagine an ellipsis, since ζητοῦσι can be a dative participle. Others think that the phrase ἀπόδωσις [repayment] from the preceding verse must be repeated. But it is better to understand the verb δώσει [he will give], since eternal life itself is not ἀπόδωσις [repayment], but χάρισμα [a gift of grace]. Awards of grace are bestowed on the godly in eternal life in place of reward, which is why the Syriac also inserts the word יהב, "gives eternal life." The arrangement, then, is this: "He will reward each one according to works. To those, on the one hand, who, persevering in doing good, seek glory, etc., He will give eternal life."

Some employ a transposition such as this: "He will reward each one according to works. To those, on the one hand, who, persevering in doing good, seek eternal life—glory, honor and immortality." But as anyone can see, this transposition is forced.

With ὑπομονὴν ἔργου ἀγαθοῦ [perseverance of good work], one should understand both "perseverance in good work," for "he who perseveres until the end will be saved" (Mat. 10:22); and putting up with persecution for the sake of good works; and patient expectation of some future glory to be revealed in its time. This ὑπομονὴ [perseverance] and patience are highly necessary for godliness, for "we must through many tribulations enter the kingdom of heaven."

Some refer that ὑπομονὴν [perseverance] to this, that they would enjoy that patience and tolerance of God that the Apostle discussed in v.4. But the earlier explanation is simpler.

When they are said to ζητεῖν δόξαν καθ' ὑπομονὴν ἔργου ἀγαθοῦ [seek glory according to perseverance of good work], it should not be understood in this sense, as if they placed confidence in their works, or sought to be justified before God and saved through and on account of works; but that they know that this is God's will, revealed in the law, that those who strive for the proposed aim of eternal life must walk in the way of the divine commandments.

This is a very beautiful description of eternal life. It will be δόξα [glory], "glory of soul and body." It will be τιμὴ [honor], because then the heavenly Father will honor those who served Christ in this life (John 12:26). It will be ἀφθαρσία [incorruptibility], because then this corruptible will put on ἀφθαρσίαν (1 Cor. 15:53).

Bellarmine, Bk. 5, *On Justification*, ch. 3: "When the Apostle said that God would reward each one according to works, he immediately linked eternal life to those who, according to patience, seek the glory and incorruptibility of good work. Therefore, he taught that eternal life is that award which is given according to the proportion and measure of the work."

We reply: ζητεῖν δόξαν καθ' ὑπομονὴν ἔργου ἀγαθοῦ [seek glory according to perseverance of good work] can be understood in two ways, either according to the Law or according to the Gospel. If according to the Law, which agrees best with the apostolic aim, then the sense will be that the divine law promises eternal life to those who obey perfectly. But since, on account of the weakness of the flesh, no one can perfectly fulfill the law in this life (Rom. 8:1), this and similar promises of the law are rendered useless to us, wherefore one must flee by faith to Christ, who is "the τέλος [end, goal] of the law" (Rom. 10:4), "in whom the promises of God are ναὶ καὶ ἀμὴν [Yes and Amen]" (2 Cor. 1:20). If according to the Gospel, which can be done through accommodation, then the sense is that, having been justified by faith in Christ, who fulfilled the law in our place, we should from now on perform good works that flow from faith and, through perseverance of good work, seek glory and honor—that is, constantly walk in good works as on a path—in order that we may at length obtain the ultimate possession of eternal life by grace, through faith. For eternal life is "the τέλος [end, goal] of faith" (1 Pet. 1:9). "Good works, however, are the way of the kingdom, not the cause of reigning." (Bernard in his treatise *On Grace and Free Will*, near the end.)

v.8 τοῖς δὲ ἐξ ἐριθείας, καὶ ἀπειθοῦσι μὲν τῇ ἀληθείᾳ, πειθομένοις δὲ τῇ ἀδικίᾳ, θυμὸς καὶ ὀργή.

v.8 But unto them that are contentious, and do not obey the truth, but obey unrighteousness, indignation and wrath, (KJV)

Here he explains...

2. The punishments of the wicked comprehended under the preceding general statement in v.6.

Ἐριθεία [contention]—some say that it comes from ἐριθεύειν or ἐριθεύεσθαι which is "to work at spinning wool."

Ἔριθοι, says Hesychius, are ἐριουργοί, "those who work with wool." Gregorius Nyssenus, in his discourse on this word in 1 Cor. 15: "Then the Son will be subjected to the Father, etc. Who will accuse Paul and say that he means with the word ἐριθείας 'a zeal for contention and a desire for revenge?' It is clear to everyone that ἡ ἔριθος—properly a handmaid who handles wool (from ἐριουργίας, a worker of wool or a woolworker)—is being named from that Scripture, and so we normally mean the skill and the ability to deal with wool."

But Nyssenus is looking back at Isaiah 38:12 and Tob. 2:12, where the words ἔριθος and ἐριθεύομα are used with that meaning.

Suidas says that ἐριθείαν is τὴν διὰ λόγων φιλονεικίαν [quarreling with words], which is why the Vulgate translates with "contention." In 2 Cor. 12:20 the words are joined together: "ζῆλοι,

θυμοὶ, ἐριθεῖαι, ἀκαταστασίαι [debates, envyings, wraths, strifes]."
Gal. 5:20: "ἔρεις, ζῆλοι, θυμοὶ, ἐριθεῖαι [variance, emulations, wrath,
strife]." James 3:16: ὅπου ζῆλος καὶ ἐρίθεια, ἐκεῖ ἀκαταστασία [where
envying and strife is, there is confusion]." From these passages, a
conclusion can be reached concerning the genuine meaning of this
word. The Syriac has the noun ‫ניצן‬, meaning "contentious, quar-
relsome." They are therefore called ἐξ ἐριθείας [from contention]
from the Hebrew phrase, "sons of quarrels, who are from contention," that is, *contentious*.

Lyra explains it thus: "The one whose soul is always contend-
ing, and with whom συντήρησις, or 'the rule of right reason,' always murmurs back to evil."

We demonstrated above that the Apostle is here dealing with
the Jews. Therefore, he accuses them of resisting and opposing the
salutary doctrine set forth in the Gospel, so that it is thus added by
way of explanation, ἀπειθοῦσι τῇ ἀληθείᾳ [they disobey the truth].

Contrary to this explanation, some have argued that with
ἀλήθειαν [truth], the Apostle in this passage does not understand
the truth of doctrine revealed in the Word, since he is dealing with
Gentiles, on whom the light of the Word did not shine, but rather
he understands the true knowledge that is naturally ingrained in
the minds of men—the meaning with which he had used this vocable in ch. 1:18 and 25. They then argue that the ones who are called
πειθόμενοι τῇ ἀδικίᾳ [obedient to unrighteousness], are those who
continually pursue unrighteousness, in the same sense as in the
preceding chapter, v.18, where he said that they were holding the
truth of God captive, as it were, in unrighteousness. Ἀδικίας [un-
righteousness], moreover, is a noun that is generally used to signify a depraved doctrine and perverse examples of behavior.

But all these things proceed from that hypothesis, that the
Apostle is now dealing with the Gentiles in this second chapter and
convicting them of sin.

Some understand the passive verb ἀποδοθήσεται [he will be re-
paid] being carried forward from v. 6. But the verb ἔσται, "there will

be" or "there will occur wrath," is more correctly stated here by ellipsis. It should be noted well that the Syriac interpreter, when he
speaks of the rewards for good works in v.7, uses the verb יְהַב, "he
will give." But when, in this verse, he speaks of the punishments
for evil works, he uses the verb נְפָרוּע, "he will weigh out," so as to
indicate a disparity between evil and good works, namely, that evil
works are deserving of punishments, and good works, though not
deserving of rewards, will be rewarded on the basis of grace.

v.9 θλίψις καὶ στενοχωρία, ἐπὶ πᾶσαν ψυχὴν ἀνθρώπου τοῦ
κατεργαζομένου τὸ κακόν, Ἰουδαίου τε πρῶτον καὶ Ἕλληνος·

*v.9 Tribulation and anguish, upon every soul of man that doeth evil,
of the Jew first, and also of the Gentile; (KJV)*

He repeats the same thing he had said in the preceding verse,
using different words for the sake of emphasis.

Namely, θλίψις ἔσται [there will be tribulation]. The antithesis
of verses 7 & 8 is repeated, but in inverse order, for there mention
was made first of good works, then of evil works; but here he mentions first evil works, then good works.

Θλίψις [tribulation] properly signifies "compression," from
θλίβειν, which is used with regard to the active compression of the
heel, and the passive pressing of grapes. It is used metaphorically
of "affliction," especially in the New Testament books and among
Church writers. Affliction, then, means θλίψιν, expressing, not so
much the action itself of afflicting, but more, the narrow places
into which one who is being afflicted is driven. It means that anxiety with which one is oppressed, or in general, the evil that is suffered. The Syriac has the noun אוּלְצָנָא, "anguish, necessity, trouble," especially the kind that is caused by craving, which agrees
beautifully with the state of the damned (Luke 16:24).

Στενοχωρία [anguish] is properly "anguish of spirit," such as
normally occurs in illnesses and terrors. Thycydides, Bk. 7, uses it
of a narrow space into which someone is driven by enemies. It is
this meaning that Plutarch uses in *Symposiacs*, Bk. 6, Q. 6, in contrast to εὐρυχωρία, "a spacious or wide place." In this metaphorical

meaning Comicus said: "My troops are now utterly confined to a narrow place."

In the same way some understand the passage of the Apostle in 2 Cor. 6:12, οὐ στενοχωρεῖσθε ἐν ἡμῖν, στενωχωρεῖσθε δὲ ἐν τοῖς σπλάγχνοις ὑμῶν, "you do not dwell narrowly in us." But there likewise, as in this passage, he is using a metaphorical meaning. It is not that, on our account, your souls are in anguish and anxiety, but the fact that you feel anguish—that comes from a sincere and filial love toward us.

The Syriac has the noun אַלְצָנוּט, from the root טוּק, "he has torn," and by way of metaphor, "he has disturbed, he has struck together." Luther translates, "*Angst* [anxiety]."

Ἰουδαίου πρῶτον [of the Jew first], for God had proclaimed His law especially to the Jews, and had bound them to His service with various benefits.

Just as in Rom. 1:16 he had said that the proclamation of the Gospel first had to be made to them because of the promise to the Fathers (Acts 13:46), so in this passage he says that the penalty for violating the law was prepared and was to be imposed on them first of all by the righteous judgment of God.

v.10 δόξα δὲ καὶ τιμὴ καὶ εἰρήνη παντὶ τῷ ἐργαζομένῳ ἀγαθόν, Ἰουδαίῳ τε πρῶτον καὶ Ἕλληνι.

v.10 But glory, honour, and peace, to every man that worketh good, to the Jew first, and also to the Gentile: (KJV)

He repeats what he had said previously in v. 7 concerning the awards for good deeds, so that he may more deeply drive that judgment of God into the souls of his hearers.

Ἡ δόξα [the glory] is in contrast to τῇ ὀργῇ [the wrath]; τιμὴ [honor] is in contrast to τῇ θλίψει [the affliction]; εἰρήνη [peace] is in contrast to τῇ στενοχωρίᾳ [the narrow place] in the preceding verses.

They will have glory in body and soul; honor with God, and

with all the angels and the blessed; peace in a conscience undisturbed by any pangs.

v.11 Οὐ γάρ ἐστι προσωποληψία παρὰ τῷ Θεῷ.

v.11 *For there is no respect of persons with God. (KJV)*

Προσωποληψία [respect of persons] is literally "the accepting of a face."

He confirms what he had said in v.6, that God would give to each one according to works:

1. From the comparison with the office of a righteous judge.

He is said (with a Hebrew phrase) "to accept the face of someone," who does something as a favor for another (Gen. 19:21, 1 Sam. 25:35, etc.). He is said "to accept a person in judgment" who does not take into account the merits of a case, but makes a judgment in a person's favor as a favor, having carefully weighed his external characteristics which strike the eyes. These external things render the person commendable to us, although they do not pertain to the case itself—things such as riches, honor, family, dignity, authority, family ties (Lev. 19:15, Deu. 1:17, 16:19, Pro. 18:5, 24:24).

Augustine, in Bk. 2. *Against Two Epistles of the Pelagians*, ch. 7, defines it as προσωποληψίαν "when one pays attention, not to the merits of the case, but to the dignity of the person."

"An acceptor of persons" is a judge who, when a case has been neglected about which a judgment should properly be made, he only takes into account the persons. And however he happens to be disposed toward them, that is how he makes a judgment concerning the dispute.

But such praise of justice is attributed to God very often in the Scriptures, that with Him there is no προσωποληψία [respecting of persons] (Deu. 10:17, 2 Chr. 19:7, Job 34:19, Acts 10:34, Gal. 2:6, Eph. 6:9, Col. 3:11 & 25, 1 Pet. 1:17).

In this passage, it is specifically applied to the distinction between Jews and Gentiles, for God pays no heed to that, either in handing out rewards or in imposing penalties.

Observe: Peter (1 Pet. 1:17-18) deduces from this—that God is ἀπροσωπολήπτης [not a respecter of persons]—a weighty exhortation to behavior that ought to be rooted in the fear of God.

It is not to be regarded as προσωποληψία [respecting of persons]— the fact that God, on account of a person having been reconciled to Him by faith in Christ, also considers his works to be pleasing, or that He distributes His gifts as He chooses.

v.12 Ὅσοι γὰρ ἀνόμως ἥμαρτον, ἀνόμως καὶ ἀπολοῦνται· καὶ ὅσοι ἐν νόμῳ ἥμαρτον, διὰ νόμου κριθήσονται.

v.12 For as many as have sinned without law shall also perish without law: and as many as have sinned in the law shall be judged by the law; (KJV)

2. He proves the righteousness of God from the outcome.

The sense is that those who sinned outside the Law of Moses, being ignorant of it, are to be damned through the law of nature; those, on the other hand, who knew the Law of Moses and still sinned against it, are to be damned by it.

By those who "sinned without the law," he understands the Gentiles, who did not have the written law. By those who "sinned in the law," he understands the Jews, who received the law that was solemnly pronounced by God. So, then, he applies separately to Jews and Gentiles that universal accusation of the human race which he had discussed earlier, for the entire human race is contained in their embrace.

The Jews are said to have sinned "in the law," not because they had transgressed the law, for they had this in common with the Gentiles, but because they were ἐν τῷ νόμῳ, "under the law" (Rom. 3:19).

v.13 Οὐ γὰρ οἱ ἀκροαταὶ τοῦ νόμου δίκαιοι παρὰ τῷ Θεῷ, ἀλλ᾽ οἱ ποιηταὶ τοῦ νόμου δικαιωθήσονται.

v.13 For not the hearers of the law are just before God, but the doers of the law shall be justified. (KJV)

He moves on to confirm the minor premise, namely, that the works of the Jews are just as unrighteous as those of the Gentiles. But he replies as if to a tacit objection. The Jews thought they were not unrighteous, since they had and heard the law and observed it externally. The Apostle replies that the law must be kept perfectly.

This matter has the Jews in view, who certainly heard the divinely received law, but did not do it, that is, they did not fulfill it perfectly, and so neither could they be justified by it.

The word order of παρὰ τῷ θεῷ [before God] is very emphatic. The hearers of the law may seem to be righteous before men, but before God—that is, in the judgment of God—not the hearers, but the doers of the law will be justified.

On each and every Sabbath the law was recited and explained to them in the synagogues. They spent all their effort on a diligent examination of the law, but they did not fulfill the things prescribed by the law.

Bellarmine, Bk. 2, *On Justification*, ch. 16, responding to this apostolic passage, says that it can be explained in three ways: "(1) 'The doers of the law will be justified,' that is, they will merit an increase of righteousness, and through this they will be justified meritoriously through works. (2) 'The doers of the law will be justified,' that is, those who truly desire to be doers of the law will see to it that they are justified. For they do not do the righteousness of the law unless they have been justified (Augustine, *On the Spirit and the Letter*, ch. 26). (3) 'The doers of the law will be justified,' that is, they will be judged as righteous in the divine judgment and will justly obtain the crown of righteousness." He claims that this exposition is more literal than the others.

Pererius, Disputation 7 on Romans chapter 2, (1) repudiates the exposition of Augustine, "since Paul is not attempting in this passage to prove that it is necessary for men first to be justified and thus to become doers of the law. Rather he chiefly intends to prove that, not hearers, but doers of the law will be justified in God's sight."

(2) He repudiates the exposition of Sotus and Stapleton, who take the apostolic passage concerning the increase of righteousness in this sense: "Those who have first been justified will then be justified by observing the law, that is, they advance further and grow in righteousness, although this exposition does not agree with Paul's aim."

(3) He approves that exposition whereby the word *justify* is understood as "to esteem and declare righteous." "In that sense, they will be pronounced and declared righteous on the Day of Judgment, and as such, they will be remunerated with eternal life—those who were not only hearers, but also doers of the law." From this he concludes that "this statement of Paul refutes as false the opinion of the heretics at that time—those who steal all the force and reckoning of righteousness from the good works of righteous men and assign it to faith alone—since justification is relegated to the hearing of the law and zeal for it (which includes faith), unless it is accompanied by the keeping of the law."

(4) He submits the exposition of Ambrose, who interprets the words of the Apostle concerning those who believe in Christ, whom the law of Moses not only predicted and promised, but also commanded the Jews to believe in Him and to obey Him. (The words of Ambrose are: "He says this because these are not the ones who are righteous—those who hear the law—but those who believe in Christ, whom the law promised. Indeed, this is what it means 'to do the law.' But no one does the law who does not believe the law and does not accept Him to whom the law bears witness. Now, the Gentile, who seems to be without the law—if he believes in Christ, he is said to have done the law. The Jew, on the other hand, is said to be a hearer of the law and not a doer, since he does not believe in the Christ who was written in the law.") He says that this exposition is both true and godly, but it does not agree with the purpose of the Apostle and the sense of his words.

We reply: (1) The Apostle teaches that whole and perfect obedience to the law is required, that knowledge only or hearing only does not suffice for a person to be justified by the law. But by no means does he teach that men can furnish that perfect obedience and so be justified by the law. He rather teaches the opposite in this Epistle and in the one to the Galatians, and here and there in Ephesians.

(2) If the law were fulfilled perfectly by us, then certainly justification would be by the law. But that conditional requirement brings nothing into existence.

(3) Therefore, the statement is a legal one, promising justification and life, but with the condition of perfect obedience. For they are said to do the law, who continue in all things that have been written in the Book of the Law (Deu. 27:28, Gal. 3:10). Such doers of the law are certainly righteous, not only before men, but also before God, and obtain life through obedience to the law (Lev. 18:5, Luke 10:28). But since such a ποιητὴς [doer] of the law does not exist, it follows that neither does a law exist that can vivify, that is, justify (Gal. 3:21).

(4) The aim of the Apostle is to teach that the Jews are not righteous by the law, since they do not satisfy the law. And in chapter 8 verse 3, he declares in general that, because of the weakness of the flesh, the perfect fulfillment of the law is ἀδύνατον [impossible] for us. Therefore we invert the argument. Not the hearers, but the doers of the law will be justified. But no one among men is a doer of the law, that is, one who fulfills it perfectly. Therefore, by the law and the works of the law no flesh is justified before God, which is the conclusion expressly stated in Rom. 3:20 and Gal. 2:16. Of course, Pererius strenuously denies this assumption. But it is demonstrated in its place with clear arguments.

(5) But if we should really accept that interpretation (that the doers of the law will be justified, that is, on the day of judgment they will be pronounced and declared righteous), it still would not yet follow that such a ποίησιν [doing] of the law is either perfect or deserving of eternal life, but only that it would be the effect and testimony of justifying faith, and based on this testimony the judgment is to be made with regard to the inner justifying faith.

The Apostle is speaking legally, not practically,[27] for the law demands the most perfect obedience—not only external obedience, but also internal. No, even more, it demands the highest integrity of the entire nature. But he makes the most effectively convincing case in this very passage that such doers of the law do not exist. He teaches how justification by the law is to be understood, that is, what must be understood by those who profess that they want to be justified by the law, namely, that it is not a matter of hearing the law and being instructed in it, but it is a matter of precisely observing that very thing that he knows to be commanded by the law (Rom. 10). Since no one does this, the following argument of the Apostle emerges: Whoever is justified by the law keeps the law. But no one keeps the law. Therefore no one is justified by the law. The major premise is proven, since it is not the hearers of the law who are righteous before God. Rather, "The doers of the law shall be justified."

v.14 Ὅταν γὰρ ἔθνη τὰ μὴ νόμον ἔχοντα φύσει τὰ τοῦ νόμου ποιῇ, οὗτοι, νόμον μὴ ἔχοντες, ἑαυτοῖς εἰσι νόμος·

v.14 *For when the Gentiles, which have not the law, do by nature the things contained in the law, these, having not the law, are a law unto themselves: (KJV)*

This statement has the Gentiles in view, who, while they did not have the written law, still had the law of nature engraved on their hearts, pointing out the difference between noble and ignoble things, prescribing the good and proscribing the bad. Thus, neither do the Gentiles have any excuse for their shameful deeds.

Some have determined that the Apostle in this passage is not describing the Gentiles as they are, but as they ought to be, in order to prove, they say, that righteousness does not consist in the sort of external observation of the law of which the Jews used to boast. He, in turn, pits the moral obedience of the Gentiles that is (or should be) rendered to the law of nature against the ceremonial righteousness of the Jews, and teaches that this moral obedience is much to be preferred to the ceremonial obedience. He proceeds

27 Latin: *de jure, non de facto*

with a sort of rhetorical concession. If the Gentiles, guided by nature without the written law and without ceremonies of the law, had rendered perfect obedience to God, then they would be righteous as far as the written law is concerned, even without the ceremonies of the law. There is, therefore, no value to the external, fictional, ceremonial righteousness of the Jews.

But it is clear that the Apostle is describing the Gentiles, not as they were before the Fall or as they could be if the Fall of their first parents hadn't intervened, but as the more sensible among them are after the Fall. Therefore, it is more correctly said that even the more sensible Gentile who, by natural instinct, does some things that are of the law and thus in some way is a doer of the law, is preferred to the Jew who, being confident in external works and ceremonies of the law, is merely a hearer of the law. But above all, the Apostle has in view the fact that the Gentiles do not have any excuse for their shameful deeds, etc.

There is an elegant antanaclasis here. The Gentiles, who do not have the law (namely, the written law) are a law unto themselves when they do by natural instinct those things that are of the law.

When he denies that the Gentiles had the law, it is understood that he is speaking about the external and solemn proclamation of the law, just as in Rom. 9:4, νομοθεσία [the giving of the law] is celebrated as a certain peculiar advantage of the Jews. Meanwhile, the Gentiles had the law inscribed on their hearts, just as it is immediately added in v.15 that, since this natural law is in reality the same as the moral law, it therefore obligated the Gentiles just as much as the Jews.

The Apostle notably says of the Gentiles, not that they do the law, that is, fulfill it perfectly (as the phrase ποιεῖν νόμον [to do the law] is understood in the preceding verse), but that they do those things that are of the law, even though they have no more than a certain small part of the external works of the law. Hence that ποιεῖν [to do] is only to be understood partially, both on account of some of the more sensible Gentiles, and with regard to the external observance of the law.

v.15 οἵτινες ἐνδείκνυνται τὸ ἔργον τοῦ νόμου γραπτὸν ἐν ταῖς καρδίαις αὐτῶν, συμμαρτυρούσης αὐτῶν τῆς συνειδήσεως, καὶ μεταξὺ ἀλλήλων τῶν λογισμῶν κατηγορούντων ἢ καὶ ἀπολογουμένων.

v.15 *Which shew the work of the law written in their hearts, their conscience also bearing witness, and their thoughts the mean while accusing or else excusing one another; (KJV)*

With τὸ ἔργον τοῦ νόμου [the work of the Law], the thing itself is understood, namely, the sentence expressed by the law. For τὸ ἔργον [the work] is in contrast to the writing of the law as an external characteristic.

Γραπτόν [written]. The Syriac explains it as a metaphor with the adjectival particle of comparison כַּ. "They display the work of the law, as written upon their heart."

This writing of the law should be distinguished from the former writing of the law, of which mention was made in Jer. 31:33. For they are different: (1) With regard to the *subject matter*. In Jeremiah, the doctrine of the Gospel is understood, but here the natural law. (2) With regard to *the efficient cause*. The former writing is from the Holy Spirit, the latter from nature. (3) With regard to *the object*. The former pertains to believers, the latter to all men in common. (4) With regard to *the effect*. The former renders people pleasing to God, the latter ἀναπολογήτους [inexcusable].

Συμμαρτυρούσης τῆς συνειδήσεως, "the conscience bearing witness together." The Vulgate does not grasp the emphasis when it simply translates "bearing witness, etc." But the Apostle is looking back at what he had said in the preceding verse, that the Gentiles φύσει, "by natural judgment," do the things which are of the law.

Μεταξὺ ἀλλήλων [between one another]. Some refer to an interval of time in this sense, that their thoughts accuse them—one after another—of vices, and they excuse the same man, due to conscience, of things wrongly or rightly done. The Vulgate translates: "between them alternately," in the sense that their thoughts sometimes accuse, sometimes excuse.

Ἀπολογουμένων [defending], namely, when the Gentiles are not conscious of any more serious external crime in themselves. The Syriac has, "with thoughts that lead out into a wide space," which is a Syrian idiom.

v.16 ἐν ἡμέρᾳ ὅτε κρινεῖ ὁ Θεὸς τὰ κρυπτὰ τῶν ἀνθρώπων κατὰ τὸ εὐαγγέλιόν μου, διὰ Ἰησοῦ Χριστοῦ.

v.16 *In the day when God shall judge the secrets of men by Jesus Christ according to my gospel.* (KJV)

Some connect this verse with the end of v.12, "they will be damned through the law," so that vv. 13-15 are inserted almost as a parenthesis. But it can also be joined together with the immediately preceding verses, since, even on the Last Day, the conscience will accuse some and excuse others.

Ἐν ἡμέρᾳ [on the day]—read "as will be manifested on the day." For in this life the inner thoughts of man are not seen, regardless of what his conscience may dictate. Some, however, connect these words with v.12, "they will be judged on that day, etc.," so that vv.13-15 are taken to be included in the parentheses.

Κατὰ τὸ εὐαγγέλιον [according to the Gospel], because the Gospel teaches that "Christ will return to judge the living and the dead" (Acts 10:42). But above all, the Apostle has this in view, that the Gospel will be the norm in that judgment, for he who believes the Gospel will be saved, while "he who does not believe will be condemned" (Mark 16:16).

With the word *Gospel*, some understand the whole doctrine that the Apostle preached and afterward put down in writing, since damnation does not properly come from the Gospel as such, but from the law.

Others say that Paul is referring to his Gospel as that Evangelical history that Luke put down in writing at his counsel and urging (2 Cor. 8:18, Philemon 24, 2 Tim. 4:11). But it is more correctly understood of the Gospel preached by the Apostle.

114

v.17 Ἴδε σὺ Ἰουδαῖος ἐπονομάζῃ καὶ ἐπαναπαύῃ τῷ νόμῳ καὶ καυχᾶσαι ἐν Θεῷ

v.17 Behold, thou art called a Jew, and restest in the law, and makest thy boast of God, (KJV)

Now the Apostle turns from the Gentiles to the Jews and upbraids them for their vain boast in that name. He demonstrates that the Jews indeed have some shadow and semblance of external righteousness, but are lacking the true inner obedience of the heart. He again uses a rhetorical figure, as in the beginning of the chapter, and accuses all the Jews under the persona of a single Jew. But first he reviews certain advantages of the Jews, so that he may afterwards demonstrate that they are just that much more ungrateful to God. "Look, you who are called by the name 'Jew,'" being such in name only, not in fact.

The Vulgate translates: "Now, if you are called a Jew," which is how the Syriac also translates: אֶן אֲנְתְּדְרִין, probably by a spurious error of the manuscript that it used which had εἰ δὲ [now, if] instead of ἰδὲ [look!]. But the approved Greek manuscripts all read ἰδὲ, and the construction would be left dangling if it read εἰ δέ.

Ἐπαναπαύῃ τῷ νόμῳ [You rest upon the Law], you rest and relax softly upon the law, figuring that it is sufficient for your salvation and that you can gain peace of conscience and salvation from it as long as you render some sort of obedience to it in an external fashion.

Καυχᾶσαι ἐν θεῷ [You boast in God], you boast that you belong to the people to whom God promised that He desired to be their God, and made a covenant with them. The Apostle has this in view, that the Gentiles are said to have been lacking the salvific knowledge of God, ἄθεοι, "without God" (Eph. 2:12).

Some distinguish between these phrases, "to boast in God" and "to boast in the Lord" (Jer. 9:24, 1 Cor. 1:31). The former, they say, includes the knowledge of God and of His law, while the latter additionally requires obedience, as men subject themselves to God with an eager will, just as servants to their lords.

A simpler answer is that ἐν [in] is used in this passage in place of περὶ [about], "you boast about God," that is, about the revelation and knowledge of God. Syriac: בַּאלָהָא.

v.18 καὶ γινώσκεις τὸ θέλημα, καὶ δοκιμάζεις τὰ διαφέροντα, κατηχούμενος ἐκ τοῦ νόμου,

v.18 And knowest his will, and approvest the things that are more excellent, being instructed out of the law; (KJV)

The Syriac adds an appendix and connects the phrase γινώσκεις τὸ θέλημα [you know the will] with the preceding καυχᾶσαι ἐν θεῷ [you boast in God], "you boast about God, that you know His will." You boast that you recognize the will of God, and that through the law you can discern between wrong and right.

The Gentiles know nothing except for the power and divinity, that is, the being of God, namely, that God exists, that He is powerful, good, just, wise. But you, in addition to this, know the will of God concerning the salvation of the human race. You know the revealed Word—how He wants to be worshiped.

Δοκιμάζεις τὰ διαφέροντα [you approve the things that are more excellent]. Τὰ διαφέροντα [the differing things] the Vulgate translates as "the more useful things;" Erasmus and Cajetan, "the extraordinary things;" others, "excellent and unique things."

But it can be deduced from the verb δοκιμάζειν [to test, approve] that in this passage it more properly means "difference" or "discrepancy." The Vulgate translation renders τὸ δοκιμάζειν with "test," which is ambiguous, since "to test" sometimes means "to explore and examine," but sometimes "to approve." In this passage, the first meaning agrees with the text, so that the sense is, "you explore what the difference is between good works and bad works." The Syriac has the verb פְּרַשׁ, "he separated, he distinguished." Luther: *"Du prüfest was das beste zu tun sey* [You test what the best thing to do is]."

Theodoret on this passage: "'You test the more useful things,' which means, you distinguish between the things that are contrary to one another." Some refer, not to the comparison of good and bad works, but to the comparison of one good work to another. "You explore those good works by which they excel and surpass, which the Gentiles did not know by the light of nature." But the former explanation agrees better with the text.

Κατηχούμενος [catechized] properly means, "having been instructed and educated with the living voice." For he is properly said to be κατηχεῖσθαι [catechized] to whom something sounds in the ears, who is taught about a certain subject with the ministry of the living voice (Acts 18:25, Gal. 6:6). It is also properly used concerning the fundamental points of a certain doctrine, which are passed down to another with the living voice. But here it generally signifies the one being instructed. The Apostle, then, is tacitly criticizing the Jews, that they have been thus far well versed in learning the fundamental points of the law, and yet they ignore and repudiate Christ, who is the τέλος, "the end of the law."

v.19 πέποιθάς τε σεαυτὸν ὁδηγὸν εἶναι τυφλῶν, φῶς τῶν ἐν σκότει,

v.19 *And art confident that thou thyself art a guide of the blind, a light of them which are in darkness, (KJV)*

You boast, not only of knowing the law correctly, but also of being able to teach others from it.

With *blindness* is understood the spiritual darkness in which all men are born by nature. Teachers are called "lights" (Mat. 5:14).

v.20 παιδευτὴν ἀφρόνων, διδάσκαλον νηπίων, ἔχοντα τὴν μόρφωσιν τῆς γνώσεως καὶ τῆς ἀληθείας ἐν τῷ νόμῳ.

v.20 *An instructor of the foolish, a teacher of babes, which hast the form of knowledge and of the truth in the law. (KJV)*

Παιδεύειν means not only "to instruct," but also "to correct and to punish," so that it is used both of doctrine and of discipline. Therefore, a παιδευτὴς ἀφρόνων [foolish] is an instructor and punisher of fools. The Syriac has the verb רדא, which likewise means not only "he taught," but also "he punished" (Luke 22:16, Acts 7:22).

With τοὺς νηπίους [babes] are understood those who, like infants, are still course and ignorant (Mat. 11:25).

With μόρφωσιν τῆς γνώσεως [form of knowledge], some understand "a certain external and superficial kind of knowledge." In this sense the Apostle (2 Tim. 3:5) calls it a μόρφωσιν τῆς εὐσεβείας, a certain vain sort of feigned piety.

Thus Theophylact explains this passage with ἐπίπλαστον εἰκόνα, "a masked image that retains an outward form of truth, but nothing more." Dominicus from Soto follows this exposition.

But it is more correctly understood as a form and norm of the true knowledge expressed in the law. For (1) the Apostle does not simply say that the Jew has μόρφωσιν τῆς γνώσεως [a form of knowledge], but also adds καὶ τῆς ἀληθείας [and of truth].

(2) He says that this form of knowledge and truth is expressed in the law. But could anyone imagine that there is in the law only some sort of superficial and ethereal kind of knowledge and truth?

(3) The Apostle has been enumerating the advantages of the Jews because of which they were flattering themselves. Those advantages were certainly not false, but true. Afterwards he then goes on to this, so that he may blame them for proving themselves unworthy of those advantages.

(4) Chrysostom, Oecumenius and Theophylact understand it from the Greek Fathers in the same way; Ambrose, from the Latin. Chrysostom, Homily 5 on Romans: "It is as if someone who has the image of a king displays nothing of his likeness, while those to whom his image is not entrusted imitate it accurately, even without a prototype."

The Syriac has the noun דּוּמְיָא which corresponds to the Hebrew דְּמוּת, meaning "perfect likeness." Luther, on the fifth chapter of Genesis: "One recognizes by diligent observation that they properly called צֶלֶם an image or a figure, while דְּמוּת, which means likeness, is the perfection of an image."

But the argument is inferred in this passage—how it can be proved that the divine law is perfect in knowledge and in truth, that is, the norm and rule of true knowledge.

v.21 Ὁ οὖν διδάσκων ἕτερον, σεαυτὸν οὐ διδάσκεις; Ὁ κηρύσσων μὴ κλέπτειν, κλέπτεις;

v.21 Thou therefore which teachest another, teachest thou not thyself? thou that preachest a man should not steal, dost thou steal? (KJV)

After enumerating some of the advantages and benefits of the Jews, he demonstrates that they were ungrateful to God for these gifts, and so, since they abused them, they yielded to ignominy, injustice and damnation. The argument of the Apostle goes like this: He who has and teaches the law, but does not do it, is unrighteous. The Jews have and teach the law, but do not do it. Therefore... He presses the minor premise and drives it home by means of antithesis. It must be noted that whatever things are here enumerated, the Jews may not do them in their deeds, but they do them in the heart through depraved lusts. He has in view v.1, τὰ αὐτὰ πράσσεις ὁ κρίνων [you who judge practice the same things].

There is an elegant antanaclasis here. Therefore, you who teach another, do you not teach yourself? For we may teach ourselves one thing, but teach another thing to others. We teach others when we set before them precepts of doctrine and behavior; we teach ourselves when we are proficient in knowledge, and when we ourselves yield to the principles that we set before others, leading an exemplary life before them.

v.22 Ὁ λέγων μὴ μοιχεύειν, μοιχεύεις; Ὁ βδελυσσόμενος τὰ εἴδωλα, ἱεροσυλεῖς;

v.22 Thou that sayest a man should not commit adultery, dost thou commit adultery? thou that abhorrest idols, dost thou commit sacrilege? (KJV)

Ἱεροσυλεῖν properly means "to rob temples," from ἱερὸν and συλεῖν. Later it is generally understood as any kind of sacrilege.

Some specifically apply it to the Jewish priests who would practice robbery against the people in the name of divine service.

It seems that the Syriac has this in view when it translates "you despoil the house of sanctity," that is, "of the sanctuary" בֵּית מַקְדְּשָׁא.

But it is more correctly understood about any of the unbelieving Jews in general who would attribute to creatures the honor due to God, and thus they would deprive God of His glory by the monstrous crime of sacrilege.

The Jews committed the crime of sacrilege, because they did not concede that God alone was just and the one who justifies him who is of faith—the one who believes that Christ alone is our righteousness before God. For since they sought righteousness in their works, they robbed God and His Son Christ Jesus of the praise that belonged to His righteousness and mercy.

v.23 Ὃς ἐν νόμῳ καυχᾶσαι, διὰ τῆς παραβάσεως τοῦ νόμου τὸν Θεὸν ἀτιμάζεις.

v.23 Thou that makest thy boast of the law, through breaking the law dishonourest thou God? (KJV)

That which he had previously called καυχᾶσαι ἐν θεῷ [to boast in God] in v.17, he calls καυχᾶσαι ἐν νόμῳ [to boast in Law] in this passage, since the Jews boasted about the law that was divinely handed down to them.

Διὰ τῆς παραβάσεως τοῦ νόμου [Through the transgression of the Law]. "Through the transgression or the violation of the law." He compares the law to definite boundaries or lines which no one should cross, while sin is the transgression of those boundaries.

Observe: Just as God is glorified through good works (Mat. 5:16), so through the sins of those who bragged about being the people of God, He is dishonored.

v.24 Τὸ γὰρ ὄνομα τοῦ Θεοῦ δι' ὑμᾶς βλασφημεῖται ἐν τοῖς ἔθνεσι, καθὼς γέγραπται.

v.24 For the name of God is blasphemed among the Gentiles through you, as it is written. (KJV)

He demonstrates the reason why he has accused them of sacrilege and dishonoring God, namely, because they were the cause of God's name being blasphemed.

The sense is, you stand in the footsteps of your wicked ancestors, and so God justly utters the same words of complaint about you as He once uttered about them. There are examples of this in Isa. 52:5, Eze. 36:23.

Chemnitz, in his *Harmony*, ch. 12, p.249: "It is a useful rule for elucidating many passages of Scripture that prophecy, that is, the Scripture, is understood to be fulfilled (1) when something occurs which the Scripture properly and simply predicted in the passage that is cited and wants this to be understood (Mat. 1:23). (2) When something similar occurs that is related to a past event (Mat. 13:35). (3) When the Scripture does not speak about a single definite deed, but relates a general doctrine, that is correctly said to be fulfilled just as many times as that which Scripture says occurs in any passage (Mat. 15:7, 13:14, etc.). (4) Many statements of Scripture speak both about the head and about the members. Therefore, they are correctly said to be fulfilled when they are accommodated either to the members or to the head (Hos. 11:1, Mat. 2:15)." The citation in this passage belongs to the second class.

v.25 Περιτομὴ μὲν γὰρ ὠφελεῖ, ἐὰν νόμον πράσσῃς, ἐὰν δὲ παραβάτης νόμου ᾖς, ἡ περιτομή σου ἀκροβυστία γέγονεν.

v.25 For circumcision verily profiteth, if thou keep the law: but if thou be a breaker of the law, thy circumcision is made uncircumcision. (KJV)

The Jews were confident especially (1) in νομοθεσία [the receiving of the Law]; (2) in περιτομῇ [circumcision]. Therefore, after discussing the first part of their vain confidence and boasting, the Apostle now proceeds to the second part. He also responds to the tacit objection concerning the advantage of circumcision that had been granted to the Jews: Circumcision and ceremonial righteousness are indeed advantageous, but only if accompanied by a circumcision of the heart and by the perfect obedience of the law.

"Circumcision is advantageous if one observes the law." The papists try to wrest out of this that the law can be fulfilled perfectly in this life, since circumcision was certainly beneficial to some.

We reply: The Apostle does not wish for his words to be taken as if it were possible for some of the Jews to fulfill the law, or as if circumcision were of no advantage to any of the Jews. Rather, he means that circumcision, when it is not used as a seal of the gracious righteousness of faith, is an obligation to obey the whole law. Gal. 5:3, "I testify again that every man who circumcises himself is obligated to observe the whole law." The covenant that was initiated in circumcision did indeed require the fulfillment of the law (Gen. 17:1). But what was lacking to the one circumcised—this the one who is circumcised by faith could take and apply to himself from the perfect satisfaction of Christ, since circumcision, on the basis of the divine institution, was a reminder and a seal of the coming blessing of the Seed. In this respect circumcision is said by the Apostle in Rom. 4:11 to be a seal of the righteousness of faith. Therefore, as many among the circumcised as would apply to themselves the satisfaction of Christ and the merit of faith, they were considered before the judgment of God as those who had fulfilled the law. Since the Jews neglected this true purpose and use of circumcision and underwent circumcision as part of a legal obedience through which they assured themselves of salvation, the Apostle rightly sets this against them: Circumcision is indeed advantageous if someone observes the law, that is, either by fulfilling the law *per se*, or by laying hold of Christ, who is the goal of the law, by faith. Since the Jews had done neither of these things, circumcision was of no value for them. As the Apostle says in this passage, circumcision had turned back into foreskin for them.

Ἀκροβυστία is "the skin on the extremity of the male member," which is cut off in circumcision. Aristotle calls it ἀκροποσθίαν from ἄκρον, "extreme," and πόσθη, "the male member." In Latin, it is called "foreskin," from the outcome, since it is "foreskinned" or "amputated" by the Jews.

Some take it from βύω, "to stop up, to block up," so that the ἀκρόβυστος is thus "the one having the covering on the extremity," that is, "having the extreme part of the male member covered, covered with the foreskin." He is contrasted with the περιτετμημένος, "the circumcised." So it is that the Chaldeans and Syrians determine that the word comes from "stopping up," עורלּותא, "the skin that covers the tip of the male member."

When it is said that ἡ περιτομή σου ἀκροβυστία γέγονεν [your circumcision has become foreskin], it has the sense that circumcision is reckoned to him as foreskin. He is thus considered as if he were not circumcised, as explained in the following verse.

v.26 Ἐὰν οὖν ἡ ἀκροβυστία τὰ δικαιώματα τοῦ νόμου φυλάσσῃ, οὐχὶ ἡ ἀκροβυστία αὐτοῦ εἰς περιτομὴν λογισθήσεται;

v.26 Therefore if the uncircumcision keep the righteousness of the law, shall not his uncircumcision be counted for circumcision? (KJV)

The Apostle concludes the comparison of the Gentile who does the law by true obedience with the Jew who brags about his ceremonial and external righteousness of the law. But he is only speaking hypothetically. If there were such a Gentile, he would far surpass a circumcised Jew.

With ἀκροβυστίαν [foreskin], he understands by metonymy "the Gentiles who have the foreskin," as elsewhere "circumcision" is used for the circumcised Jews (Gal. 2:7-8).

Ἐὰν τὰ δικαιώματα τοῦ νόμου φυλάσσῃ [if he keeps the righteous requirements of the Law], if he furnishes that which God in His law prescribes as just and right.

Τὰ δικαιώματα [The righteousnesses] in the Old Testament are typically called "commands," that is, "the justifying instruments[28]," since, if they were perfectly obeyed, they would justify a man.

But how could Gentiles, who had foreskins, have kept the law? We reply: Either the Apostle is speaking about Gentiles who were converted to Christ, who walked in obedience to the divine commandments by faith, even without circumcision; or he is only speaking hypothetically. If there were such a Gentile, which there could have been, except that, through the Fall of our first parents, the whole nature of man has been corrupted by sin.

---

28 Latin: *justificamenta*

Instead of the verb λογισθήσεται [he will be reckoned], Chrysostom reads μετατραπήσεται [he will be converted] and adds, "οὐκ εἶπε λογισθήσεται, ἀλλὰ τραπήσεται, ὅπερ ἐμφατικώτερον ἦν [he did not say 'he will be reckoned,' but 'he will be bent,' which was more emphatic]." But the sense is that the foreskin will be reckoned for circumcision, that is, the one who has the foreskin will be considered as circumcised. If he observes the law, he will be just as pleasing to God as if he were circumcised.

v.27 Καὶ κρινεῖ ἡ ἐκ φύσεως ἀκροβυστία, τὸν νόμον τελοῦσα, σὲ τὸν διὰ γράμματος καὶ περιτομῆς παραβάτην νόμου;

v.27 And shall not uncircumcision which is by nature, if it fulfil the law, judge thee, who by the letter and circumcision dost transgress the law? (KJV)

By a sort of comparison he attributes the judgment of the one who is worse to the one who is better and preferred.

Κρινεῖ σὲ, "he will judge and condemn you," for it is customary for κρίνειν [to judge] to be used in place of the composite κατακρίνειν [to condemn] (Mat. 12:41).

With τὴν ἐκ φύσεως ἀκροβυστίαν [the foreskin by nature] are understood the Gentiles who have the foreskin by nature, who had no other law but the natural one.

With τὸ γράμμα [the letter], some understand the fact that the Jews had the written law, which the Gentiles lacked. For this reason, φύσις καὶ γράμμα [nature and letter], natural law and written law, are contrasted with one another, just as ἀκροβυστία καὶ περιτομὴ [foreskin and circumcision] are contrasted. But γράμμα καὶ περιτομὴ [letter and circumcision] are more correctly combined by hendiadys, so that the sense is, "through a literal or external circumcision." For as is clear from v.29, the Apostle understands with the word *letter* an external matter, but with the word *spirit*, he understands an internal matter.

By hearing the written law and by undergoing circumcision, they profess themselves Jews and boast about both of these things. Yet meanwhile they break the law.

v.28 Οὐ γὰρ ὁ ἐν τῷ φανερῷ Ἰουδαῖός ἐστιν, οὐδὲ ἡ ἐν τῷ φανερῷ ἐν σαρκὶ περιτομή.

v.28 For he is not a Jew, which is one outwardly; neither is that circumcision, which is outward in the flesh: (KJV)

He demonstrates what he had set forth above, that external and ceremonial righteousness is worth nothing before the judgment of God. What is required is an inner purity of heart, perfect obedience to the law and integrity of the whole nature.

ὁ ἐν τῷ φανερῷ [he who in the open], that is, he who according to the flesh is born of Jewish parents; he who by external profession has joined himself to the Jewish people; he who observes the ceremonies of the law.

"Is not a Jew," namely, a true Jew before God, belonging to the chosen people of God and the divine covenant.

v.29 ἀλλ' ὁ ἐν τῷ κρυπτῷ Ἰουδαῖος, καὶ περιτομὴ καρδίας ἐν πνεύματι, οὐ γράμματι, οὗ ὁ ἔπαινος οὐκ ἐξ ἀνθρώπων ἀλλ' ἐκ τοῦ Θεοῦ.

v.29 But he is a Jew, which is one inwardly; and circumcision is that of the heart, in the spirit, and not in the letter; whose praise is not of men, but of God. (KJV)

Ὁ ἐν τῷ κρυπτῷ [he who in the secret], he who by the inner faith of the heart embraces the Messiah who was promised to the Jews; who has been joined to the chosen people of God by a spiritual bond; who has been regenerated internally through the Holy Spirit and in this way has become a son of God and an heir of eternal life. Only God sees that this man worships God rightly in the heart, and thus acknowledges him as His own and praises him with this name.

Ἡ περιτομὴ καρδίας [the circumcision of heart] is the inner regeneration and renewal of the heart, including the amputation of shameful desires (Deu. 10:16, 30:6; Jer. 4:4, 9:26; Col. 2:11).

Ἐν πνεύματι [in spirit], either with regard to "the Holy Spirit" working effectively with power (Col. 2:11); or with regard to the subject, "in spirit," that is, internally; or with regard to the manner, "in spirit," that is, spiritually, since it involves new spiritual motives. For that circumcision that takes place ἐν γράμματι [in letter]—according to the external ceremony of the written law—is being contrasted with this spiritual circumcision.

"Whose praise is from God," who alone views the heart; "not from men," who judge only according to the outward appearance.

We infer from this passage, contrary to the papists, that circumcision in the Old Testament was an efficacious and salutary means by which infants were received into the covenant of grace and were made participants in regeneration and renewal.

The true Jew, says the Apostle, is the one who has a circumcised heart. And in the end, that is the true circumcision—that which occurs in spirit, in the heart. But the circumcised Israelite infants were true Jews, and their circumcision was a true circumcision, as long as they did not resist the working of the Holy Spirit through actual impenitence and unbelief. Therefore they were circumcised by the Spirit in their hearts, that is, regenerated and renewed. Otherwise, not only would they fail to stand apart from the Gentiles before God, but they would be even worse than Gentiles, since they would be hiding the foreskin of the heart with the circumcision of the flesh.

That, in turn, must finally be judged a true circumcision that has the praise, not from men, but from God—that which God Himself administers internally in the heart, not that which men apply on the outside. Yet the circumcision of infants is such (Deu. 30:6) that God "will circumcise the heart of your seed." Therefore, it is a true and salutary circumcision that has been joined with the circumcision of the heart.

Notes on the Epistle to the Romans: Chapter 3

v.1 Τί οὖν τὸ περισσὸν τοῦ Ἰουδαίου; ἢ τίς ἡ ὠφέλεια τῆς περιτομῆς;

v.1 What advantage then hath the Jew? or what profit is there of circumcision? (KJV)

The Apostle runs to meet the tacit objection: If the Jews are just as sinful and are accused by the law just as much as the Gentiles (as in the preceding chapter, v.12); if the Gentiles can be just as pleasing to God through faith in Christ without circumcision as the circumcised Jews (as asserted in v.26); if he who is outwardly a Jew is not a true Jew, and if that circumcision done in the flesh is not a true circumcision (v.28), what, then, is the advantage of the Jews or the benefit of circumcision?

Τὸ περισσὸν is "the overflow." In this passage it denotes "advantage." The Syriac has the noun יַתִירוּתֵהּ, which means "the excellence" of the Jews. Luther: *"Was haben die Jüden Vorteils? [What advantage do the Jews have?]"* In other manuscripts it has: *"Warumb wird das Jüdenthumb so hoch gehalten* [Why is Jewishness considered so highly]?"

v.2 Πολὺ κατὰ πάντα τρόπον. Πρῶτον μὲν γὰρ ὅτι ἐπιστεύθησαν τὰ λόγια τοῦ Θεοῦ.

v.2 Much every way: chiefly, because that unto them were committed the oracles of God. (KJV)

Πρῶτον [first], namely, περισσεύουσιν [they abound]. He begins to enumerate specific advantages, and yet he lists no more than one. He expounds the rest later on in chapter 9:4. For he runs first to meet the objection that could be directed against this response.

Erasmus states that τὸ πρῶτον [first] pertains only to the order of the discourse, but it is more correctly referred to the position and dignity of the advantages. Thus the Syriac translates, סַגִי, "much."

Ἐπιστεύθησαν [they were entrusted], namely, αὐτοὶ τὰ λόγια τοῦ θεοῦ [with the words of God]. The order of construction has been inverted, "the utterances of God have been entrusted to them." A similar phrase is found in 1 Tim. 1:11: κατὰ τὸ εὐαγγέλιον [according to the Gospel], etc., ὅ ἐπιστεύθην ἐγώ [with which I was entrusted].

Lyranus, through ignorance of the phrase, understands it as if the utterances of God were believed by the Jews, and in this they surpass the Gentiles. The Syriac likewise translates less aptly, "that the words of God were rendered faithful."

With τὰ λόγια τοῦ θεοῦ [the words of God], (1) some seem to understand the words of the divine law that were pronounced by the mouth of God on Mt. Sinai and engraved on the tablets of the Decalogue, which had, by divine command, been kept by the Jews in the ark of the covenant.

(2) Some understand more generally the utterances of God first preached with the living voice through Moses and the Prophets, and afterward put into writing by the will of God—the utterances through which God manifested Himself to the Patriarchs, Moses and the Prophets and to the whole Israelite people, both proclaiming and explaining the law to them and promising them the Messiah, who is the τέλος [end, goal] of the law. Those who understand the apostolic phrase in this way have in mind God's command to Moses and the Prophets in which He ordered them to write down the particular chapters of the heavenly doctrine as they were divinely revealed, and to commend these books to the Jewish Church and to the Levites, so that they might put them beside the ark (Deu. 31:24; Jos. 24:26; Isa. 8:1, 30:8; Jer. 30:2).

Anselm on this passage: "Since we are convinced that the Scriptures are true which they handed down to us, and we received the books of divine authority from no other nation."

Johann Driedo calls the Jews "the slaves charged with carrying our Scriptures,"[29] and adds, "Although they have the Scriptures in common with us, they are enemies of our faith. While they do not understand the truth of the Scriptures, yet they unwillingly

---

29 Latin: *Capsarios Scripturarum nostrarum*

retain a testimony to the truth by holding and preserving the same books."

(3) Most simply, one should understand with this phrase not only the word ἀκουστὸν [heard], but also ὁρατόν [seen]. For he does not say that τὸν λόγον τοῦ θεοῦ [the word of God] was entrusted to the Jews, nor does he say that τὰ μυστήρια τοῦ θεοῦ [the mysteries of God] were entrusted to them, but he uses the sort of vocable that embraces both the Word and those visible Sacraments that are signs of invisible grace, when he says that τὰ λόγια τοῦ θεοῦ [the words of God] were entrusted to them. But he primarily and chiefly has in mind the Word, of which the Sacraments are seals, so to speak.

v.3 Τί γὰρ εἰ ἠπίστησάν τινες; Μὴ ἡ ἀπιστία αὐτῶν τὴν πίστιν τοῦ Θεοῦ καταργήσει;

v.3 For what if some did not believe? shall their unbelief make the faith of God without effect? (KJV)

He runs to meet the objection: *What benefit are* τὰ λόγια τοῦ θεοῦ [the words of God] *to the Jews, since they do not have faith?* The Apostle gives two answers: (1) Only some of them were unbelievers; (2) their unbelief does not nullify the faithfulness of God.

Τὶ γὰρ [for what]. An aposiopesis, for ἐροῦμεν [shall we say] or something similar is assumed.

With πίστιν τοῦ θεοῦ [the faithfulness of God] he understands the constancy of God in keeping His promises. He denies that this is rendered invalid by and on account of the unbelief of men. For καταργεῖν means "to abolish, to render idle and ineffective." The sense, then, is that, although some did not keep faith, nonetheless the faithfulness of God is not shaken in the least on account of that; it does not take anything away from the constancy of God in keeping His promises. God does not for that reason stop being the God of this people. And even less can this outcome of theirs be ascribed to the word of His promises.

This must be used to oppose the Calvinists, who make the pres-

130

ence of the body and blood of Christ in the Holy Supper dependant on the faith of man. It ought to be used against the papists as well, who imagine that the covenant of God, which He entered into with us in Baptism, is rendered invalid through the sins committed after Baptism, so that no further consolation can be sought from Baptism in the true conversion to God.

v.4 Μὴ γένοιτο. Γινέσθω δὲ ὁ Θεὸς ἀληθής, πᾶς δὲ ἄνθρωπος ψεύστης, καθὼς γέγραπται, Ὅπως ἂν δικαιωθῇς ἐν τοῖς λόγοις σου, Καὶ νικήσῃς ἐν τῷ κρίνεσθαί σε.

v.4 God forbid: yea, let God be true, but every man a liar; as it is written, That thou mightest be justified in thy sayings, and mightest overcome when thou art judged. (KJV)

Μὴ γένοιτο. "May it not happen!" In common speech we say, "far be it![30]" namely, that we should say this or state that. The Syriac translates חַס, "may you be propitious," or "may he restrain"—understanding "God," as we Germans say, "*Behüt uns Gott!* [May God preserve us!]" Joshua 22:29, מִמֶּנּוּ לָנוּ חָלִילָה, "far be it to us, from us." חלל means, among other things, "he profaned, he polluted." Hence חָלִילָה with a paragogic ה is a word of prohibition and abomination, "let it be to me a profane thing, may God prohibit this" (Gen. 18:25, 44:7; 2 Sam. 20:20).

Γενέσθω ὁ θεὸς ἀληθής [May God be true]. "May God be" or "be declared and said to be the Judge." Mat. 5:45, "That you may be," that is, be recognized as "children of the heavenly Father." John 15:8, "you will be," that is, be recognized as, "my disciples."

Πᾶς δὲ ἄνθρωπος ψευστής. "Every man is a liar," fickle and false. It is to be understood regarding the nature of man (such as it is after the Fall) which is being restored in those who are being renewed by the Holy Spirit. But this can hardly be applied to the Evangelists and Apostles who have been directly enlightened and inspired by the Holy Spirit. This is said in opposition to Albert Pighius, who insults us thus in Bk. 1, *Ecclesiastical Hierarchy*, ch. 2, p.8: "Who is it who makes you certain that all those things are true

30 Latin: *absit*

and certain that Mark and Luke write about Christ, when they did not see these things personally, but merely believed the stories of others? Likewise, even if we believe that Matthew and John were present for the sayings and acts of Christ, we do not believe everything they wrote, for they could have had a lapse of memory, or they could have lied."

Καθὼς γέγραπται [as it is written] (Psa. 51:6).

Ὅπως ἂν δικαιωθῇς ἐν τοῖς λόγοις σου, "that you may be justified," that is, that you may be acknowledged as righteous "in your words," by imposing the well-deserved penalties with which you have threatened sinners.

Καὶ νικήσῃς [and that you may conquer]. In Hebrew, תִּזְכֶּה, "that you may remain pure and clean." For he who is found to be pure and clean in the judgment wins the case and conquers his adversary.

Ἐν τῷ κρίνεσθαί σε [when You judge]. This corresponds to the Hebrew בְּשָׁפְטֶךָ, "in Your judging, when You judge." As in the preceding part, בְּדָבְרֶךָ, "in Your speaking," that is, when You speak.

Some say that is more correctly translated, "when You judge," since the passage is cited from Psa. 57, where it has the active בְּשָׁפְטֶךָ, just as in 1 Sam. 5: "Give us a king לְשָׁפְטֵנוּ that he may judge us." For it is another form of the passive, as in Psa. 109: בהשפטו, ἐν κρίνεσθαι αὐτὸν, "when he is judged."

Luther translates it with a passive, "when you are judged," which agrees (1) with David's aim. For the royal Prophet wants to teach that God does injury to no one and that His judgments are just, no matter what men wickedly conclude about them and wrongly judge. (2) With the apostolic citation in this passage, ἐν τῷ κρίνεσθαί σε [in Your judging], which the Vulgate translates, "when you are judged." (3) With the Syriac version, which has לָךְ כַּדְרִינִין, "when they judge you." (4) With the rules of grammar, for other similar examples also occur elsewhere in which an active infinitive is used instead of a passive (Gen. 4:26, Pro. 25:7, Phi. 1:23).

v.5 Εἰ δὲ ἡ ἀδικία ἡμῶν Θεοῦ δικαιοσύνην συνίστησι, τί ἐροῦμεν;

132

Μὴ ἄδικος ὁ Θεός, ὁ ἐπιφέρων τὴν ὀργήν, (κατ᾽ ἄνθρωπον λέγω.)

v.5 But if our unrighteousness commend the righteousness of God, what shall we say? Is God unrighteous who taketh vengeance? (I speak as a man) (KJV)

He proposes another exception, the occasion for which arises out of the words of David. If the unrighteousness of men serves for the manifestation and confirmation of divine justice, then it would follow that God is unjustly angry at the unrighteousness of men. But the former proposition is true, for unless men had sinned, God could not manifest His righteousness in punishments. Therefore, the latter proposition must also be true.

Εἰ δὲ ἡ ἀδικία ἡμῶν Θεοῦ δικαιοσύνην συνίστησι [But if our unrighteousness constitutes God's righteousness], "constitutes," that is, establishes, confirms and supports. Hesychius: "illuminates, commends." The Syriac has the verb מְקִים, "establishes." Luther: *"preisets* [praises it]."

With ἀδικίαν ἡμῶν [our unrighteousness] he understands our treachery, with a generic noun used instead of a specific; with δικαιοσύνην θεοῦ [the righteousness of God] he understands the faithfulness, truth and constancy of God.

Ὁ ἐπιφέρων τὴν ὀργήν, "sending in wrath," that is, the punishment signified by metonymy with the noun "wrath." Syriac: "he who causes His wrath to come."

Κατ᾽ ἄνθρωπον λέγω [I speak according to man]. This phrase of the Apostle is used in two ways: (1) To signify that he is proposing something crassly, according to human custom, so that even the more crude can understand (Rom. 6:19, Gal. 3:15). (2) To signify that he is speaking according to their judgment—of those who are mere men, not yet renewed by the Holy Spirit. It is used in this latter sense in this passage. "I am speaking according to man," that is, I am producing a form of argument used by profane men; I am speaking according to the judgment, not of a godly and renewed man, but of the obstinate and hardened Jew. Thus in 1 Cor. 3:3, "to walk according to man" is to walk according to the flesh.

v.6 Μὴ γένοιτο: Ἐπεὶ πῶς κρινεῖ ὁ Θεὸς τὸν κόσμον;

v.6 God forbid: for then how shall God judge the world? (KJV)

The Apostle responds to the proposed objection with vehemence and by a reduction to absurdity. If God justly judges the world, then He is certainly not unjustly angry at the unrighteousness of men.

Some understand it generally about God's continual act of governance (Gen. 18:25, John 5:22).

Others understand it specifically about the Last Judgment. The verb in the future tense favors this exposition. But the phrase "if He were unjust" must be assumed, so that it follows from the proposed objection.

v.7 Εἰ γὰρ ἡ ἀλήθεια τοῦ Θεοῦ ἐν ἐμῷ ψεύσματι ἐπερίσσευσεν εἰς τὴν δόξαν αὐτοῦ, τί ἔτι κἀγὼ ὡς ἁμαρτωλὸς κρίνομαι.

v.7 For if the truth of God hath more abounded through my lie unto his glory; why yet am I also judged as a sinner? (KJV)

Some imagine a third objection here. *If sins lead to the glory of God, then not only should they not be punished* (as the preceding objection also inferred), *but He should be lenient toward them.* But it is more correctly stated that the Apostle is responding to the proposed objection by a reduction to absurdity. As the cause, so the effect, and vice versa. If, therefore, the sins of men promote and commend the righteousness of God, or even reveal it, as the proposed objections intends, then they would be righteous works in and of themselves, and thus sins would not be sins; such people would be unjustly condemned as sinners.

Περισσεύειν is "to abound, to excel." This same meaning is found in Mat. 5:20 and 1 The. 4:1.

v.8 Καὶ μὴ, (καθὼς βλασφημούμεθα, καὶ καθὼς φασί τινες ἡμᾶς λέγειν,) ὅτι ποιήσωμεν τὰ κακὰ, ἵνα ἔλθῃ τὰ ἀγαθά; Ὧν τὸ κρίμα ἔνδικόν ἐστι.

v.8 And not rather, (as we be slanderously reported, and as some af-

firm that we say,) Let us do evil, that good may come? whose damnation is just. (KJV)

The Apostle, who is pleased to curse the blasphemy of those who attribute this doctrine to the Gospel and its teachers, announces the just penalty for blasphemies and sees fit to give them no other response.

Observe how old are those calumnies which are derived from the doctrine of free justification by faith, as if through it the zeal for good works were prohibited; they were already leveled by some men at the time of the Apostles. But it is called "blasphemy" by the Apostle, because it abounds in the ignominy of God Himself, by whom the doctrine of the Gospel has been revealed.

Ἵνα ἔλθῃ τὰ ἀγαθὰ [that the good things may come], so that the wisdom and power of God may become manifest, in that He knows how to bring good out of evil.

One asks, based on this passage, *if it is permissible to consent to the lesser evil in order to avoid the greater?* We reply: One must distinguish between the evil of guilt and of punishment, or between the evil of sin and the evil of suffering[31].

This distinction is found in Tertullian, Bk. 2. *Against Marcion*, ch. 14. With regard to "the evil of punishment," it is permissible to consent to the lesser in order to avoid the greater, as when sailors in danger of shipwreck jump into the sea. But in "the evil of guilt," that is not permissible.

Augustine, *On Lying*, ch. 19: "Let us not commit the lesser evil, lest others commit the greater with a broad limit—or worse, with no limit!"

Cajetan on this passage: "No sin, neither the smallest nor one of medium size, is desirable or should be committed in order that the more serious sins may be avoided."

Some distinguish between an ordinary act and a case of extraordinary necessity. To be sure, ordinarily, evil should not be

---

31 Latin: *inter mala culpae et poenae, sive inter mala delicti et mala supplicii*

done in order to avoid other greater evil; but in a case of necessity, where you are not able to advise either against the least or against the greatest, it is preferable to permit the lesser. But it is one thing to permit something against one's will, and another to consent to it voluntarily. There cannot be a case of necessity of this kind in which a person ought to consent to lesser sins for the sake of avoiding greater ones.

But this axiom must be opposed—that one must do evil in order that good may result. This is found in Aristotle, in so many words, Bk. 3, *Ethics*, ch. 1. It is done among the papists who tolerate brothels in order to promote the chastity of honest virgins and wives.

But, you say, God Himself permitted divorce among the Jews in the Old Testament due to their hardness of heart (Mat. 19:8). We reply: Even then He did not consent to that casual divorce nor approve of it, but publicly and perpetually accused and condemned it with the voice of His law.

v.9 Τί οὖν; Προεχόμεθα; Οὐ πάντως. Προῃτιασάμεθα γὰρ Ἰουδαίους τε καὶ Ἕλληνας πάντας ὑφ' ἁμαρτίαν εἶναι.

v.9 What then? are we better than they? No, in no wise: for we have before proved both Jews and Gentiles, that they are all under sin; (KJV)

Another response to the objection proposed at the beginning of the chapter, that, as far as righteousness before God is concerned, the Jews have no advantage over the Gentiles. And, if they are considered in and of themselves to be outside of a state of grace with regard to their corrupt nature, it has already been pronounced by the mouth of the Prophets that they are no better than the rest.

Τί οὖν; προεχόμεθα; [What, then? Are we better?] Some join both parts together. "What, then?" or "In what ways, then, are we better than they?" This is how the Latin interpreter translates it, as well as the Syrian interpreter. But the Greek manuscripts separate these parts in two. "What, then? We are not any better, are we?" This is how Luther translates. The verb ἐροῦμεν [shall we say], or something similar, is thus assumed. "What shall we say, then?"

Προεχόμεθα [Are we better?]. The Apostle is speaking in the persona of Jewish people, for he himself was also a Hebrew (2 Cor. 11:22, Phi. 3:5), whence also, according to the custom of the Jews, he calls Abraham his father (Rom. 4:1); and the Jews he calls his brothers, his "relatives according to the flesh" (chapter 9:3).

Προεχόμεθα [Are we better?], that is, by nature and with respect to righteousness before God. In verse 1 he had put it this way: τὶ οὖν περισσὸν τοῦ Ἰουδαίου [what, advantage, then of the Jew]. Here he expresses it with the verb προεχόμεθα. The Syriac translates in both places with יַתִּירָא, which means "excellence."

Οὐ πάντως [not at all]. The οὐ [not] is transposed with πάντως [at all], "absolutely not, in no way, by no means," as the Vulgate correctly translates. The Syriac has omitted it.

He uses a similar expression in 1 Cor. 5:10.

Προῃτιασάμεθα [we have before proved]. The Vulgate translates, "we pled our case earlier." Αἰτιᾶσθαι is formed from αἰτία [cause], which means "to present a case, to say that there is a case." In Demosth., περὶ στεφάνου, αἰτίαν ἡγεῖσθαι [concerning a crown, to consider a cause] and αἰτιᾶσθαι τὴν τύχην [to accuse the fortune] are used instead. Therefore προῃτιασάμεθα is the same as ἠλέγξαμεν [we examined]. As the Greek scholars say, "we have argued the cases," that is, "the reasons that have been given," or even "we have awarded a case." Luther: "Wir haben bewiesen [We have demonstrated]."

Some think that αἰτιᾶσθαι [to prove] is formed from αἰτίαμα; or rather, αἰτίαμα, which means "complaint" or "accusation," derived from αἰτιᾶσθαι, so that the sense is: We incriminated earlier, that is, we leveled that charge earlier against Jews and Greeks. In other words, "earlier we accused the Jews and the Greeks." But the prior explanation agrees more with the text. The Apostle had succeeded in demonstrating in the two preceding chapters that both Jews and Greeks are sinners. The Syriac has the verb פסק, which means "he cut away, he cut up," and, by way of metaphor, "he decided, he decreed, he determined."

Πάντας ὑφ' ἁμαρτίαν εἶναι [that all are under sin], that all are under the yoke of sin, sold under sin, etc., weighed down with the burden of sin and therefore subject to the curse and condemnation that is due for sins.

v.10 Καθὼς γέγραπται ὅτι Οὐκ ἔστι δίκαιος οὐδὲ εἷς.

v.10 *As it is written, There is none righteous, no, not one: (KJV)*

Origen, in his commentary on this passage: "The Apostle presents an example for the teachers of the Church, that the things that they speak to the people, they are to set forth, not as drawn from their own conclusions, but as they are fortified by divine testimonies."

The saying that is cited in this verse is from Psa. 14:3, Psa. 53:2. The rest of the sayings that follow are adduced from various Scripture passages. So the Latin interpreter was wrong to force all these things into Psalm 14, which even Bellarmine himself acknowledges in Bk. 2, *On the Word of God*, ch. 2, where he says: "They (those who state that the Jews erased some things from the Hebrew manuscripts out of hatred toward the Christians) object that in Psalm 13 (according to the Latin numbering) there are eight verses missing which, nevertheless, are cited by the Apostle in Romans 3 and are there in the Septuagint. This (they say) results from the malice of the Jews, who removed these verses from the Hebrew in order to demonstrate that our Apostle did not faithfully present the testimony of the Psalm. But Blessed Jerome (Bk. 16, *On Isaiah*) responds to this objection, which had been made also to him long ago. He says that these verses do not properly belong to Psalm 13, but are cited by the Apostle from various passages of Scripture, then moved by the Apostle into the Psalter from somewhere else. For the first and the second of those verses are found in Psalm 5; the third in Psalm 139; the fourth in Psalm 9; the fifth, sixth and seventh are from Isaiah 59; and the last, from Psalm 35. And in the same place Jerome adds that these verses are not in the Septuagint translation, nor did any Greek author see fit to expound them in his commentaries on these verses. Origen also, in his commentary on Romans 3, says that the Apostle took these verses from various passages of Scripture. With these words he clearly means that those verses are found neither in the Hebrew text, nor in the translation of the elders in the Septuagint."

But if such is the case, why does the Church allow these verses in the Vulgate edition? Bellarmine responds: "Because they are some part of Scripture, and because they cannot be removed without disturbing and offending the people, since they have been there now for a long time." But neither response is satisfactory. Not the first, because, while they are indeed part of Scripture, they do not belong to that passage. Not the second, because only such an offense has been taken that cannot and should not prejudice the truth.

But no matter how much the sayings cited from the Psalms and the Prophet Isaiah are properly spoken about the wicked, they are still correctly appropriated by the Apostle to all men, since by nature, that is, before they are regenerated and renewed by the Spirit of God, all people after the Fall are wicked (Tit. 3:3). In the same way the words of the Apostle must be understood, not only of actual sins, but also of original sin, for it is the source of all actual sins, and it resides in every part of a man.

v.11 Οὐκ ἔστιν ὁ συνιῶν, Οὐκ ἔστιν ὁ ἐκζητῶν τὸν Θεόν.

v.11 There is none that understandeth, there is none that seeketh after God. (KJV)

This passage is found in Psa. 14:2 and in Psa. 53:3, although slightly different. Κύριος ἐκ τοῦ οὐρανοῦ διέκυψεν ἐπὶ τοὺς υἱοὺς τῶν ἀνθρώπων τοῦ ἰδεῖν, εἰ ἔστι συνιῶν; ἢ ἐκζητῶν τὸν θεόν [The Lord stooped down from heaven to look upon the sons of men, if there is anyone who understands, or anyone who seeks God]. But since it immediately follows, "all turned aside, etc.," from that it is understood that no one has been found by God who understands or who seeks God.

These can be joined together etiologically: No one is righteous, for there is no one who understands or seeks after God. But they are more correctly taken copulatively, so that the corruption of both mind and will is understood to be described.

Ἐκζητῶν τὸν θεὸν, "diligently seeking God," concerned with due zeal for the true knowledge of God and for the true worship of Him. The Syriac has the verb בְּעָה, "he has studied carefully." Furthermore, the phrase "to seek after God" is used in three ways in the Scriptures: (1) It means "to consult God in a doubtful matter" (2 Kin. 22:13), which used to be done either with the priestly Urim and Thumim, or through the Prophets as messengers of the divine will (1 Sam. 9:9). (2) "To implore God's help" (Job 5:8). (3) "To worship God zealously and with the full consent of the will" (2 Chr. 14:4). This is how it is used in this passage.

v.12 Πάντες ἐξέκλιναν, Ἅμα ἠχρειώθησαν· Οὐκ ἔστι ποιῶν χρηστότητα, Οὐκ ἔστιν ἕως ἑνός.

v.12 They are all gone out of the way, they are together become unprofitable; there is none that doeth good, no, not one. (KJV)

This verse is found in Psa. 14:3 and Psa. 53:4. The corruption of human nature has already been described with negative words. It is now described with positive words in order to indicate that original sin does not only involve a lack of the righteousness that is owed, but also a depraved desire and a character full of vice.

Πάντες ἐξέκλιναν, "all turned aside" and wandered away from the right path. The divine law prescribes the way in which we should go, turning aside neither to the right nor to the left. Sin is a turning aside from that way, a deviation from the path of righteousness prescribed in the law. But it is not only the turning aside of actual sin that is understood; it is also original sin's turning aside from original righteousness[32].

Ἅμα ἠχριώθησαν, "at the same time they became useless," namely, for doing good. In Hebrew it is נֶאֱלָחוּ, which Arias renders "they became rancid;" Pagninus, "they stunk;" others, "they festered as with pus." The root is אלח in the Niphal, "to completely putrefy," and by way of metaphor, "he was corrupted and contaminated" (Job 15:16). A festering wound is an indicator of corruption and death. The corruption is, therefore, signified by the sin of our

---

32 Latin: *justitia concreata*

first-formed parents which has been introduced to all people, together with spiritual death.

The Targum translates Psalm 14:4, אִסְתְּנִיפוּ, "they were contaminated."

Ἕως ἑνός, "up to one." Some determine that this should be taken exclusively, so that one Man is excluded from that number, namely, Christ, who alone is free from sin. This is certainly true, but it cannot be proven from this phrase. For in Hebrew it is אֶחָד ם אֵין גַּ, "not also one," that is, "not even one." But the royal Prophet is speaking about ψιλοῖς ἀνθρώποις [mere men], born from corrupt parents according to a common nature, from whose number Christ the θεάνθρωπος [God-Man] is excepted, having been born of a virgin, without male seed, and therefore free from all sin.

v.13 Τάφος ἀνεῳγμένος ὁ λάρυγξ αὐτῶν, Ταῖς γλώσσαις αὐτῶν ἐδολιοῦσαν. Ἰὸς ἀσπίδων ὑπὸ τὰ χείλη αὐτῶν.

v.13 *Their throat is an open sepulchre; with their tongues they have used deceit; the poison of asps is under their lips: (KJV)*

The first part of this verse is found in Psa. 5:10; the latter in Psa. 140:4.

Τάφος ἀνεῳγμένος [open grave], etc. This expresses beautifully the metaphor of the Hebrew verb נֶאֱלָחוּ, "they thoroughly decayed." Just as the most horrible and putrid odors emanate from a grave, so from the mouth of the wicked proceed perverse and putrid utterances.

The Syriac has a plural: "Their throats are open graves."

Ταῖς γλώσσαις αὐτῶν ἐδολιοῦσαν [with their tongues they deceived], instead of ἐδολιοῦν, a Chaldean or Asiatic irregularity.

In Hebrew, it is יַחֲלִיקוּן, "they flatter with their tongue," which Psalm 55:12 expresses in this way: חָלְקוּ, "they made their mouth smooth as butter," that is, they use flattering words in order to deceive others, and thus they act deceitfully with their tongues.

Ἰὸς ἀσπίδων [poison of asps]. In Hebrew the vocable is עַכְשׁוּב,

which means "ptyaden," that is, that snake that shoots its venom from a distance, so called from the verb πτύειν [to spit].

Observe: Their insults and calumnies are compared to the venom of snakes, because they draw their origin from the infernal serpent, and a cure is only found for them with the greatest difficulty. It is also said with respect to the preceding metaphor. Their throat is an open grave, because venomous serpents also dwell in graves.

v.14 ῟Ων τὸ στόμα ἀρᾶς καὶ πικρίας γέμει.

v.14 Whose mouth is full of cursing and bitterness: (KJV)

This verse is found in Psa. 10:7.

Ἀρᾶ is "an imprecation, a curse, a dreadful saying." In Hebrew it is אָלָה, "an oath," and that which accompanies it, "imprecation." The Targum has וְיטוּל, "their mouth is full of curses." The Syriac also uses this noun for this passage.

Πικρία means "bitterness." In Hebrew it is מִרְמוּת, "deceit," in place of which the Septuagint interpreters seem to have read מְרֹותֹות, "bitternesses."

v.15 Ὀξεῖς οἱ πόδες αὐτῶν ἐκχέαι αἷμα.

v.15 Their feet are swift to shed blood: (KJV)

This verse is found in Isa. 59:7, where in the Hebrew is added נָקִי, "innocent blood." The LXX: οἱ δὲ πόδες αὐτῶν ἐπὶ πονηρίαν τρέχουσι, ταχεινοὶ ἐκχέαι αἷμα [And their feet rush into evil, swift to shed blood].

In the same place is added, "Their thoughts are thoughts of iniquity."

v.16 Σύντριμμα καὶ ταλαιπωρία ἐν ταῖς ὁδοῖς αὐτῶν.

v.16 Destruction and misery are in their ways: (KJV)

This verse is found in Isaiah in the passage cited.

Σύντριμμα is "grinding together, mixing together, breaking together," from the verb συντρίβεσθαι, "to crush together," and metaphorically, "to crush together with pain and sadness." Luther translates "*Unfall* [mishap]," namely, in that they prepare evil for others.

Ταλαιπωρία is "misery." Luther: "*Hertzleidt*" [heartache].

In Hebrew: שֹׁד וָשֶׁבֶר, "desolation and breaking apart in their ways."

v.17 Καὶ ὁδὸν εἰρήνης οὐκ ἔγνωσαν.

v.17 And the way of peace have they not known: (KJV)

This passage is from Isa. 59:8, ὁδὸν εἰρήνης οὐκ οἴδασι. This is "the way of peace" that leads to peace and eternal happiness (Luke 1:79). By nature this way of peace is known to no man; it is only revealed to us in the Gospel.

In the same place is added: "And there is no discernment in their ways; their paths have curved inward on them. No one who treads on their paths knows peace."

v.18 Οὐκ ἔστι φόβος Θεοῦ ἀπέναντι τῶν ὀφθαλμῶν αὐτῶν.

v.18 There is no fear of God before their eyes. (KJV)

This verse is from Psalm 36:2, except that there it has the singular number.

In the last passage, he mentioned a lack of divine fear, since all the sins already enumerated arise from this defect.

v.19 Οἴδαμεν δὲ ὅτι ὅσα ὁ νόμος λέγει, τοῖς ἐν τῷ νόμῳ λαλεῖ, ἵνα πᾶν στόμα φραγῇ καὶ ὑπόδικος γένηται πᾶς ὁ κόσμος τῷ Θεῷ.

v.19 Now we know that what things soever the law saith, it saith to them who are under the law: that every mouth may be stopped, and all the world may become guilty before God. (KJV)

The aim is to prove that those most severe judgments and accusations of David and Isaiah principally have the Jews in view, since they were selected from the books of the Old Testament that had been entrusted to the Jewish people.

Observe: (1) All the books of the Old Testament, no matter when they were written, go by the name of "the Law." And there is an elegant antanaclasis in the word νόμος [law]. For in the first sense it means the Scripture composed of the Law of Moses and the books of the Prophets. In another sense it means the Mosaic state established by the Law of Moses.

(2) The law is said in this passage to "speak." Therefore, it is not "the mute and dead letter," as the papists blaspheme. Alb. Pighius, *Controversies*, 3: "If you were to claim that these things refer to the judgment of the Scriptures, it proves that you are lacking in common sense. For the Scriptures are mute judges." Gregory of Valencia, Bk. 9, *Analogy of Faith*, ch. 6: "The Word of God is much broader than the Scripture, nor is it bound to mute letters."

Ἵνα πᾶν στόμα φραγῇ [that every mouth may be stopped], "in order that every mouth," that is, the mouth of all people, both Jews and Gentiles, "may be stopped up," that is, in order that no one may be able to boast about his own righteousness before God, but that all should be forced to humble themselves before God. Φράττειν is properly "to surround, to protect and shut in with a hedge," whence φραγμὸς, "a hedge" (2 Cor. 11:10, Heb. 11:33).

Καὶ ὑπόδικος γένηται πᾶς ὁ κόσμος τῷ Θεῷ [and the whole world become accountable to God] is a judicial phrase, "so that all men may acknowledge that they are under the judgment of God," that is, under a curse and condemnation. The Syriac has the verb חב in the passive, "he was guilty of debt, obliged."

v.20 Διότι ἐξ ἔργων νόμου οὐ δικαιωθήσεται πᾶσα σὰρξ ἐνώπιον αὐτοῦ, διὰ γὰρ νόμου ἐπίγνωσις ἁμαρτίας.

v.20 *Therefore by the deeds of the law there shall no flesh be justified in his sight: for by the law is the knowledge of sin.* (KJV)

This is the conclusion of the entire disputation that began in v.18 of the first chapter. The law accuses men and damns them on account of sin. Therefore, there is no reason why anyone should hope to be justified by the law or the works of the law.

Διότι [therefore] is rendered causally by Luther: *"Darumb das kein Fleisch durch des Gesetzes Werck für ihm gerecht seyn mag* [Therefore, no flesh may be righteous before Him through the work of the law]." It can also be translated illatively: "Consequently, he is not justified, etc."

With the word *flesh,* the entire man is understood, according to the synecdoche that is employed. Verse 28 is expounded in this way. Therefore, it is frivolous what Dominicus a Soto tried to prove in this passage from the word *flesh*—that Paul is dealing with the man who lacks the aid of the divine Spirit, and thus only excludes from justification the works that are done before faith, solely by the powers of free will.

Οὐ δικαιωθήσεται πᾶσα σὰρξ is a Hebrew phrase, "all flesh will not be justified" (Mat. 24:22). With "the works of the law," by which the Apostle denies that man is justified before God, some papists understand only the works of the ceremonial law. Joh. Paulus Windeck., in his disputation *On Justification,* Friburg, in the year 1610, th. 33, attempts to prove with a number of arguments that this exposition is not improbable. But Augustine has already expressly refuted this explanation on several occasions, in his book *On the Spirit and the Letter,* ch. 8, and in Epistle 200.

Indeed, this interpretation is being abandoned in modern times by a majority of papists. Cornelius a Lapide on this passage: "When the Apostle separates faith from works here and in every place, he understands not only the works of the ceremonial and civil law, but also of the moral law. For he is speaking of that law that has been inscribed on the hearts of man by nature (Rom. 2:15), that accuses all men of sin (3:10), that damns the whole world (v.9), and from which comes the recognition of sin (v.19). Yet these things are not consistent with the ceremonial law, but with the moral law."

But that interpretation is no better in which they say that, with the works of the law, "only those works that precede faith and that are done solely by the powers of free will are excluded from the act of justification" (Bellarmine, Bk. 1, *On Justification,* ch. 19). Or "only those works are excluded that are done without grace, without the gift of the Holy Spirit, by men who have not yet been reborn" (Duraeus, *Against Whitaker*, Bk. 8, f. 253).

For (1) the Apostle absolutely and simply, without any additional limitation, excludes the works of the law from the act of justification. But the works of the reborn are likewise works of the law, since they are done according to the norm of the law (Psa. 119:35, Rom. 7:22, 25, etc.).

(2) Paul, when he excludes works from justification, is not writing to Jews who are not yet converted or baptized, but to those whose faith, he teaches, is proclaimed in the whole world (Rom. 1:8). Yet he nevertheless denies that they are justified by the works of the law—not only those that they had done before their conversion to Christ and prior to their rebirth, but also those that they did afterwards, when they were in Christ, under grace.

(3) In order to prove that we are justified by faith without works, he adduces the example of Abraham—and of him, not when he was still dwelling in the idolatrous city of Ur, or when he was first summoned from there, but now, after he had been converted and while he was living a godly life, the Apostle declares that "he was not justified by works" (Rom. 4:2,3,5). But the rule and example correspond to him most precisely. Therefore, the apostolic pronouncement—that no flesh shall be justified by the works of the law—is general, excluding also the works of the reborn.

(4) The Apostle sets forth such a manner of justification in which all boasting must be excluded (Rom. 3:27, 4:2). But if the reborn are justified by the works done while under grace, then all boasting is not yet excluded, for the reborn are driven to good works by the Holy Spirit in such a way that they also perform them. Therefore, it must not be stated that the good works of the reborn play a part in the act of justification. Chrysostom, Homily 9 on the Epistle to the Romans: "He is saved by faith who has no works of which he should boast; he who is properly adorned with deeds does not become righteous by them, but by faith. This is wonderful and manifests above all the power of faith."

(5) The Apostle sets forth such a justification that a man may be certain of it (Rom. 4:15). But if we are justified by works, then we could never be certain of the grace of God, for even the most holy men are forced to admit that the righteousness of works is imperfect, and that sin clings to them.

(6) Paul denies that men are justified by works of the law for the very reason that the law cannot be perfectly fulfilled (Rom. 7:14). But even the reborn themselves are forced to admit that they cannot fulfill the law perfectly. Therefore... Many arguments can be sought from the Epistle to the Galatians opposing the false apostles who were not fighting to defend the works done before faith and without faith in Christ, but the works of the reborn, by which they taught that man is justified before God. For they had been converted to Christ. This is made especially clear from chapter 2:16 of that Epistle, where Paul excludes both his own works and those of believers from the act of justification. It is also clear from the Epistle to the Ephesians 2:8, where the praise of justification is removed from those works for which "we were created in Christ Jesus that we should walk" in them.

Likewise it is clear from the analogy of faith that teaches: (a) that the good works of the reborn are imperfect and unclean, and thus they cannot justify us, but rather they themselves need justification. (b) That works cannot be added to divine grace as a συναίτια [a joint cause], since "if by grace, then no longer by works" (Rom. 11:6); nor to the merit of Christ, since "He has trod the wine press alone" (Isa. 63:3); nor to faith, since "we are justified by faith without works" (Rom. 3:28). (c) That works are excluded from election, therefore also from justification. The status of things is inverted if a man is said to be justified by works after faith, since, as soon as a person truly believes in Christ, he is justified before God, so that works do not come before a person is justified, but follow after a person has been justified. Augustine, *De Fide et Operibus*, ch. 14, says that the unanimous confession of the saints excludes works from the act of justification and from the foundation of our confidence before God (Exo. 34:7; Job 9:28; Psa. 130:2; Psa. 143:2; Isa. 64:6; Dan. 9:7; Rom. 7:14; 1 John 1:8). (d) That the merit of justification and salvation is removed even from the works of righteousness (Titus 3:5).

The papists take this to mean (1) that those works are excluded that are works of the law, that is, works that the law extracts from a person by means of threats, not works that are done by faith and love.

We reply: The works that are extracted from a person by threats cannot properly be called works of the law, since the law requires love for God from the whole heart, from the whole soul, etc., and hence also obedience that flows out of perfect love, not obedience that is extracted by fear of punishment. The law certainly threatens punishment to the disobedient, but obedience extracted by threats is not the perfect obedience of the law. Thus is established what kind of obedience the law requires.

Therefore, although the works of the reborn are not, in this sense, works of the law—for the law does not extract them by threatening and terrifying, since they are "fruits of the Spirit" (Gal. 5:22) and proceed "from a willing spirit" (Psa. 110:3) and are done by the reborn readily and with love—nevertheless in another sense they are and are said to be works of the law, and by the title of "works of the law" they are excluded from the act of justification, clearly because the reborn do not follow the judgment of reason or their own intention in the exercise of good works. Instead, they follow the norm and the prescription of the divine law (Rom. 7:25), and they mortify the flesh by taking into account the commandments, promises, threats, rewards and punishments, so that the flesh may be subject to the Spirit and not resist Him in doing good works. Therefore, they are still "works of the law," not because the law is an efficient cause, but because it is the object of obedience.

(2) That those works are excluded from the act of justification because they are opposed to grace. But the works of the reborn, inasmuch as they are done from grace, are not opposed to grace.

We reply: The works of the reborn are obviously not opposed to grace in an absolute or simple way, since they are done from the grace that regenerates and renews a man. Nonetheless, they are opposed to grace in the act of justification (Rom. 11:6), because, although the grace of regeneration confers both things on a man, namely, both justification and renewal, nevertheless justification is not renewal, nor does it consist in renewal, but these two benefits are distinct, and consequently one must speak differently about things that are different. Nor should the papists deny that this apostolic contrast between works and faith in the act of justification also pertains to the works of grace. For Bellarmine, Bk. 2, *On Grace and Free Will*, ch. 10, proves with many examples that "election is entirely free and depends only on the grace and mercy of God, without any previewing[33] of works."

Here, one likewise might babble: The grace of the electing God and the works of the reborn are not opposed to one another, for the works of the reborn arise from the grace of the electing God. Eph. 1:4, "We were elected that we might be holy." Therefore election does not depend only on the grace of God without the previewing of works. However Bellarmine may wish to respond to this sophistry, let him also consider the same a response to his own argument by which he attempts to prove that the works of the reborn, since they are works of grace, cannot be opposed to justifying grace in the act of justification. Bellarmine writes this same thing in Bk. 2, *On Repentance*, ch. 12: "Merit that is worthy in and of itself,[34] namely, righteousness, is opposed to grace." I assume he means that the good works of the reborn are meritorious, so that they are entirely worthy, since Bellarmine teaches the same in Bk. 5, *On Justification*, ch. 16. Therefore, the good works of the reborn are opposed to grace!

(3) That the righteousness "of the law" consists in the good works that the law prescribes to be done. This the Apostle does not reject, but rather commends (Rom. 2:13,26; 8:4). The righteousness that is "by the law" or "in the law" consists in those good works that men do without the grace of faith, aided only by knowledge of the law. This righteousness alone does the Apostle exclude, and he sets it against faith when he excludes the works of the law.

---

33 Latin: *praevisione*
34 Latin: *meritum ex condigno*

We reply: The Apostle makes the general proclamation, "by works of the law no flesh is justified" (in this verse); "man is justified by faith, without works" (v.28); "the righteousness of God through faith in Christ, without the law, has been manifested to all and upon all who believe" (v.22); "the law is not of faith, and thus no one is justified in the law" (Gal. 3:12). Therefore, while the Apostle does not simply reject the righteousness of the law, he nevertheless excludes it from the act of justification, because it is imperfect, nor does it agree with each and every part of the norm and rule prescribed in the law. Thus the true and apostolic distinction is between the righteousness of the law and the righteousness of the Gospel; between the righteousness of faith and that of works. The former, that is, the righteousness of the law and of works, is excluded from the act of justification, while only and alone the latter, that is, the righteousness of the Gospel and of faith, is said by him to have a place in the act of justification.

The Photinians state: "Paul added that we are justified without the works of the law for this reason, in order to indicate that the Apostle is speaking about the works required by the law, and thus about the perpetual and most perfect observation of the divine precepts, as the law requires. But since no one is able to furnish the kind of obedience that the law requires, therefore," they say, "the Apostle submits that we are justified by faith, that is, by trust and by that obedience—as much as anyone is able to furnish, and inasmuch as he seeks and strives daily to furnish as much obedience as possible without the works of the law, that is, even though for the moment he is unable to fulfill the whole law perfectly, as he should."

We reply: (1) It is correctly said that the works of the law do not justify, for the very reason that the law requires perfect obedience which no one is able to furnish in the infirmity of this life. (2) But it should not be inferred from that that imperfect obedience somehow aids in the act of our justification before God. The opposite should, rather, be inferred. Since the righteousness of works, namely, the obedience to the law furnished by us, is imperfect, therefore we cannot be justified before God through it. (3) It is a false hypothesis that with the word *faith*, by which the Apostle teaches that we are justified before God, not only trust is understood, but also the obedience to the law furnished by us.

v.21 Νυνὶ δὲ χωρὶς νόμου δικαιοσύνη Θεοῦ πεφανέρωται, μαρτυρουμένη ὑπὸ τοῦ νόμου καὶ τῶν προφητῶν,

v.21 But now the righteousness of God without the law is manifested, being witnessed by the law and the prophets; (KJV)

Now that the Apostle has taught that all men—both Jews and Greeks—are sinners before God, he returns to the principal proposition set forth in ch. 1:17, that the righteousness that counts before God is to be sought from the Gospel, not from the law.

He calls "the righteousness of God" that which, in another place, he calls "the righteousness of faith," as he declares in the very next verse. With the verb φανεροῦσθαι [to be manifested] he indicates (1) that this righteousness is a mystery that is hidden to human reason. (2) That this righteousness certainly already existed during Old Testament times, but now, that is, in the New Testament, it has been manifested, for unless it had already existed long ago in the Old Testament, it could not now be said to be manifested in the New Testament. Augustine presses this reasoning in Bk. 2, *On Original Sin And Grace Against the Pelagians*, ch. 25. (3) That the light of evangelical doctrine is brighter in the New Testament than it was in the Old (Rom. 13:12).

Ambrose in his commentary takes the word "righteousness" here in a legal sense and says that it is manifested without the law because the righteousness of God forgave them whom the law held as guilty, for He did that without the law. The law punishes sinners; it does not absolve them. But in the following verse the Apostle declares sufficiently clearly that he is speaking about evangelical righteousness.

There is an elegant antanaclasis in the double repetition of the word νόμου [law]. "The righteousness of God is manifested without the law," that is, without the works of the law, and yet it is "attested by the witness of the law," that is, by the books of Moses and of the Prophets (Gen. 22:18, Isa. 53:11, Jer. 23:6, etc.).

Τὸ χωρὶς νόμου [without law]. Origen refers this to the verb πεφανέρωται [has been manifested], but Augustine more correctly refers it to the phrase δικαιοσύνη θεοῦ [righteousness of God]. Origen says that "in the earlier words the natural law is understood. In the latter words the law of Moses is understood, since the article is added." But that rule, that the article is always added to the law of Moses, is not universal (Rom. 3:20, 7:7).

Augustine, *On the Spirit and the Letter*, ch. 9: "The righteousness of God is without the law because God confers it through the Spirit of grace on the believer without the assistance of the law, that is, without being helped by the law. For through the law He shows man his infirmity, so that, fleeing to the mercy of God through faith, he may be healed."

Now, when it is said that the righteousness of God does not only now begin in the New Testament, but is "manifested," and when it is said to have the witness of the Law and the Prophets, this should be set against the Photinians, who deny that the Old Testament Fathers were justified and made heirs of eternal life by faith in Christ.

v.22 δικαιοσύνη δὲ Θεοῦ διὰ πίστεως Ἰησοῦ Χριστοῦ, εἰς πάντας καὶ ἐπὶ πάντας τοὺς πιστεύοντας. Οὐ γάρ ἐστι διαστολή.

v.22 Even the righteousness of God which is by faith of Jesus Christ unto all and upon all them that believe: for there is no difference: (KJV)

"Upon all who believe," whether they are Gentiles or Jews.

v.23 πάντες γὰρ ἥμαρτον, καὶ ὑστεροῦνται τῆς δόξης τοῦ Θεοῦ,

v.23 For all have sinned, and come short of the glory of God; (KJV)

"All sinned," that is, "are sinners" (John 3:6, Rom. 5:12), since the active verb among the Hebrews signifies at once a condition and a quality. 2 Sam. 14:14, "By dying, we die," that is, "we are mortals." Psa. 14:1, men are said "to corrupt their way," to do a work that is to be despised, etc., where these things are to be understood regarding the evil of original sin.

(1) The particle *all*, inasmuch as it is universal, includes all men, without any discrimination for sex, age or nationality. It includes Jews and Gentiles, who are born into this world according to the common course of nature. This is to be taught against the papists, who exempt Mary from the number of sinners; against the Calvinists, who teach that children of believing parents are born holy; against the Photinians, who deny original sin.

(2) Where sin is not yet rightly known, the grace of Christ is neither sweet nor does it find any place. For this reason, the Apostle advances the doctrine of sin before this careful treatment of justification.

(3) Since all are sinners, therefore no one is justified by the law, by their works, by their own merits.

With δόξαν τοῦ θεοῦ [glory of God], (1) Schmaltz., on p.42 of his refutation of Dr. Franzius' *On Original Sin*, understands "that supreme happiness which they who are dear to God enjoy both in this and in the future age, as in chapter 5:2. And in 15:7, the same happiness is referred to as 'the future glory of God.'" He presses this exposition so as not to be forced to concede that men are born with original sin, which is the absence of the divine image. But it can rightly be called into doubt whether, in Rom. 15:7, "the glory of God" should be understood with that meaning, since there he means rather "the glorification of God."

(2) Related to this exposition of Schmaltzus is that in which the phrase "the glory of God" is understood concerning the glory which God confers on man. For God glorifies man not with bare words, but by conferring blessedness on him.

(3) Some understand it concerning the glory that man received in the first creation, when he was formed in the image of God, that is, of the glorious image of God which consists "in true righteousness and holiness" (Eph. 4:24).

(4) Costerus takes it for the grace of God that makes a soul noble and glorious (In *Enchiridion*, p. 266).

(5) Some explain it concerning the righteous works by which they are able to elucidate and promote the glory of God.

(6) Blessed Luther takes it most simply about boasting before God, so that the sense is: No man can boast before the judgment of God that he has kept the law perfectly and has no sin. For since they have offended God, sinners do not have glory, but rather trouble and disgrace, as Chrysostom comments on this passage.

But some things can be combined from these interpretations for very good reason. For it amounts to the same thing, whether one says that men fall short of the glory of the divine image in which they were formed in Adam, or of the righteousness that avails before God, or of boasting, or of eternal life itself. For all these things are so closely connected to one another that one follows the other.

Some explain the verb ὑστεροῦνται [they come short] to mean that they are excluded from the glory of God; others, that they are unable to reach the glory of God; others, that they lack, or they need the glory of God; others, that they fall short of the glory of God, etc. Origen on this passage: "From this, that all had been made to be under sin, the effects are also without a doubt foreign to the glory of God, for they had neither been able to grasp it in any way nor earn it." But this diversity of interpretation arises from the fact that different people are using the vocable τῆς δόξης [of the glory] differently.

v.24 δικαιούμενοι δωρεὰν τῇ αὐτοῦ χάριτι, διὰ τῆς ἀπολυτρώσεως τῆς ἐν Χριστῷ Ἰησοῦ

v.24 Being justified freely by his grace through the redemption that is in Christ Jesus: (KJV)

Δικαιούμενοι, "as those who are justified." The participle depends on the preceding verb ὑστεροῦνται [they lack].

The verb δικαιοῦσθαι [to be justified] has a forensic meaning, "to be pronounced righteous, to be absolved," since the whole act of our justification is described with forensic terms. *The defendant* is man the sinner; *the plaintiff*, or the accuser, is the law and the devil; *the witness* is the conscience; *the advocate* is Christ; *the judge* is God. Both accusation and condemnation are contrasted with this justification.

Therefore, the papists err when they define justification as "the infusion of righteousness" (Bellarmine, Bk. 1, *On Justification*, ch. 1; Costerus in *Enchiridion*., ch. 6).

Δωρεὰν [as a gift] is used in three ways in the Scriptures. (1) It is contrasted with "the payment of a price" (Gen. 29:15, Exo. 21:2, Num. 11:1, 2 Kin. 24:24, Mat. 10:8, 2 Cor. 11:7, Rev. 21:5). (2) It means "without just cause, rashly out of levity or petulance" (Psa. 35:19, Psa. 69:5, Psa. 109:3, Psa. 119:161, Pro. 24:28, Pro. 26:2, Gal. 2, the last verse). (3) It is contrasted with "merit," whether good or bad (1 Kin. 19:5, 25:31; 2 Kin. 2:31; Eze. 16:10, Eze. 14, last verse; Sirach 29:8 and 10; Jer. 15:13; Lam. 3:52; 2 The. 3:8).

Out of these meanings, the first and the third agree with this passage. "We are justified freely," that is, without the intervention of a price paid by us, without our merit—indeed, contrary to our merit. For as David's enemies are said to have hated him "freely"[35]— both because there was no merit or cause in David on account of which his adversaries should have hated him; and because there was a cause in David why they shouldn't have hated him—so also God justifies us freely, both because there is no merit or cause in us on account of which we should be justified; and because, on the contrary, there is, rather, in us merit and cause of damnation, because of which God could have cast us away from His face.

Augustine, Sermon 15, *On the Apostolic Words*, and on these words in Psa. 56: "You save them for nothing. You find no reason for which You should save; but You do find much reason for which You should damn. And nevertheless You receive us on the basis of mercy, on account of Christ."

Ambrose on this passage: "We are justified freely, that is, by the gift of God, while we do nothing—we neither earn anything by

---

35 Latin: *gratis*

rendering payment, that is, with the works that precede, nor do we compensate with the works that follow."

Τῇ αὐτοῦ χάριτι [by His grace]. With "grace" he understands the gracious favor of God and the mercy founded in Christ, as is evident (1) from the synonyms. For as justification is here attributed to the grace of God, so elsewhere it is attributed to "the mercy of God" (Eph. 2:4, Titus 3:5, 1 Pet. 1:3, etc.); to "love" (1 John 3:16, Rom. 5:8); to φιλανθρωπία [philanthropy] (Titus 3:4). (2) From the comparison. Grace, in the article of justification, is contrasted with "works" (Rom. 11:6, Eph. 2:8); with "debt" (Rom. 4:4-5); with "merit" (Eph. 1:6); with "the law" (Rom. 3:21, 6:14; Gal. 2:21, 5:4, etc.). (3) From the etymology. חנן means "to show favor, to receive into grace, to show mercy out of grace" (Exo. 33:19, Rom. 9:15, Gen. 6:8, Heb. 11:7, 2 Kin. 13:23, etc.). Χάρις is related to the verb χαρίζεσθαι, "to forgive out of grace" (Luke 7:42; 2 Cor. 2:9, 12:13), and to the verb χαριτοῦν, "to consider someone pleasing and beloved" (Eph. 1:6, etc.). (4) From the effects, properties and circumstances of that grace. In Gal. 1:15, "the calling" is attributed to it. But that is a work of divine mercy (Rom. 9:11, Eph. 1:4, etc.). In Heb. 4:16, we are commanded to "approach the throne of grace." But that "throne of grace "is nothing other than the mercy of God set forth for us in Christ, the Mercy Seat. In John 1:16-17, that grace is said to come down to us from the fullness of the merits of Christ. It is contrasted with the wrath that the law of Moses pronounces. It is said to be "in place of grace," that is, it befalls us with no merit of our own. Or, to put it another way: On account of Christ, who is the only Man in grace (Rom. 5:15), we, too, are said to be received by God into grace. (5) From the absurdity that would result if it did not have this meaning. Rom. 5:20, "Where sin abounded, grace abounded more." Imagine that "grace" meant "infused righteousness," and in the abundance of sin you will have an abundance of inherent righteousness. Rom. 6:15, "Shall we sin, since we are not under law, but under grace?" If, in this apostolic treatment, grace meant "an infused condition," then there would be no passage that could object to this.

The apostolic passage must especially be noted in 2 Tim. 1:9-

10, from whence such an argument arises. We are justified in time by that same grace by which we were also elected from eternity. But that grace by which we were elected from eternity is the gracious mercy of God in Christ (Eph. 1:4). Therefore, since Bellarmine himself defines the eternal grace of God thus (Bk. 1, *On Grace and Free Will*, ch. 2), that it is "the love of God with which God loved us before the world was made, from eternity itself," he will not be able to deny that the grace of justification is also the gracious favor and love of God.

These things are so certain and clear that some of the papists themselves acknowledge the truth of them. Albertus Pighius, Bk. 5, *On Free Will*: "We shall seek a varied understanding of 'grace,' not from the schools, but from the divine Scriptures, seeing that in the schools they generally imagine that the grace of God is a certain quality of our soul that was not created by God, whether it be the same thing as the condition of charity or distinct from it. I consider all these things to be false and to have no authority from the Scriptures." Pererius, Disputation 13 on Romans ch. 3, n. 53: "The noun 'grace,' when it says here that they are justified '*gratis*, by His grace,' although it can signify that supernatural and inherent divine quality infused by God into the soul of man by which a man is righteous and acceptable to God, it nevertheless appears rather in this passage to signify the gracious goodness and kindness of God toward man. For Paul contrasts the grace of God with the works of men, signifying, not that due righteousness is somehow rendered by the merits of men, but rather that, on account of the infinite kindness and free mercy of God, righteousness is given to man, with no preceding good merits of men, and indeed, with many bad merits."

Bellarmine, Bk. 1, *On Grace and Free Will*, ch. 7, admits that "those Scriptures that place charity after grace must be understood so that 'grace' signifies the benevolence of God toward us, not some sort of quality that exists in us." But from the logical sequence of the text, it is evident that, in the apostolic treatment of our justification before God, the Apostle is dealing with grace as it comes before charity. Therefore...

The papists think that "grace" means "the infused condition of righteousness." The Council of Trent, Session 6, Canon. 11: "Anathema," they say, "to those who assert that the grace by which we are justified is only the favor of God."

In the chapter on Baptism in the Roman Catechism, p. 310: "Grace is the divine quality that dwells in the soul; it is like a certain splendor and light that erases all the spots from our souls and renders them more beautiful and more splendid."

Bellarmine, Bk. 1, *On Grace and Free Will*, ch. 3: "It is the common conclusion of theologians that grace is the supernatural condition infused in us by God by which the soul is adorned and perfected and truly rendered pleasing and acceptable to God." Bk. 2, *On Justification*, ch. 3: "Justifying grace is not just the favor of God, but a gift that dwells in the soul." Here he also makes the following connections to this apostolic passage:

(1) "The favor of God is sufficiently explained with the word 'gratis,' for he who justifies 'gratis' certainly justifies from benevolence and generosity. Thus that addition, 'by grace,' must signify, not favor itself, but something else, that is, the effect of His favor, namely, righteousness that has been given and infused by Him. This is the formal cause of justification."

We reply: It is not uncommon for the Scripture, for the sake of greater emphasis, to explain one word with another, or to join together two synonymous words, or to add an adverb to a noun of the same meaning, for the sake of adding certainty to a thing and for the sake of emphasizing it (Mat. 2:10, Luke 2:9, etc.). But in this passage, that addition is lacking the necessary rationale. For since the grace of the God who justifies us not only gives us the remission of sins and imputes the righteousness of Christ to us, but it also begins new motives by the Holy Spirit—that is, both justification and renewal—therefore grace and the gift that comes by grace are joined together by a single connection. And lest someone should imagine that we are justified because we are now pleasing to God on account of those new motives, the particle "gratis" is added, which corresponds to the חִנָּם of the Hebrews, so that the sense is that we are justified before God without any of our merit— indeed, contrary to our merit—so that the cause of our gracious acceptance is not in us, but in God.

Martin Chemnitz, in Part 2 of his *Loci*, p. 737, states this with a most beautiful arrangement: "It is said of Joseph that he found grace in the eyes of his lord (Gen. 39:4). But it is added that he loved him 'because he was blessed,' that is, on account of the exceptional virtues that Potiphar noticed in Joseph. Therefore, lest anyone begin to think that we are also justified by the grace of God in the same way, the Apostle adds the particle 'gratis,' in order to demonstrate that, in justification, God does not take into account any dignity or merit or anything else that dwells in us so that on account of that He receives us into grace. Rather, although He finds in us a reason why He could damn us, He receives us to eternal life by His free goodness alone." Therefore, the particle δωρεὰν [as a gift], far from undermining our exposition, greatly confirms it.

(2) "The preposition 'through' (*per*) cannot be accommodated to favor and benevolence; it indicates the *formal* or the *meritorious* or the *instrumental* cause. For we would not rightly say, 'God justifies us through His favor or through His benevolence.' But we would rightly say, 'God justifies us through indwelling grace, through the merit of the Son, through faith and the Sacraments.'"

We reply: (1) The preposition "through" (*per*) is not found in the Greek text; it simply says τῇ χάριτι [the dative form of "the grace"]. (2) The preposition "through" very often denotes an efficient cause in the Scriptures (John 1:3; Rom. 6:4, 11:35; 1 Cor. 1:9; Heb. 2:10). (3) Titus 3:5, God is said to have saved us κατὰ τὸν αὐτοῦ ἔλεον [according to His mercy], where an infused condition cannot be understood with "mercy." (4) The Syriac translates בְּטַיְבוּתָא, "in grace" or "by grace."

(3) "The benevolence of God is not vain, but entirely furnishes and effects that good thing that it desires for someone. Therefore, when God justifies, He does not only make a nice wish, but He also makes righteous and holy."

We reply: The question is not whether the free mercy of God—who receives believers into grace for the sake of Christ—and the gift of renewal through the Holy Spirit are always joined together, for none of us denies that, since it is certain that no one is reconciled to God through faith in Christ without at the same time being renewed through the Holy Spirit. But this is the point in question, whether we are received into grace and accepted into eternal life on account of that gift of renewal; or, in other words, whether that gift of renewal is to be understood when we are said to be justified and saved by the grace of God. This we deny. Therefore, the benevolence of the God who justifies us is not vain, but altogether furnishes that good thing that it desires for us.

For (1) God justifies us by imputing the righteousness of Christ. It is clear that this imputation is not putative or imaginary, but real and efficacious, based on the imputation that has been made of our sins to Christ. (2) The same grace of the justifying God gives us the Holy Spirit, through whom our nature begins to be renewed. But in this renewal, neither our merit nor the substance of our righteousness can be placed before God, since that renewal is not perfect, but should daily increase and will be perfected later on, in the next life.

Διὰ τῆς ἀπολυτρώσεως [through the redemption]. Ἀπολύτρωσις is properly "the redemption of a captive through the payment of a λύτρῳ, or price, for his head." As Lucian says of Achilles: Χρημάτων ὀλίγων τὸν Ἕκτυρος νεκρὸν ἀπελύτρωσας [You redeemed the corpse of Hector for a little money].

Chrysostom notes that it is called ἀπολύτρωσιν, not ἡμυλύπρωσιν, since it is a full and perfect redemption. Therefore, in the work of redemption, Mary must not be joined to Christ, nor should our own merits be combined with the merit of Christ.

This vocable reminds us of (1) that miserable captivity in which we were held as prisoners in Satan's kingdom on account of sin; (2) that precious λύτρον [price] with which Christ redeemed us from that hostile captivity and power—His own blood. 1 Tim. 2:6: "He gave Himself as a ἀντίλυτρον [repayment]"; (3) that intimate bond of gratitude by which we are therefore bound to Christ as our Redeemer and Lord.

Therefore, the grace of God when He justifies is not absolute, but is founded on the merit of Christ. But one must judge in the same way concerning election, which, of course, is nothing else than preordained justification and glorification (2 Tim. 1:9-10).

v.25 ὃν προέθετο ὁ Θεὸς ἱλαστήριον διὰ τῆς πίστεως ἐν τῷ αὐτοῦ αἵματι, εἰς ἔνδειξιν τῆς δικαιοσύνης αὐτοῦ διὰ τὴν πάρεσιν τῶν προγεγονότων ἁμαρτημάτων,

v.25 Whom God hath set forth to be a propitiation through faith in his blood, to declare his righteousness for the remission of sins that are past, through the forbearance of God; (KJV)

Προέθετο [He set forth], namely, in His eternal counsel and decree (1 Pet. 1:20). He has revealed this eternal counsel of His in the word of the Gospel. For in it, Christ is set before us, to be received by us by means of a true faith.

Ἱλαστήριον is "a means of appeasing, [36] a propitiatorium." The Syriac has the noun חוּסָיָא, from the root חוס, "he spared." The LXX uses this noun for the lid covering the ark of the covenant, which Moses calls כַּפֹּרֶת. According to the last verse of Hebrews 4, it was a type of Christ (1) with regard to the efficient cause, namely, the divine decree. For just as the Mosaic Propitiatorium was established by divine mandate, so also Christ was established as our Mediator in the eternal counsel of the Father (1 Pet. 1:20); (2) with regard to the effect and fourfold use. It was used, first, for the purpose of *revealing the divine will*. The Propitiatorium was the seat of divine oracles (Exo. 25:22). So also Christ has revealed to us the counsel of God regarding our salvation (John 1:18). It was used, secondly, for *propitiation*, from which the "Propitiatorium" derives its name, because it was a symbol of the gracious presence of God, who was pleased with His people in the promised Messiah. So also Christ is "the ἱλασμὸς (propitiation) for our sins" (1 John 2:2), for through Him the heavenly Father is pleased with us. Thirdly, it was used for

---

36 Latin: *placamentum, propitiatorium*

the purpose of *covering*. The Propitiatorium was the lid of the ark in which the tablets of the Law of Moses were kept. So also Christ covers the multitude and the magnitude of our sins committed against the tablets of the law, lest they come into the view of God; in addition, He also covers up the curse of the Law by His obedience and affords to believers a desirable shelter against the fire of divine wrath, as in the case of the tax collector when he prays in true repentance (Luke 18:12, ἱλάσθητί μοι [be propitious to me]). Fourthly, it was used for *sprinkling*. Both the Propitiatorium and the people of Israel were sprinkled with the blood of the sacrifices (Lev. 16:14-15). So also the expiation of our sins takes place through the sprinkling of the blood of Christ, by which they are effectively cleansed and washed away before the judgment of God (Heb. 9:12-14, 10:3-4, etc.; 1 Pet. 1:1; Rev. 1:6).

This propitiation through the blood of Christ was beautifully prefigured in the Propitiatorium of the Old Testament. (1) In the Old Testament, there was only one Propitiatorium. So also Christ is the one and only Mediator and Propitiator in the New Testament (1 Tim. 2:4). (2) Access to the Propitiatorium was blocked to no one. For although it was only once per year that the high priest would enter the Holy of Holies, where the Propitiatorium was, nevertheless they would pray daily with their face turned toward the Propitiatorium. So also Christ is our Propitiator, not only because of merit, but also because of efficacy. Therefore, we can and should daily "approach the Throne of Grace with confidence" (Heb. 4:16). (3) The Propitiatorium was, by way of type, that very thing through which they would be reconciled to God. So also Christ is that very thing by which and through which we are pleasing to God, namely, the oblation, the victim and the sacrifice. (4) Reconciliation could not take place by any other way except through the Propitiatorium. So also there neither is nor can there be any propitiation of our sins except in this one and only Mediator of ours. (5) It was with a grateful spirit that the Israelites acknowledged this benefit of God that was furnished to them in the Propitiatorium. So also we are constrained by that expiation of sins to perpetual gratitude to Christ.

The Photinians object that "that lid is called a Propitiatorium, not because it placated God toward the people of Israel, but because God, in rendering Himself propitious and placated on it, answered their prayers. So also Christ is called the Propitiatorium, not because He has placated God toward us, but because God, in showing Himself to be most pleased with us in Christ, has revealed His will through Him." (Socinus, *Contra Covetum*, p.126, Schmaltz. in Exam. 157, *Errorum Errore* 47, p.15.)

We reply: (1) The Apostle immediately adds that this Propitiatorium has been set forth to us in the blood of Christ, clearly teaching that Christ is our ἱλασμὸν [propitiation] and ἱλαστήριον [Propitiatorium] for this very reason, that He has expiated our sins by the shedding of His blood and has rendered God propitious toward us. (2) There is often something greater in the antitype than in the type. Christ is our ἱλαστήριον in a far greater way than that type of the Mosaic Propitiatorium. (3) That lid could not have been called a ἱλαστήριον, nor would God have shown Himself to be propitious and pleased on it unless He had had Christ in view, who, by His death and by the shedding of His blood, has placated God toward us, and by whose merit our sins are covered before the judgment of God.

Ἐν τῷ αἵματι [in the blood]. The Syriac refers this to the neighboring phrase, namely, to the noun πίστεως [faith], for it is translated this way, "through faith in His blood." But it is more correctly referred to the more remote word, namely, to the noun ἱλαστήριον, so that the Propitiatorium is understood as being set forth to us in the blood of Christ.

With the word "blood," the sacrifice on the altar of the cross is understood as the offering for us, and indeed, the suffering and death of Christ are joined together with the shedding of blood on the altar of the cross. But the fact that the Apostle mentions blood is not to be taken exclusively, as Piscator wants, as if only the passive obedience of Christ were the meritorious cause of our justification. Rather, the Apostle has in view, first, the type of the sacrifices in the Old Testament, since, just as the blood of animals was shed in the sacrifices for bodily—that is, Levitical—cleansing, so also the blood of Christ that was prefigured with the blood of the sacrifices, cleanses our conscience from dead works (Heb. 9:13-14). Secondly, he has in view the type of the sprinkling of the Propitiatorium with the blood of the sacrifices, by which was signified that our Propitiatorium in the New Testament was likewise to be sprinkled, not with the blood of another, but with His own blood. Thirdly, he has in view the complement of both the passive and the active obedience provided to the heavenly Father in His death and suffering (Phi. 2:9). Never was it more clearly revealed that God has loved us than in His own suffering and wounds.

Εἰς ἔνδειξιν τῆς δικαιοσύνης αὐτοῦ [for demonstration of His righteousness]. With the noun "righteousness" (1) some understand the truthfulness of God in keeping promises, since Christ the Mediator was promised in the Law and the Prophets. Therefore, by furnishing Him, God demonstrated that He is righteous, truthful and constant in keeping promises.

(2) Others understand the righteousness acquired by the suffering and the merit of Christ, which is imputed to us by faith, which is called "the righteousness of God" in the preceding verse 22. This is how Blessed Luther views it with his translation: "*damit er die Gerechtigkeit / die für ihm gilt / darbiete* [so that He might furnish the righteousness that avails before Him]."

(3) Still others understand the righteousness of God manifested in the suffering of Christ, so that the text should therefore be rendered in this way: In order that He might demonstrate His righteousness by punishing our sins in Christ and by demonstrating, in that very act, that He does not remit sins except by the intervention of a perfect satisfaction—which is proper for divine justice. Likewise, that, content with the satisfaction provided through Christ, He remits sins to those who believe in Him, nor does He demand their own payment from them—which, likewise, agrees with divine justice. None of these explanations is at odds with the analogy of faith, although, due to the word ἐνδείξεως [demonstration], the last one seems to agree most with the text.

Διὰ τὴν πάρεσιν τῶν προγεγονότων ἁμαρτημάτων [on account of the remission of the sins that occurred beforehand]. Πάρεσις [remission] properly signifies "the loosing of bonds," and thus it means that sins are a sort of spiritual bond by which a man is rendered inept for that which is good, while at the same time being bound to temporal and eternal punishment.

Observe that, in the remission of sins, not only does God's mercy show itself, but also God's righteousness. For He does not remit sin rashly, as if He didn't care about it. Neither does He remit sin unjustly, as if He were fond of it. Nor does He remit sin unknowingly, as if He were ignorant of it, or as if it were hidden during His examination. Instead, He remits sin in view of the full satisfaction provided by Christ, apprehended by believers through faith.

But why does he mention the sins committed beforehand? Not to deny that the remission of the sins that are committed by the reborn after they have received grace also takes place through Christ; nor to teach that Christ made satisfaction only for original sin. But (1) he wanted to indicate that the power of the merit of Christ extends to the sins committed under the Old Testament, and that Christ did not only make satisfaction for the sins committed after His offering on the cross, but also for those that were perpetrated already beforehand, from the time of the Fall of our first parents. For the suffering of Christ was beneficial before it took place; and His benefits avail both forwards and backwards (Rev. 13:8).

(2) And consequently, to demonstrate that "it was impossible for the blood of bulls and goats to take away sins" (Heb. 10:4). Otherwise, there would have been no need for another sacrifice prefigured by them. Through the figures of the paschal lamb, the sacrifices, and the Propitiatorium, the future satisfaction of Christ was foreshadowed in the Old Testament and applied to believers through faith.

(3) He also wanted to run to meet the Epicurean notion, lest someone should think that, by the remission of sins, license is being given to sin. Our Old Man has been crucified with Christ in order that the body of sin may be abolished, lest afterwards we should be enslaved again to sin (Rom. 6:6).

(4) And he would set before us a solid consolation, that we should certainly obtain the remission of the present infirmities that still cling to us, since so many and such great preceding sins were remitted to us by grace (Rom. 5:8).

v.26 ἐν τῇ ἀνοχῇ τοῦ Θεοῦ, πρὸς ἔνδειξιν τῆς δικαιοσύνης αὐτοῦ ἐν τῷ νῦν καιρῷ, εἰς τὸ εἶναι αὐτὸν δίκαιον καὶ δικαιοῦντα τὸν ἐκ πίστεως Ἰησοῦ.

v.26 *To declare, I say, at this time his righteousness: that he might be just, and the justifier of him which believeth in Jesus.* (KJV)

The Syriac joins this together with the word προγεγονότων [occurred beforehand] in the preceding verse. For it translates this way: "On account of the sins which we sinned from the beginning, through the latitude that God gave us for His forbearance." So the sense would be that those sins were permitted through "the tolerance of God" (Acts 17:30).

Luther places the text in the same order. *"In dem daß er Sünde vergibt / welche bis anher blieben waren unter Göttlicher Gedult* [In that He forgives sins which until now had remained under divine patience]."

But it can be explained in another way, that sin could not be taken away through the law nor through any good work. Instead, it was to be remitted by grace, for the sake of Christ. Indeed, the aim of the Apostle is clearly to show that, for the sake of the future sacrifice of Christ, God was patient toward sinners even in the Old Testament, and remitted sins to the penitent on account of it.

Εἰς τὸ εἶναι αὐτὸν δίκαιον καὶ δικαιοῦντα [that He might be just and the Justifier]. An elegant play on words, from which Augustine astutely infers in his book *On the Spirit and the Letter*, ch. 9: "In this apostolic dissertation, 'righteousness' is understood, not in that God is righteous, but in that He justifies the ungodly."

Τὸν ἐκ πίστεως Ἰησοῦ, "the one who is by faith of Christ," that is, "the one who believes in Christ." For just as οἱ ἐκ περιτομῆς [those by circumcision] are "circumcised," so also those who are ἐκ πίστεως Ἰησοῦ [by faith of Jesus] are "believers" in Christ.

In this passage the causes and the object of our justification before God are expressed.

1. *The chief efficient cause* is the grace of God, that is, God's free favor that takes our misery into account.

2. *The meritorious cause* is Christ in the office of redemption, which the Apostle describes with three very significant words. First, with the word ἀπολύτρωσιν [redemption], which has in view the spiritual captivity in Satan's kingdom from which we have been redeemed by the precious λύτρῳ [price] of Christ. Second, with the word ἱλαστήριον [Propitiatorium], which has in view the lid of the ark of the covenant in the Old Testament. Third, with the phrase the αἷμα τοῦ χριστοῦ [blood of Christ], which, by way of synecdoche, signifies the entire obedience of Christ, active as well as passive.

3. *The instrumental cause* is faith, that receiving (ληπτικόν) means that embraces the benefits of Christ offered in Word and Sacraments, which are the imparting (δοτικοῖς) means.

4. *The formal cause* is πάρεσις, the remission of sins, which is joined by an indivisible connection with the imputation of the righteousness of Christ (Rom. 4:3).

5. *The final cause* with respect to God is ἔνδειξις τῆς δικαιοσύνης αὐτοῦ [the demonstration of His righteousness]. In justification, or the remission of sins, God remains just in that He justly punishes our sins in Christ, who received them upon Himself; and He justifies believers by means of the righteousness of Christ that has been imputed to them.

The object of justification is man the sinner, but only such a one as believes in Christ, that is, who acknowledges his sins from the Law, who seriously grieves over them, and who by faith applies to himself the promise of the remission of sins for the sake of Christ.

v.27 Ποῦ οὖν ἡ καύχησις; Ἐξεκλείσθη. Διὰ ποίου νόμου; Τῶν ἔργων; Οὐχί, ἀλλὰ διὰ νόμου πίστεως.

v.27 Where is boasting then? It is excluded. By what law? of works? Nay: but by the law of faith. (KJV)

Ποῦ ἡ καύχησις [where the boasting?], that is, of one's own righteousness. Indeed, such boasting must have a basis in truth; it may not consist in the bare opinion of the mind.

In the Vulgate translation the pronoun "your" is added, from which Bellarmine deduces (Bk. 1, *On Justification*, ch. 19): "Only those works are to be excluded from the act of justification that are done without grace, by the powers of free will. Not all boasting," he says, "is being excluded by the Apostle, but only that which arises from works of free will done without grace, for he adds: Where is your boasting, in that you boast in yourself and not in the Lord? But we do boast in the Lord on the basis of works done from faith. This is not forbidden."

We reply: (1) In the Greek text, the pronoun σου [your] is not added; (2) neither is it added in the Syriac text; (3) neither in any of the Latin manuscripts. (4) One must distinguish between "the boasting of a good conscience," which is permissible, and "the boasting of one's own righteousness before the judgment of God," which is not permissible (1 Cor. 4:4). (5) He teaches that we are justified "by the law of faith," that is, by the doctrine of the Gospel, which is free on account of Christ, not by works. Absolutely all human boasting is excluded from justification, "that God alone may be just and the one who justifies Him who is by faith" (v.26). (6) What the Apostle says broadly in this passage, that "boasting is excluded," he applies in the next chapter to Abraham as he stood in the midst of doing good works, denying that he had a boast of righteousness before God. (7) If the reborn were justified by their works, they would still have a certain boast by which they may boast partly in God, partly in themselves, since they act by God in perfecting good works in such a way that they themselves are also acting. But one must boast only in the Lord (Jer. 9:24; Dan. 9:7,18; Luke 17:10; 2 Cor. 1:17). (8) A clear example that absolutely all boasting of one's own righteousness—inherent and actual—is excluded, is set forth in the Pharisee (Luke 18:11), who certainly gave thanks to God with this word, "that he is righteous," and thus acknowledged that righteousness had been infused in him by God. Nonetheless, "he did not go down to his house justified" (v.14).

Ἐξεκλείσθη. "Was excluded." The Syriac has אֶתְבַּטַל from the root בטל, "it was abolished, made vain, useless." Luther: *"Er ist aus* [it is out]," and in other manuscripts, *"Er ist nichts* [it is nothing]."

There is an elegant antanaclasis in the different meanings of the word νόμου [law] as it is twice repeated. For although it is properly and customarily assigned to the doctrine of works, here it is assigned to the Gospel, that is, the doctrine of faith, by which all boasting is therefore and for this reason excluded, inasmuch as the Gospel teaches that the righteousness that avails before God is to be sought in Christ alone.

In what sense, then, does the Apostle insist that boasting is excluded by the law of deeds, since the law of deeds accuses everyone of sin and damns them? We reply: He has in mind the preconceived notion of the Jews in which they thought that the law was given to them to this end, that they might be justified and saved through it. With this mist covering their mind, they did not realize that boasting about their own righteousness as if it availed before the judgment of God is excluded by the law of deeds.

Some think that this is a new argument for proving the conclusion, assumed from the final goal. The final goal of our justification is the sole glory of the one true God. Therefore, we are not justified partly by faith and partly by works, but by faith alone. The rationale of the connection is that, if we were justified either wholly or partially by our works, then the glory of righteousness would not be attributed only to God. But the particle οὖν [therefore] shows that this exclusion of boasting is being deduced from the demonstrated justification by faith alone. Since all men are sinners and are justified freely by the grace of God through faith, without works, therefore all boasting about one's own righteousness is excluded before the judgment of God.

v.28 Λογιζόμεθα, οὖν πίστει δικαιοῦσθαι ἄνθρωπον, χωρὶς ἔργων νόμου.

v.28 *Therefore we conclude that a man is justified by faith without the deeds of the law. (KJV)*

The verb λογιζόμεθα [we conclude] is translated less suitably in the Vulgate as "we think."[37] Augustine (*On the Spirit and the Letter*, ch. 13) more correctly renders it as "we reckon."[38] Theophylact, writing on this passage, understands the thought as συλλογιζόμεθα, "we reckon by means of argumentation." Xenophon, Bk. 1, *Cyropaedia*: ἐκείνων δὲ ἐπελάθου, ἅποτε ἐγὼ καὶ σὺ ἐλογιζόμεθα, "which we have concluded by firm reasoning." There is great emphasis on this verb, for it means "we conclude based on the reasoning discussed at both ends, and by subtraction, as with a calculation; we infer from the things that were presented before, reckoning a sum as when numbers are added together."

The Apostle thus indicates two things with this verb: (1) That he is inferring this conclusion from the things that came before. (2) That this conclusion is not a theory, but is clearly proven.[39] Luther: "*So halten wir es nun dafür* [So we therefore now hold]."

The papists raise a thunderous objection against Luther on this passage, because in the German version he added the exclusive particle "*allein* [alone]." But (1) this translation clearly expresses the genuine, proper and native conclusion of the Apostle. It is the same thing, "to be justified by faith without works," and "not to be justified except through faith" (Gal. 2:16), that is, 'to be justified by faith alone.' (2) It agrees with the native idiom of the German language. For this is the idiom of the German language, that when two or more things are being contrasted, the exclusive is added to that which is being affirmed for the sake of greater emphasis and clarity (Luther, Vol. 5, *Jen. Germ.*, f.140). (3) He did this in keeping with the example of the Syriac version (Rom. 4:5); the Greek version (Gen. 3:11, Deu. 6:13, Mat. 4:10); the Latin version (Lev. 21:2; Deu. 6:13, 10:20, 12:32, 22:27, 32:39; 1 Sam. 10:19, 18:8; 2 Kin. 7:7, 19:11, 23:9; 2 Chr. 20:12; Est. 3:2, 4:13; Job 17:1; Dan. 11:4; Zec. 8:19); the Italic (Gal. 2:16); the German editions before Luther (Norib., AD 1483), which are held at Confluentia and Spira.

v.29 Ἦ Ἰουδαίων ὁ Θεὸς μόνον; Οὐχὶ δὲ καὶ ἐθνῶν; Ναί, καὶ ἐθνῶν,

---

37 Latin: *arbitramur*
38 Latin: *colligimus*
39 Latin: *non Topica, sed apodictica*

v.29 Is he the God of the Jews only? is he not also of the Gentiles? Yes, of the Gentiles also: (KJV)

A new argument for proving the conclusion. If justification were by the law and the works of the law, then God would only be the Savior of the Jews, since the law was given only to the Jews.

v.30 ἐπείπερ εἷς ὁ Θεός, ὃς δικαιώσει περιτομὴν ἐκ πίστεως καὶ ἀκροβυστίαν διὰ τῆς πίστεως.

v.30 Seeing it is one God, which shall justify the circumcision by faith, and uncircumcision through faith. (KJV)

If God were to justify the Jews in one way and the Gentiles in another, He would not be "one," that is, always resembling Himself. Both the consequence and the antecedent of such as assertion are absurd. Therefore, He justifies them both in one and the same way, namely, by faith.

Origen is mistaken when he derives a diverse way of justifying from the uncertain difference in the particles ἐκ [from] and διὰ [through], since the aim of the Apostle is obviously the opposite, namely, to establish a single way of justifying.

v.31 Νόμον οὖν καταργοῦμεν διὰ τῆς πίστεως; Μὴ γένοιτο! Ἀλλὰ νόμον ἱστῶμεν.

v.31 Do we then make void the law through faith? God forbid: yea, we establish the law. (KJV)

The point is this: Even though justification is not by works of the law, nevertheless we do not repudiate the law on that account.

We certainly do not καταργοῦμεν, "destroy" the law—render it useless and idle—by teaching that we are justified by faith without the works of the law. The Syriac has the verb בטל, the same verb it used to translate ἐξεκλείσθη [it was excluded] in v. 27.

Ἱστῶμεν, "we make firm, we erect,[40] etc." The Vulgate, less suitably, "we establish.[41]" For "to set up" is used of those things that do

---

40 Latin: *Stabilimus, erigimus*
41 Latin: *statuimus*

not yet exist, as in Virgil: "The city that I establish." But "to make firm" means the confirmation of those things that are.

But how is the law made firm through faith?

(1) Because faith, that is, the doctrine of the Gospel, shows us Christ, who is the τέλος, "the end of the law" (Rom. 10:4), and the one who furnishes perfect obedience to the law in our place.

(2) Because believers use the law "lawfully" (νομίκως), acknowledging from it the extreme corruption of their nature, unlike the hypocrites who stray from the true sense and usage of the law, judging that merely any kind of external obedience is prescribed in it.

(3) Because τὸ δικαίωμα [the righteousness] of the law is fulfilled in the believers (Rom. 8:4), since the righteousness of Christ, which is the perfect fulfillment of the law, is imputed to them through faith. Luther on this passage: "*Der Glaube erfüllet alle Gesetze / die Wercke erfüllen kein Titel des Gesetzes* [Faith fulfills every law; works do not fulfill even a tittle of the Law]."

(4) Because believers, who have been justified by faith, are being renewed by the Holy Spirit so that they begin to furnish a voluntary and interior obedience. Thus by faith they arrive at works, that is, at the obedience of the law. They do not arrive at faith and justification by works, as the hypocrites attempt to do in vain.

Notes on the Epistle to the Romans: Chapter 4

The Apostle confirms in this chapter what he had said above in 3:21, that the righteousness of God by which we justified has been proven by the testimony of the Law and the Prophets. For he sets forth first the example of Abraham, and second, the testimony of David; the first is from the Law, that is, the Books of Moses, while the second is drawn from the Prophets.

v. 1 Τί οὖν ἐροῦμεν Ἀβραὰμ τὸν πατέρα ἡμῶν εὑρηκέναι κατὰ σάρκα;

v.1 What shall we say then that Abraham our father, as pertaining to the flesh, hath found? (KJV)

The Apostle proves the gracious justification by faith from the example of Abraham, who, even while living a life of good works, was not justified before God by works, but by faith.

This is why he adduces the example of Abraham: (1) Because the Jews, in seeking righteousness in their works, boasted greatly about "Father Abraham" (Mat. 3:9). He therefore summons them back to consider the manner of justification that was set forth in the example of Abraham.

(2) Because Abraham is described as being endowed with notable virtues and adorned with a great heap of good works. Therefore, the Apostle wants it to be understood that, if Abraham was justified by faith and not by works, much less should others seek the righteousness that avails before God in their works.

(3) In order that, by adducing a testimony in favor of justification by faith from the first and most ancient writing of the Church, namely, the First Book of Moses, he may by that very antiquity—which is highly valued by all men of sound judgment—confirm the godly and refute the pseudo-apostles.

With regard to the qualifying phrase[42] κατὰ σάρκα [according to flesh] being placed at the end, some think it modifies the more remote, that is, the subject, which is "Abraham," whom they think

42 *prosdiorismos*

the Apostle is calling "father according to the flesh" in the same sense in which he later calls the Jews "his brothers, relatives according to the flesh" (Rom. 9:3), namely, because, according to the flesh, he was descended from Abraham just as the rest of the Jews were. So Origen, Ambrose and Lyranus interpret this passage.

But it is more correctly understood to modify the nearer, that is, the predicate explained in the verb εὑρηκέναι [to have found], as the natural progression shows.

With "flesh," some understand "the circumcision of the flesh," so that the sense is as follows: The law of Moses provides so little for salvation that not even Abraham—that notable Patriarch, the Father of all Jews—could have obtained anything according to the flesh, that is, through the circumcision of the flesh, unless he were reconciled and justified by faith in God. According to this reasoning, it is a reference to 2:28, where external circumcision is called περιτομὴ ἐν σαρκί [circumcision in flesh] (Eph. 2:11).

Others expound κατὰ σάρκα [according to flesh] as ἐξ ἔργων [by works], which is how the Apostle himself expounds it in the following verse, so that the sense is: What boast shall we say that Abraham obtained before God through works or by works? Surely we will not say, nor could we say, that Abraham discovered the praise of righteousness with God by works, or that he was justified by works! The Apostle thus has in view with this phrase that which he had said in the preceding chapter, 3:20, "By works of the law no flesh will be justified."

In any case, the matter turns out the same, since circumcision, insofar as the pseudo-apostles urged it as part of the righteousness that avails before God, pertains to works.

The Syriac translates בַּבְסַר, "in the flesh."

It is certain that κατὰ σάρκα [according to flesh] cannot be understood in this passage in the same sense as it is used in Rom. 8:12-13, since Abraham had already been reborn when it says of him that "faith was imputed to him for righteousness." Nor can it be gathered from this qualifying phrase that he is only dealing in this passage with works done without faith and the grace of the Holy Spirit, since the Apostle is speaking about Abraham as he was in the midst of living a life of good works. With σάρκα [flesh], then, we are to understand "the circumcision of the flesh" and all the works in which the pseudo-apostles sought the glory of righteousness, which is signified with the noun σαρκὸς [flesh] because, since the reborn are still partially σαρκικοὶ [fleshly] (Rom. 7:14), even in their flesh good does not dwell (v.18). Since they are neither perfectly good nor purely spiritual, thus also no one can be justified before God by works.

For what is said in Greek with the words Ἀβραὰμ τὸν πατέρα ἡμῶν [Abraham our father], the Syriac has רֵישָׁא רַאבְהָתָא, "chief of the fathers." For this sense, the Greeks usually use the word Πατριάρχης [Patriarch].

v.2 Εἰ γὰρ, Ἀβραὰμ ἐξ ἔργων ἐδικαιώθη, ἔχει καύχημα, ἀλλ᾽ οὐ πρὸς τὸν Θεόν.

v.2 *For if Abraham were justified by works, he hath whereof to glory; but not before God. (KJV)*

Some form the argument this way: If Abraham was justified by works, he has a boast with men, but not with God. Yet he does not only have a boast with men, but also with God. Therefore, he was not justified by works. Thus the majority of the ancients.

Others say the opposite: If he was justified by works, he has a boast with God. But he does not have such a boast. Therefore, he was not justified by works.

We would permit the former argument, only without the papistic addition, "not by preceding works." Still, the vocable καύχημα [boast] favors the latter argument, since it does not properly mean "glory," as the Vulgate renders this passage, but "boasting." Paul never excludes "glory" from justification, but "boasting" is expressly excluded in Rom. 3:27, from which it can be easily surmised that boasting is not being differentiated by the Apostle as if there were one kind of boasting with men and another with God—as if he denied the latter while granting the former. Rather, boasting is absolutely excluded, since in this argument there can be no boasting except with God.

Some see an objection being set forth to the conclusion expressed in the preceding verse: How can it be denied that Abraham discovered something according to the flesh, since he had secured the praise of righteousness? The Apostle responds that Abraham received the praise of righteousness by works with men, but not with God.

It is more correctly asserted that the Apostle is continuing to elaborate the argument he began in v.1, so that the sense is: If Abraham had been justified by works, then he would have a καύχημα [boast], that is, an occasion for boasting. But he did not have a καύχημα [boast] with God. (For that must be repeated from the obvious connection with the earlier part of this verse.) Therefore, he was not justified by works. He had said in v.28 of the preceding chapter, "Boasting is entirely excluded," and in v.23 of the same chapter, "All fall short of the glory of God." He applies that specifically to Abraham and teaches that he, too, fell short of the glory of his own inherent and actual righteousness with God, from which he infers that Abraham was not justified by works before the judgment of God.

Chrysostom, Homily 8 on the Epistle to the Romans: Βούλεται δεῖξαι, ὅτι καὶ ἐκεῖνος ἐκ πίστεως ἐδικαιώθη, ὅπερ ἦν περιουσία νίκης πολλῆς. Τὸ μὲν γὰρ ἔργα μὴ ἔχοντα ἐκ πίστεως δικαιωθῆναι τινὰ, οὐδὲν ἀπεικός· τὸ δὲ κομῶντα ἐν κατορθώμασι μὴ ἐντεῦθεν, ἀλλ᾽ἀπὸ πίστεως γενέσθαι δίκαιον, τοῦτο ἦν θαυμαστὸν, καὶ μάλιστα τῆς πίστεως τὴν ἰσχὺν ἐμφαῖνον. "He wants to show that even Abraham, who had just returned from a great victory, was justified by faith. Now, if he who is lacking works is justified by faith, there is nothing absurd about that. But that he who abounded in good works was not made righteous by them, but by faith—this was truly remarkable and made the power of faith especially manifest."

Cornelius a Lapide, writing on this passage, twists the text in this way: "If Abraham was justified by works, that is, if Abraham had only that righteousness that is by the works of the law or of nature to the exclusion of faith, etc."

Bellarmine agrees with this. Bk. 1, *On Justification*, ch. 19: "When the Apostle says that Abraham was justified by faith, not by works, he does not reject the works done by faith, but rather affirms that they were not done without faith, because if they had been, then they never would have justified him. Therefore, he excludes the works that Abraham might have done apart from faith."

We reply: (1) We demonstrated above that the Apostle excludes absolutely all works—even those that are done by the reborn—from the act of justification. (2) This very point is also clearly evident from the example of Abraham, which was adduced for that very purpose. The Apostle is not talking about the works that Abraham might have done without faith; he is expressly dealing with the works done by Abraham in the midst of living a godly life, and he denies that Abraham was justified before God by them. Rather, he teaches that Abraham was justified "by believing, not by doing" (verses 3 and 4); "that faith was imputed to him for righteousness" (same reference); "that he was justified not through the law, but by faith" (verses 13 and 16). (3) Between Paul and the pseudo-apostles there was no question about works done without faith, since the pseudo-apostles likewise taught faith in Christ. Rather, the question was, whether we are justified by means of faith and by works at the same time, or whether we are justified by means of faith without works. Therefore, since the Apostle proves his thesis of *justification by faith without works* through the example of Abraham, it is thus plainly apparent that he is not talking about works without faith, but about works done from faith. (4) When the Scripture says of Abraham that "faith was imputed to him for righteousness," it is speaking about Abraham, not as he still remained in Ur of the Chaldeans, but as one who had already been converted to the true God and who was already occupied in the pursuit of good works.

Emanuel a Sa draws this conclusion: "As one who has been justified, he has a boast with God, as if he were to say that justification will indeed be with God." But what need is there for that, since Paul is clearly not discussing anything but justification with God?

Toletus argues that καύχημα [boast] is not called "boasting" (1) "because it is not a valid assertion, namely, that such a one has reason to boast, for a man does not have any reason to boast in himself since he has nothing that he did not receive." We reply: It is false to say that Paul concedes that Abraham had a reason to boast. For this is the argument: If Abraham had been justified by works, then he would have had a reason to boast. But he has none. It is evident in the proposition that that phrase "with God," expressed only one time, is understood to be repeated also in the first part. If we were to agree with others that the answer is given by the Apostle through a distinction, then it is false that man has no reason to boast—if he is justified by works. For Paul demonstrates the opposite, since he denies that boasting is excluded by the law of works; rather, it is excluded by the law of faith.

(2) "Because καύχημα [a boast] is not the same thing as καύχησις [boasting] at the end of the preceding chapter. It means the same thing as praise and approval." We reply: Cajetan and Justinian state the opposite; they take it as "boasting." Καυχᾶσθαι does not mean "to be praised," but "to praise oneself," that is, "to boast." Καύχημα and καύχησις [boast and boasting], like ποίημα and ποίησις [deed and doing], do not differ with regard to substance, but only with regard to manner. Καύχημα denotes "the subject matter and the occasion of boasting;" καύχησις denotes "the act itself of boasting."

Observe that it is one thing to boast "with God," and another thing to boast "in God." To boast "with God" is to attribute the praise of the righteousness that avails before God to his works; to boast "in God" is to set aside the praise of the righteousness that avails before God by his works. It is to boast, not in himself, not in his works, but only in the mercy of God shown to us in Christ. So he cannot infer from the fact that we are enjoined to "boast in the Lord" that we should seek the righteousness that avails before God in the works that are done from faith and in grace, or that we should place confidence in it. On the contrary, all our confidence and all boasting of righteousness should be placed only in the mercy of God and in the merit of Christ alone. Gal. 6:14, "Far be it from me to boast, except in the cross of Christ." 1 Cor. 4:4, "I am not aware of anything for myself."

v.3 Τί γὰρ ἡ Γραφὴ λέγει; Ἐπίστευσε δὲ Ἀβραὰμ τῷ Θεῷ, καὶ ἐλογίσθη αὐτῷ εἰς δικαιοσύνην.

v.3 *For what saith the scripture? Abraham believed God, and it was counted unto him for righteousness.* (KJV)

The confirmation of the main proposition: Abraham was justified by faith. Therefore, not by works.

Faith is said to be "imputed for righteousness," because it is that medium, and really, the only thing on our part by which we apprehend Christ and His benefits so that His righteousness is imputed to us. Therefore it is the same thing, that faith is imputed for righteousness as it apprehends the benefits of Christ offered in the Word of promise; and that Christ is our righteousness before God as He is apprehended by faith.

Bellarmine, Bk. 2, *On Justification*, ch. 9, impugns this exposition of the text, which also conforms to the analogy of faith. "Faith," he says, "was certainly reckoned to Abraham for righteousness, as the Apostle says. But we do not admit the interpretation that the phrase 'faith is reckoned for righteousness' means that the righteousness of Christ is imputed to us if we apprehend Him by faith. This interpretation opposes the Apostle, first, because the Apostle says that faith itself is imputed for righteousness. But faith is not the righteousness of Christ, that is, that by which Christ is righteous. Rather, it is our righteousness, that is, that by which we are righteous by the gift of God. Then, because the word 'impute' in this passage does not mean a bare estimation, but an estimation which corresponds to the truth in the matter itself, as is clear from the words, 'To him who works, wages are not imputed according to grace, but according to debt.' For it is certain that, to him who works, wages are owed, not only by opinion and estimation, but truly and properly."

We reply: (1) One must distinguish between the faculty of believing, kindled in the heart of a believer by the Holy Spirit through the Word, and believing itself, so to speak. "For with the heart one believes for righteousness" (Rom. 10:10).

(2) Faith in the latter sense has been understood as a confident

apprehending of the merit and righteousness of Christ, which He merited for us by doing and by suffering.

(3) This faith is obviously not the righteousness itself of Christ, and yet it does still receive it and applies it to itself. Thus there is a relationship between the righteousness of Christ and faith, insofar as faith apprehends it. Therefore faith is said to be imputed for righteousness, because that which we apprehend by faith is imputed to us for righteousness.

(4) The Scripture says both things, that "faith is imputed to us for righteousness," and that "Christ is our righteousness" (Jer. 23:6, 33:16). "In Him we have righteousness" (Isa. 45:23). "He has been made righteousness for us by God" (1 Cor. 1:30). "In Him we become righteousness" (2 Cor. 5:21). Therefore, since Christ and faith are called at the same time "our righteousness," it follows that faith is called and is our righteousness for this reason, that it apprehends the righteousness of Christ and makes it our own.

(5) Faith is not the righteousness of Christ—that by which Christ is essentially righteous. Rather, it is our righteousness, though not a righteousness inhering in us, but one that is imputed to us for righteousness, since it apprehends the righteousness acquired for us by Christ. Therefore, what he says in Rom. 3:22, that "the righteousness of God is through faith in Jesus Christ to all and upon all who believe," is an explanation of the phrase, "Faith is imputed to us for righteousness."

(6) "Imputation" means entirely the kind of estimation that has its basis in truth. For as truly as our sins were imputed to Christ so that he might make satisfaction for them, so truly is the righteousness of Christ also imputed to us believers so that we are justified by it before God. But from that it cannot be inferred that we are justified before God by an inherent righteousness, since that righteousness of Christ which faith apprehends does not inhere in us, but is imputed to us.

(7) The Apostle sets forth two kinds of imputation: one that is according to debt, another that is according to grace. The imputa-

tion that takes place in the justification of man before God pertains to the latter kind, as the Apostle expressly teaches, and has its basis not in man himself—for he is ungodly, that is, a miserable sinner who is subject to damnation by debt and according to the strict severity of justice—but in the grace and mercy of God, etc.

Socinus, in his book *Quod Evang.*, p.20, explains this Pauline phrase, "faith is imputed to us for righteousness," to mean that believers in God are considered to be righteous people. We reply: If he is declaring that they are considered to be righteous people by God due to their own inherent righteousness, then he begs the question and contradicts the apostolic text; if due to a foreign righteousness, then he is refuting himself, since he is unable to identify any other righteousness except for the righteousness of Christ which is imputed to us by faith.

Some argue that faith is imputed for righteousness in this way and for this reason, that God considers faith to be the entire righteousness of the law. But (1) the Scripture never teaches that God considers faith to be the entire righteousness of the law. (2) Our faith is imperfect, and even if it were entirely perfect, it would only be a certain part of the righteousness of the law. (3) Therefore, faith is imputed for righteousness, not considered *qualitatively*, as if, in and of itself, it were so highly esteemed in God's judgment that God pronounces us righteous on account of it; but considered *relatively*, insofar as it apprehends Christ, who is our righteousness before God.

Against our explanation regarding the imputation of faith for righteousness, the papists set forth the example of Phinehas, whose work is said to have been imputed to him for righteousness (Psa. 106:31), where the basis of imputation is declared to be in Phinehas himself.

We reply: (1) The deed of Phinehas is unique, not something that is set forth for imitation. But concerning the imputation of faith that was made to Abraham, the Apostle says that it was written "for our sake to whom it would be imputed" (Rom. 4:23). The Psalmist says of Phinehas that "it was imputed to him for righteousness from generation to generation." But concerning the imputation that was made to Abraham, it is said in v. 12 that it pertains, not to those who are descended from him by carnal generation, but who "walk in his footsteps" of faith. (2) The Apostle declares two kinds of imputation in v. 4: one according to debt, the other according to grace. The former has a basis in him to whom it is imputed. But the imputation of faith does not pertain to the former kind; it pertains to the latter. (3) The Psalmist is talking about the deed and work of Phinehas and about the righteousness of the deed. For since that deed was externally aggressive and connected with a certain vice, for that reason it had need of divine approval and a declaration of righteousness. But the Apostle is talking about believers; he teaches that faith is imputed to them for righteousness. And he is talking about the righteousness of the person. (4) A man cannot be justified before God by one certain deed, since the law requires perfect and absolute obedience in great quantity. Thus the deed of Phinehas could not be reckoned as the righteousness of the person before God. (5) The matter itself shows that there is a clear difference between the imputation of a heroic deed and the imputation of faith. The deed of Phinehas was reckoned for righteousness, that is, he was considered a righteous man by God. But the righteousness of Christ is not imputed to us by faith in such a way that it is considered to be righteous, but as it is ascribed to us, so that it is counted as our righteousness before God.

Καὶ ἐλογίσθη [and it was imputed]. Gen. 15:6 has the active verb וַיַּחְשְׁבֶהָ, "and he imputed." The Apostle, following the LXX translators, correctly renders it in the passive, "and it was imputed to him."

v.4 Τῷ δὲ ἐργαζομένῳ ὁ μισθὸς οὐ λογίζεται κατὰ χάριν, ἀλλὰ κατὰ τὸ ὀφείλημα.

v.4 Now to him that worketh is the reward not reckoned of grace, but of debt. (KJV)

v.5 Τῷ δὲ μὴ ἐργαζομένῳ, πιστεύοντι δὲ ἐπὶ τὸν δικαιοῦντα τὸν ἀσεβῆ, λογίζεται ἡ πίστις αὐτοῦ εἰς δικαιοσύνην.

v.5 But to him that worketh not, but believeth on him that justifieth the ungodly, his faith is counted for righteousness. (KJV)

Just as ὁ ἐργαζόμενος is "he who works," not considered simply, but with a condition and a view toward wages—he who has earned something by his labor—, so ὁ μὴ ἐργαζόμενος [he who does not work] is not he who has and does absolutely no work, but he who, although he does them, does not trust in them, nor does he seek the praise of a righteousness that avails before God in his works. Rather, he believes that he is justified freely through faith. Luther: *"dem der da nicht mit Wercken umbgehet* [to him who does not deal in works]." Abraham "had worked" and "was working," but he was not working in the way that was necessary for someone to be justified with God. Therefore, he is said to be "not working," because, even though he abounded in good works, these works were still no motivating factor—nor could they be—so that he should be reconciled to God.

The Apostle thus contrasts "believing" and "working," so that he should be understood as "not working." Not, of course, that he does not work in any way, but because he does not do those things by which he is able to be righteous, namely, because it was required that he should never sin.

If wages are not imputed to the one who works based on grace, but based on debt, then it seems to follow that, when wages are promised for the good works of the reborn, it must be understood not as wages of grace, but of debt. We reply: When the Apostle says that "wages are given to the one who works, not based on grace, but based on debt," he understands with "the one who works" the one who truly merits something by his labor, whose works are truly meritorious, namely, where there is a fair proportion between work and wages. In that case, nothing is given to the one who works based on grace, but he is paid what he is owed. But when wages are promised for the good works of the reborn, then those works are not—nor can they be called—meritorious, since there is no proportion or comparison between the works of the reborn and the infinite rewards promised for them. Therefore, they are not the wages of debt, but of grace.

Schmalc., in his book *On the Satisfaction of Christ*, p.219: "The words of Paul, 'to the one who works, wages are given as a debt,' should be understood as if a promise were added." We reply: A "debt of promise" is one thing—and improperly so called, since a promise is free in and of itself; "a debt of right" is another thing. The Apostle is here talking, not about a debt of promise, which can coexist with the wages of grace, but about a debt of right.

The Apostle mentions two kinds of imputation in this passage: one "according to debt," the other "according to grace." The imputation according to debt takes into consideration the one who works; the imputation according to grace takes into consideration the one who believes. The former has its basis in the man himself to whom the imputation is made; the latter has its basis not in him to whom the imputation is made, but in the grace, mercy and favor of the one who imputes.

Piscator denies the first kind of imputation, and for this reason he assumes the verb δίδοται [is given] in the latter part of v.4. The papists deny the second kind of imputation, and thus disregard the imputed righteousness of Christ. But the evidence of the apostolic text proves both kinds of imputation.

With ἀσεβῆ [ungodly], the ungodly is not understood as remaining securely in his ungodliness without repentance (Pro. 17:15), but as he comes out of it through repentance and faith. This one is judged as righteous before the judgment of God through the imputed righteousness of Christ and is absolved from sins, since compensation has been made for his sins through the satisfaction of Christ. Therefore, such a penitent and believing man, who is certainly ungodly and sinful in himself, is nonetheless righteous in Christ through faith.

v.6 Καθάπερ καὶ Δαβὶδ λέγει τὸν μακαρισμὸν τοῦ ἀνθρώπου, ᾧ ὁ Θεὸς λογίζεται δικαιοσύνην χωρὶς ἔργων,

v.6 Even as David also describeth the blessedness of the man, unto whom God imputeth righteousness without works, (KJV)

The Apostle combines the testimony of David with the example of Abraham, (1) "so that every word may be established by the mouth of two or three witnesses" (Deu. 19:15); (2) because the Jews boasted of David (to whom the promise of the Messiah had been given in a special way) just as much as they boasted of Abraham; (3) because David was "a man after God's heart." Therefore, if he testifies concerning himself that he was justified by faith and not by works, then the same must be stated all the more concerning everyone else.

The argument of the Apostle is this: The justification of a man consists in the same thing in which his μακαρισμὸς [blessedness] consists. But the μακαρισμὸς [blessedness] of a man consists in the imputation of righteousness, as David testifies. Therefore, justification also consists in the imputation of righteousness, namely, through faith (as he had taught in the preceding vv. 3 & 5), and certainly without works.

David says that it is "the μακαρισμὸν [blessedness] of that man," that is, he pronounces that man to be blessed.

But observe that μακαρισμὸν [blessedness] and δικαίωσιν [justification] are understood here by the Apostle as equivalent expressions. Therefore, there are not distinct causes of justification and of salvation; the cause of each is altogether the same.

With τὴν δικαιοσύνην [the righteousness], the papists deny that "the righteousness of Christ" is to be understood, but the opposite is clearly evident from the following distinction: Either our inherent and actual righteousness or the righteousness of Christ must be understood in this passage. But the former is impossible:

(1) Because the righteousness that avails before God must be perfect and must conform to the whole law, since God is a righteous Judge who judges according to truth. But our inherent and actual righteousness is imperfect.

(2) Because that righteousness of which the Apostle is speaking is said to be imputed to us. But inherent righteousness is not imputed to us, but 'infused,' as they say.

(3) Because that righteousness that is imputed to us is not ours (Rom. 10:3, Phi. 3:9). But inherent and actual righteousness is ours—inherent, because of the subject; actual, because of the act, if not entirely, then at least in part.

(4) Because this imputation of righteousness happens "according to grace" (v.4). But inherent righteousness is not imputed according to grace, but according to debt. (v. 5).

(5) Because that righteousness that is imputed to us "has been manifested without the law" (Rom. 3:21), which is why we are said to be justified by the Gospel, not by the law; by believing, not by doing; by faith, without works; by grace, not by works. But inherent righteousness pertains entirely to the law, for it consists chiefly in love, which is the πλήρωμα [fulfillment] of the law (Rom. 13:10).

(6) The righteousness that is imputed to us and by which we are justified before God is in Christ and becomes ours through imputation, even as "Christ was made sin for us" through imputation (2 Cor. 5:21). But inherent righteousness is not "in Christ;" it is "in us."

(7) The imputation of righteousness is defined by the Apostle as "the remission of sins" (v. 8). But inherent righteousness is not the remission itself or the non-imputation of sins.

(8) The righteousness that is imputed to us is considered "apart from works" (Rom. 3:28). But inherent righteousness is not considered apart from works. Therefore, only the latter possibility remains.

Λογίζεσθαι [to impute] corresponding to the Hebrew חשב, which the Syriac also uses in this passage, means "to make a credit, to impute." That imputation of righteousness (1) is not a bare opinion or some sort of putative figment, but is a real and true action. Moreover, it is clear from 1 Kin. 1:21, Mark 15:28, Rom. 2:26, and Philemon 18 that a certain real and true imputation is made, the basis of which exists not in the one imputing, but in him to whom the imputation happens. (2) Its basis is in the judgment and will of the God who imputes, not in us—in whom there is an opposing basis, not for righteousness, but for wrath, if God wanted to enter into judgment with us. (3) It is not the real infusion of some sort of condition or quality or act, but the real application of the righteousness of Christ, furnished outside of us but ascribed to us through faith. (4) With this imputation of the righteousness of Christ is combined *the non-imputation of sin*. Christ made perfect satisfaction for our sins and furnished perfect obedience to the law in our place. This satisfaction and obedience of Christ become ours through imputation. (5) In this imputation there are two actions. The first is God's, who imputes to us believers and regards as our own the satisfaction of Christ, that is, the fulfillment of the law and the payment of the penalty due for our sins, as if we had thus fulfilled the law ourselves and had paid the due penalties for our sins. The second is ours, for the satisfaction of Christ is imputed and applied to us at that moment when we firmly believe[43] that God receives us into grace, remits to us our sins and reckons us as righteous for the sake of Christ. (6) Imputation is considered either *with regard to the person* to whom the imputation is made, or *with regard to the thing* that is imputed. When our sin is said to be imputed to Christ and the righteousness of Christ imputed to us (2 Cor. 5:21), it means that our sin, which is in us and not in Christ, is transferred to Christ by the decree and estimation of God, that is, it is esteemed as if it were in Christ. Then, in turn, the righteousness of Christ, which is in Christ and not in us, is transferred to us by the decree and estimation of God, that is, it is esteemed and understood as if it were in us. (7) There are two modes of this imputation that takes place in justification. One is *negative*[44]; it is the non-imputation of that which exists in man and could have been imputed. It consists in the forgetting and the not taking notice of sin, and in the dismissal of guilt. The other is *positive*[45]; it is the attribution of that which does not exist in man and that he has not earned, as if it did exist in him, namely, when God considers us to be truly righteous people for the sake of the obedience of Christ, although we are not inherently such people in and of ourselves. (8) Since

---

43 Latin: *statuimus*
44 Στερητικὸς, *privativus*
45 Θετικὸς, *positivus*

God is said to impute righteousness to us, it should be taken in two ways. First, *with regard to the cause*; second, *with regard to the effect*. For this expression first indicates that the righteousness of Christ is transferred to the believer, even as our unrighteousness has been transferred to Christ. So then, this is the proper cause of our righteousness before God. Second, it shows the effect, namely, that someone who in himself is not righteous by perfect inherent righteousness is considered to be righteous, even as Christ, who was not subjectively and inherently unrighteous, was considered to be unrighteous.

v.7 Μακάριοι, ὧν ἀφέθησαν αἱ ἀνομίαι, Καὶ ὧν ἐπεκαλύφθησαν αἱ ἁμαρτίαι.

v.7 Saying, Blessed are they whose iniquities are forgiven, and whose sins are covered. (KJV)

v.8 Μακάριος ἀνὴρ, ᾧ οὐ μὴ λογίσηται Κύριος ἁμαρτίαν.

v.8 Blessed is the man to whom the Lord will not impute sin. (KJV)

At the end of the preceding verse, the participle εἴπων [saying] is assumed, which the Syriac expresses with כד אמר.

Ἄφεσις τῶν ἀνομίων [forgiveness of iniquities] is described by David and the Apostle as ἐπικάλυψιν τῶν ἁμαρτίων [the covering of sins]. And when God remits sins, He is said to μὴ λογίζεσθαι, to "not impute" them. Therefore, "the remission of sins" does not mean the total annihilation of them, so that no part of them remains present in the flesh. Rather, it means the full and perfect release from guilt.

This is also clear from the following bases: Scripture testifies (1) that sin still dwells in the flesh of the reborn (Rom. 7:14); (2) that there is a struggle between the flesh and the spirit in the reborn (Gal. 5:17); (3) that the inner man in the reborn is still in need of daily renewal (2 Cor. 4:16) and thus their renewal is not yet perfect; (4) that the saints need to pray daily for the remission of sins (Psa. 32:6, Mat. 6:11, 1 John 1:8); (5) that the children of believers are born in and with original sin (Psa. 51:7, John 3:6, Eph. 2:3); (6)

that baptized infants are still subject to sickness and death (Rom. 5:12); (7) that the reborn are admonished to wash their feet (John 13:10), to purge the old leaven (1 Cor. 5:7), to cleanse themselves from all the impurities of flesh and spirit (2 Cor. 7:1), to crucify the flesh with its desires (Gal. 5:27).

The papists make the following objections: (1) כָּסָה is the same thing as נָשָׂא, "to lift, to remove, to bear," since these vocables are considered to be equivalents.

We reply: כסה is never understood in Scripture in any way other than as "the covering of that which is still present," which is why Paul, following the LXX interpreters, renders it with ἐπικαλύπτειν [to cover]. Pro. 10:12, 1 Pet. 4:5: "Love covers sins." It does not, however, completely destroy and abolish them. The Apostle renders the word נָשָׂא in this passage with ἀφίημι, "I dismiss, I forgive, I free from debt," which is also how Psa. 85:3 is translated. Therefore, a "lifting up[46]" of guilt is meant in this passage, not the total annihilation of it (Gen. 4:12, 50:17; Num. 14:19).

(2) "Nothing can be covered up from God, unless it is entirely destroyed" (Bellarmine, 2, *On Justification*, ch. 9). "If sins are covered, God either sees them or does not see them. If He sees them, how have they been covered in His sight? If He does not see them, how does that apostolic statement stand, 'All things are bare and open to His eyes' (Heb. 4:13)?" (Becanus, *On Justification*, ch. 1).

We reply: (1) Sins in the sight of God are said to be covered, not properly, but anthropopathically. For just as stains are covered with a garment that is thrown on top, so our sins are covered before the judgment of God with the righteousness of Christ. Just as the Propitiatorium covered the tablets of the Decalogue that had been placed in the ark, so the righteousness of Christ covers our sins committed against the law. (2) Therefore, the sense is this: Sins are said to be covered before the judgment of God when God does not impute them, not as if He did not see them in any way. (3) God is said to "forget" our sins (Eze. 18:22), to "hurl them into the depth of the sea" (Micah 7:19), not to "observe iniquities" (Psa.

46 Latin: *sublatio*

130:3), to "cast sins behind His back" (Isa. 38:17), to "remove them far away from us" (Psa. 103:12), to "hide His face" from sins (Psa. 51:11). All these things are spoken anthropopathically about the releasing from guilt. But if someone wants to take them in a proper sense and infer from them the total abolition of sin in every way, then he will entangle himself in many absurdities.

Augustine on Psa. 31: "*Blessed are they whose iniquities have been remitted and whose sins have been covered.* Not in whom sins are not found, but whose sins have been covered. Sins have been buried deep, covered, abolished. If God covered sins, then He did not wish to notice them. If He did not wish to notice, then He did not wish to punish. If He did not wish to acknowledge them, He preferred to ignore them." And later: "Nor should you understand what he said in this way, that sins have been buried deep as if they were there and alive (as if they were there in such a way as to still be alive). In what way, then, did he say that sins were covered? They were covered so that they should not be seen. For what did it mean for God to see sins, if not to punish sins?" He says the same thing in Treatise 41 on John: "Is it possible that, since iniquity has been erased, no infirmity remains? If it did not remain, then we would live without sin. But who would dare say such a thing?"

v.9 Ὁ μακαρισμὸς οὖν οὗτος, ἐπὶ τὴν περιτομήν, ἢ καὶ ἐπὶ τὴν ἀκροβυστίαν; Λέγομεν γὰρ ὅτι Ἐλογίσθη τῷ Ἀβραὰμ ἡ πίστις εἰς δικαιοσύνην.

v.9 *Cometh this blessedness then upon the circumcision only, or upon the uncircumcision also? for we say that faith was reckoned to Abraham for righteousness. (KJV)*

Now follows the application of the example produced at the beginning of the chapter. For the Apostle begins to confirm that righteousness is imputed by God—not only to Jews, but also to Gentiles—in the same way in which righteousness was imputed to Abraham, namely, by faith.

The exclusive particle "only" must be assumed in the first part of the verse and of the contrast. *Does this blessedness really only befall the circumcised, or does it also befall the uncircumcised? That is, does this manner of justification have only the Jews in view, or does it apply to the Gentiles, too?* The Apostle answers that he has both in view by giving consideration to the situation at the time when it says that faith was imputed to Abraham for righteousness, namely, before he received circumcision.

v.10 Πῶς οὖν ἐλογίσθη; Ἐν περιτομῇ ὄντι, ἢ ἐν ἀκροβυστίᾳ; Οὐκ ἐν περιτομῇ, ἀλλ᾽ ἐν ἀκροβυστίᾳ.

v.10 How was it then reckoned? when he was in circumcision, or in uncircumcision? Not in circumcision, but in uncircumcision. (KJV)

Πῶς [how?], that is, "in what state," as is understood from the preceding words. The sequence of events in the Mosaic history (Gen. 15:6, 17:10) shows that righteousness was imputed to Abraham when he was not yet circumcised.

v.11 Καὶ σημεῖον ἔλαβε περιτομῆς σφραγῖδα τῆς δικαιοσύνης τῆς πίστεως τῆς ἐν τῇ ἀκροβυστίᾳ, εἰς τὸ εἶναι αὐτὸν πατέρα πάντων τῶν πιστευόντων δι᾽ ἀκροβυστίας, εἰς τὸ λογισθῆναι καὶ αὐτοῖς τὴν δικαιοσύνην.

v.11 And he received the sign of circumcision, a seal of the righteousness of the faith which he had yet being uncircumcised: that he might be the father of all them that believe, though they be not circumcised; that righteousness might be imputed unto them also: (KJV)

The sense is this: Abraham certainly received circumcision, which was a sign of the covenant. But circumcision did not justify him, since he was righteous before he received circumcision. Moreover, "circumcision was a seal of the righteousness of faith, which he had already in the foreskin," that is, it was the sign and confirmation of that divine benefit, that he should be freely justified by faith in the coming Messiah even at that time when he still had a foreskin, so that he might be, for that reason, "the father of all who believe while in the foreskin, so that righteousness may also be imputed to them." In other words, God pronounced Abraham righteous before circumcision so that he might be the spiritual father of those who still have the foreskin, in order that they might thus believe in Christ by the example of Abraham and be justified through faith.

Σημεῖον περιτομῆς ἔλαβε [He received a sign of circumcision]. "He received circumcision, which was a sign," namely, "of the covenant," which is also how the Syriac translates. This explanation agrees with the words of institution (Gen. 17:11): "This will be the sign of the covenant."

With the word σφραγῖδος [seal], (1) the Apostle runs to meet the question, *Why did Abraham receive circumcision, since righteousness had already been imputed to him before?*

(2) He explains what kind of sign circumcision was, namely, not merely "signifying," but "sealing" and "confirming." For this reason the Syriac inserted the particle ᾿ exegetically. "He received the sign of circumcision even as a seal of righteousness, of faith," that is, "this circumcision" or "this sign was a seal of righteousness," as several interpreters have correctly translated.

Origen concludes about this passage that "circumcision is called a seal of the righteousness of faith because it finished and sealed the righteousness of faith which was to be revealed in its time." We reply: This explanation does not agree with the apostolic text, because Abraham was not hoping for the righteousness of faith at some time in the future in the same way he was awaiting the advent, incarnation and suffering of the Messiah. But he was truly rendered a participant in that righteousness through faith, as the Apostle teaches in the preceding verse, and underwent circumcision as a seal of the righteousness of faith.

Chrysostom and Theophylact state that "circumcision is called a sign of the righteousness of faith for this reason, that it was given to Abraham as a sign and testimony of the righteousness which he had acquired through faith."

Lyranus on this passage: "Abraham received circumcision so that it might be a seal of the righteousness that was concealed in his mind."

Τῆς ἐν τῇ ἀκροβυστίᾳ [which in the foreskin]. It can refer both to "righteousness" as the more remote, and to "faith" as the nearer antecedent. Luther referred it to the nearer, *welchen Glauben er noch in der Vorhaut hatte* [which faith he had already in the foreskin]." It amounts to the same thing, because righteousness and faith are joined together by an indivisible connection.

Εἰς τὸ εἶναι αὐτὸν πατέρα πάντων πιστευόντων δι' ἀκροβυστίας [so that he might be father of all who believe through foreskin].

Abraham is "the father of believers," not causally and effectively, nor by natural generation, but as an example with respect to the righteousness of faith and true godliness. In 2 Kings 2:12, [Elijah] is called father, not by generation, but by imitation.

Note the meaning of the particle διὰ [through] instead of ἐν [in]. A similar expression occurs in 1 Tim. 2:15: "She will be saved διὰ τῆς τεκνογονίας [through childbirth]," that is, ἐν τῇ τεκνογονίᾳ [in childbirth].

Εἰς τὸ λογισθῆναι καὶ αὐτοῖς τὴν δικαιοσύνην, "so that righteousness may also be imputed to them," that is, so that they, too, may be justified in the same way in which Abraham was justified, namely, by faith in Christ.

We conclude from this passage against the papists:

(1) That circumcision was the saving means through which grace was provided and applied and sealed to believers. For circumcision was applied, not only to Abraham and his adult domestic servants, but also to Isaac and the rest of the Israelite infants. Therefore, certainly also to them it was a seal of the righteousness of faith. Yet this was not through carnal birth, according to which they were "children of wrath" (Eph. 2:3). Nor did they receive faith and regeneration through hearing the Word. Therefore, it is necessary for them to have gained it through the Sacrament of circumcision.

The papists object that "the promise of remission of sins and eternal life was not attached to circumcision, since Abraham, to

194

whom circumcision was first commanded, was entirely righteous[47] before receiving it (Gen. 12, Rom. 4)" (Bellarmine, Bk. 2, *De Sacramentis*, ch. 17).

We reply: This objection thoroughly contradicts David, Paul, and Christ Himself. David declares that all the saints need the remission of sins (Psa. 32:6). Paul teaches that for Abraham, even in the midst of living a life of good works, justification consists in the remission of sins (Rom. 4:7). Christ testifies that all the reborn need daily remission of sins (Mat. 6:12). Therefore, it is not permissible to conclude that, since Abraham was righteous before circumcision, he therefore did not need the promise of the remission of sins to be confirmed through the Sacrament of circumcision. For while the grace of God and the righteousness of faith were not conferred on Abraham for the first time through circumcision, it was nevertheless a conferring instrument with respect to the increase and confirmation of faith and other gifts that accompany regeneration. The same can be said with the example of the preached Word and the Sacrament of Baptism, both of which are effective means for kindling faith, regenerating, confirming and increasing, even though the ones who hear the Word and are baptized at some point are the same ones who were already regenerated earlier by faith.

(2) That the Sacraments are σφραγῖδες, "signs and seals," sealing the promise of divine grace being held out to believers. For it is the nature of a seal to testify, confirm and seal that to which it is attached. But circumcision is called in this passage "a seal of the righteousness of faith." Therefore, it sealed and confirmed that to which it was attached, namely the promise of grace. But the same thing that is said of circumcision can also be applied to the Sacraments of the New Testament, since in this general purpose the Sacraments agree with one another, even if the efficacy of the New Testament Sacraments is greater than that of the Old Testament.

The papists object: (1) "Those things that are said of circumcision alone cannot be referred to all the Sacraments." We reply: As in the efficient cause, so also in the generic final cause, all the Sac-

47 Latin: *justissimus*

raments agree. But to be a seal of the righteousness of faith belongs to the purpose of circumcision.

(2) "Circumcision is called a seal of the righteousness of faith, but not a seal of divine promises." We reply: Coordinate things are not to be placed in opposition to one another. A divine promise and the righteousness of faith are coordinates, since they are mutually related to one another; faith depends on the divine promises as on an immovable fulcrum, and the divine promises require faith, apart from which they profit no one (Rom. 4:13). Thus also circumcision and the rest of the Sacraments, properly speaking, are called seals of the righteousness of faith. For the promise of grace, like a seal attached to a letter, is confirmed for them, so that any of those who believe can be made more certain of it.

(3) "This privilege belonged to Abraham only and cannot be transferred to others, as if circumcision testified to the righteousness of anyone who is circumcised." We reply: Circumcision benefits in this way, not insofar as it was undergone by Abraham, but insofar as it was divinely instituted for the whole people of Israel, as the remaining sayings that speak of the power and efficacy of circumcision demonstrate. For this reason, Augustine (Bk. 8, *On Baptism Against the Donatists* ch. 24) states that "this Sacrament was a seal of the righteousness of faith also for Isaac, who was circumcised on the eighth day of his birth." If circumcision were not also for the rest of the Israelites a seal of the covenant and of the divine promises, how could they have sought effective consolations from it? (1 Sam. 17:26, 36; 14:6) We therefore draw this conclusion: To those whom the covenant and the covenantal promise have in view, to them also pertains the seal of the covenant and of the promise. But the covenant and the covenantal promise pertain, not only to Abraham, but also to the seed of Abraham (Gen. 17:7). Therefore...

From where, then, do they prove that it pertains only to Abraham? They answer:

(1) "Paul joins these two together, that Abraham received the sign of circumcision, and that he was the father of all believers. But those who came after Abraham were not the fathers of all believ-

ers." We reply: The Apostle sets forth Abraham as a model of justification. But the seal of the righteousness of faith through the ordinary Sacrament also pertains to justification. Therefore, it cannot refer to Abraham only.

The opposite cannot be proved from the alleged argument, or else we could argue in the same way: The Apostle joins these two things together, that Abraham received the sign of circumcision and that he was the father of all believers. But those who come after Abraham are not the fathers of all believers. Therefore, the sign of circumcision does not pertain to them. From the order of events in the text, it is clear that the Apostle appeals to Abraham as the father of all believers for this purpose and with this aim. Therefore, we rather invert the argument in this way: Since Abraham is set forth as the father of believers and a model of justification, it cannot refer to Abraham alone. But since the righteousness of faith was sealed through the ordinary Sacrament of circumcision, Abraham is set forth as the father of all believers and as a model of justification. Therefore...

The Sacraments that have been instituted belong to the whole Church, and the nature of them is one and the same with respect to each and every one of the believers. Consequently, just as circumcision is not one thing while the righteousness of faith is another, so also the seal of the promises was no different in Abraham than it was in the rest of the believing Israelites.

(2) "He distinguishes slightly between 'sign' and 'seal,' so as to indicate that circumcision is a sign to all, but not a seal." We reply: We showed above that these two things are joined together exegetically. Circumcision is considered either with respect to infants or with respect to adults. Circumcision was both a sign and a seal for the infants, not only potentially, but also actually. For, since they did not resist the Holy Spirit with actual impenitence and unbelief, therefore divine grace was not only set before them in the Sacraments, but was also infallibly applied and sealed to them. But with respect to adults, the Sacraments were actually seals only to those who were truly believing, while they were potentially seals

for everyone, for God has arranged the Sacraments to that end, that they should offer the promise of grace to everyone, and apply and therefore seal it through faith. Although this effect, by accident, did not occur in every case, nevertheless it does not in any way detract from the efficacy of the Sacraments as considered with regard to the principal act.

(3) "Scripture never calls circumcision a seal except in this passage where it treats of Abraham. This is a clear argument that circumcision was a seal for Abraham alone." We reply: That which is attributed to Abraham, insofar as he believed, is correctly attributed to all believers. For it is for this very reason that Abraham is said to be "the father of all believers." But it is attributed to Abraham, insofar as he believed, that circumcision was to him a seal of the righteousness of faith. Therefore, it is rightly attributed to all those who followed his footsteps of faith in the Old Testament, namely, that circumcision was to them a seal of the righteousness of faith, just as in the New Testament, Baptism is such a seal.

v.12 καὶ πατέρα περιτομῆς τοῖς οὐκ ἐκ περιτομῆς μόνον, ἀλλὰ καὶ τοῖς στοιχοῦσι τοῖς ἴχνεσι τῆς ἐν τῇ ἀκροβυστίᾳ πίστεως τοῦ πατρὸς ἡμῶν Ἀβραάμ.

v.12 *And the father of circumcision to them who are not of the circumcision only, but who also walk in the steps of that faith of our father Abraham, which he had being yet uncircumcised. (KJV)*

Just as in the preceding verse he applied the example of Abraham to the uncircumcised believers, that is, the Gentiles, so in this verse he applies it to the circumcised believers, that is, the Jews. He is their father, too, but only if they walk in his footsteps of faith. This, then, is what the Apostle wants to say: Just as Abraham is the father of the believers among the Gentiles, since righteousness was imputed to him while still in the foreskin, so also he is the father of the believers among the Jews, since he received circumcision as a seal of the righteousness of faith.

Τοῖς στοιχοῦσι τοῖς ἴχνεσι πίστεως, "who walk in the footsteps of faith," that is, who imitate the faith of Abraham. And so, for this reason, it is as if they walk in his footsteps, because they believe according to his example of faith.

Πίστις ἐν τῇ ἀκροβυστίᾳ [faith in the foreskin]. It is called the faith which Abraham had before undergoing circumcision. It is for good reason that the Apostle presses this against those who wanted to be justified before God by circumcision and works.

Observe that the genuine children of Abraham are described thus, that they are not only his natural children ἐκ περιτομῆς [by circumcision], "circumcised in the flesh" in an external way, but they also "walk in the footsteps of his faith."

v.13 Οὐ γὰρ διὰ νόμου ἡ ἐπαγγελία τῷ Ἀβραάμ, ἢ τῷ σπέρματι αὐτοῦ, τὸ κληρονόμον αὐτὸν εἶναι τοῦ κόσμου, ἀλλὰ διὰ δικαιοσύνης πίστεως.

v.13 For the promise, that he should be the heir of the world, was not to Abraham, or to his seed, through the law, but through the righteousness of faith. (KJV)

Some refer this to the principal proposition. Abraham obtained the inheritance of eternal life not by the law, but by faith in the promise of God. Therefore, in the same way his posterity are justified and saved, namely, not by the law nor by the works of the law, but by faith. But others refer it to the verse just before, so that the reason why Abraham's seed is not reckoned to him by carnal propagation, but by faith, is that Abraham himself was made a participant in that promise by believing, and in this way he became the father of all nations.

Οὐ γὰρ διὰ νόμου [for not through law], namely δέδοται [was given] or γέγονε [came] ἡ ἐπαγγελία τῷ Ἀβραὰμ [the promise to Abraham]. Thus the Syriac adds the verb אתה. Διὰ νόμου [through law], "through the righteousness of the law," as is apparent from the antithesis that follows, "but through the righteousness of faith."

Some expound διὰ νόμου [through law] as "under the condition of doing the works of the law." This exposition ends up in the same place as the earlier one, although the earlier one agrees better with the text.

With τὸν κόσμον [the world], Salmeron, Cornelius a Lapide, Beza, Paraeus, etc., understand "the believers in the world," since, in v.11, Abraham is called the father of all believers.

We reply: (1) Abraham is not the heir, but the father of believers. Therefore, with the noun "world," of which Abraham is said to have been made the heir, the believers in the world cannot be meant. (2) The noun "world" in the Scriptures is not understood as only the believers in the world. It either refers broadly and generally to all the men in the world, or specifically to the ungodly and unbelieving.

Some understand with the noun "world" the spiritual benefits received by faith. (1) Because the saints, who enjoy these benefits, are scattered throughout the whole world. (2) Because the kingdom of Christ, which consists in these benefits, is in the whole world. (3) Because those benefits have been disseminated throughout the whole world by the preaching of the Gospel. (4) Because these benefits do not only equal the whole world, but even surpass it. (5) Because all the possessions of the world properly belong to believers, since, of course, only they use them rightly. (6) The Scripture is speaking about spiritual benefits under the type of earthly things.

Others, with the noun "world," understand Christ, whose co-heirs are the saints, to whom the inheritance of the world has been given (Psa. 2:8).

But the noun "world" hardly ever occurs in the Scriptures where it is understood to be either the benefits of Christ distributed in the world or Christ Himself as the Savior of the world.

Therefore, the simplest understanding of "the world" is the heavenly inheritance, foreshadowed by the possession of the land of Canaan as the most excellent part of the world. This interpretation is deduced (1) from the following verse, where "the inheritance of eternal life" is to be understood with the word κληρονόμοι [heirs]; (2) from the fact that in Heb. 6:5, the heavenly inheritance is called μέλλων αἰών [the coming age]; (3) because Rev. 21:1 calls it "the new heaven and the new earth."

v.14 Εἰ γὰρ οἱ ἐκ νόμου, κληρονόμοι, κεκένωται ἡ πίστις, καὶ κατήργηται ἡ ἐπαγγελία·

v.14 For if they which are of the law be heirs, faith is made void, and the promise made of none effect: (KJV)

Οἱ ἐκ νόμου [those by law], namely, those who εἰσι [are], those who fulfill the law perfectly and seek to be justified by works.

Κληρονόμοι [heirs], namely, of eternal life. This inheritance is connected with justification, since those who have been justified by faith are adopted as God's children and inscribed as heirs of eternal life.

The promise of the Gospel is not apprehended by works, but by faith. Righteousness is from the promise of the Gospel. Therefore, righteousness is not by works, but by faith. If only those who perfectly fulfill the law can be heirs of eternal life, then faith is made void and the promise is rendered ineffective and is abolished. The rationale for the connection is that, since no one perfectly fulfills the law, and if, then, the promise depends on the condition of works and perfect obedience, then the law is of no benefit to anyone for salvation.

v.15 ὁ γὰρ νόμος ὀργὴν κατεργάζεται· οὗ γὰρ οὐκ ἔστι νόμος, οὐδὲ παράβασις.

v.15 Because the law worketh wrath: for where no law is, there is no transgression. (KJV)

The Apostle confirms that the inheritance is not by the law. For God does not confer the inheritance of eternal life on those with whom He is angry; He only confers it on those whom He has adopted as sons by grace. He also explains at the same time the reason why the promise cannot be apprehended by the law and by the works of the law—because, since the law is not observed by anyone, it does not convey υἱοθεσίαν [adoption] nor the heavenly inheritance. On the contrary, it announces wrath.

The law κατεργάζεται ὀργὴν [works wrath]. It not only announces the curse and punishment, but it also effectively produces it (1) by requiring perfect obedience, which is impossible for man in the infirmity of this life after the Fall; (2) by showing sins; (3) by announcing the curse; (4) by stirring up terrors of conscience; (5) by pressing a man down to hell itself with its weight. Yet this is attributed to the law by accident, insofar as men transgress it with sins. For in and of itself, it is a word of life and salvation.

Luther adds the exclusive particle: *"Das Gesetz richtet nur Zorn an* [The law works *only* wrath]." The papists assail him as a falsifier of the Biblical text because of this word. But Luther desired to express emphatically the mind of the Apostle. This is the question that the Apostle is dealing with, whether justification is by the law or by faith, to which he replies that it is not by the law, since the law works wrath. Therefore, since the law does not justify but works wrath, the exclusive could be added to the latter part in this direct contrast. The law works only wrath, because these two things are directly opposed to one another: "to justify," that is, to absolve from sin, and "to work wrath," that is, to accuse of sin and to damn sin.

"Where there is no law, there is no transgression."

This is to be taken generally—where there is no law, neither inscribed internally on the heart nor proclaimed to man externally.

The Photinians use this to deny original sin. We reply: The Apostle does not say, "Where there is no knowledge of the law there is no sin," since there also exist sins of ignorance. Rather, he speaks in this way: "Where there is no law, there is no sin." Infants are without the law in this sense, that they do not know the law (Rom. 2:12). And yet they are not without the law, in that they are not free from the accusation by which the law discloses and damns all ἀνομίαν [lawlessness].

v.16 Διὰ τοῦτο ἐκ πίστεως, ἵνα κατὰ χάριν, εἰς τὸ εἶναι βεβαίαν τὴν ἐπαγγελίαν παντὶ τῷ σπέρματι, οὐ τῷ ἐκ τοῦ νόμου μόνον, ἀλλὰ καὶ τῷ ἐκ πίστεως Ἀβραάμ, ὅς ἐστι πατὴρ πάντων ἡμῶν.

v.16 Therefore it is of faith, that it might be by grace; to the end the promise might be sure to all the seed; not to that only which is of the law, but to that also which is of the faith of Abraham; who is the father of us all, (KJV)

Διὰ τοῦτο ἐκ πίστεως [On account of this, by faith], namely, the inheritance from v.13 is "by faith."

Since he has demonstrated that righteousness and the inheritance of eternal life cannot come about for us by the law, he asserts that it is ἐκ πίστεως [by faith].

Ἵνα κατὰ χάριν [in order that according to grace]. The Syriac adds בזכ, "that we may be justified by grace." It is referred more correctly to the promise, which is said to be κατὰ χάριν [according to grace], since it is the promise of grace and is made freely.

Εἰς τὸ εἶναι βεβαίαν τὴν ἐπαγγελίαν [So that the promise may be firm]. For if justification were by works, the promise would not be firm for us; it would be useless, since works are not perfect, nor do they fully satisfy the law.

Observe: Certainty and firmness are here attributed to the promise, not only with respect to God, in that it is certain due to the truthfulness and omnipotence of the One who promises; but it is also entirely firm and certain for us, insofar as we embrace it by faith and apply it to ourselves. Therefore, when faith apprehends the promise and confidently relies upon it, then faith is thoroughly opposed to doubt.

Πάντι τῷ σπέρματι [to all the seed], that is, to all the children and posterity of Abraham, namely, to all believers, since in v. 11 he had called Abraham the father of all believers.

Οὐ τῷ ἐκ τοῦ νόμου μόνον [Not only to the one who is by the law]. The believers among the Jews are called "the seed of Abraham ἐκ τοῦ νόμου [by the law]," because of the law of circumcision, to which they were subject, but also as they obtained the faith that was attached to it.

The believers among the Gentiles are called "the seed of Abraham" ἐκ πίστεως [by faith], because it was only by faith that they resembled Abraham, inasmuch as they were uncircumcised.

The sense, then, is that it is "by faith" for this reason, so that the promise may be firm, not only to those who believe and at the same time are circumcised, but also to those who are counted among Abraham's children with respect only to faith, without circumcision.

v.17 (καθὼς γέγραπται. ὅτι Πατέρα πολλῶν ἐθνῶν τέθεικά σε)· κατέναντι οὗ ἐπίστευσε, Θεοῦ τοῦ ζῳοποιοῦντος τοὺς νεκροὺς, καὶ καλοῦντος τὰ μὴ ὄντα ὡς ὄντα.

v.17 (As it is written, I have made thee a father of many nations,) before him whom he believed, even God, who quickeneth the dead, and calleth those things which be not as though they were. (KJV)

Those words κατέναντι θεοῦ [before God] belong to the preceding verse, which is why the parentheses are included in the Greek text. Abraham is the father of all of us—how? "Before God," that is, not according to the flesh, but according to the counsel and ordination of God, who lit the way for us by showing us Abraham with his faith, wanting us to walk in his footsteps.

The passage cited is from Gen. 17:6. The Apostle adduces this passage in order to prove that, in the very institution of circumcision, Abraham is called the father also of those who believe among the Gentiles.

Erasmus, following Chrysostom and Theophylact, explains the particle κατέναντι θεοῦ [before God] as "according to the example or likeness of God." It is better explained as "before God," meaning that Abraham is not called the father of believers because of a carnal relationship, but because of the spiritual relationship that exists before God and renders us pleasing to Him.

Οὗ ἐπίστευσε, "whom he believed." Luther refers this phrase to the nearest preceding words. *"Ich habe dich gesetzt zum Vater vieler Heyden für GOtt/dem du gegleubet hast* [I have made you a father of many nations before God, in whom you have believed]." The Syriac translates the same way, "in whom you have believed."

Τοῦ ζωοποιοῦντος τοὺς νεκρούς [who makes the dead alive]. With "the vivification of the dead" some understand the resurrection of the Gentiles from the spiritual death of sin. But, properly speaking, it is more correctly understood as the resurrection of the body (Heb. 11:9).

How is God said to call τὰ μὴ ὄντα ὡς ὄντα [the things that are not as existing]? To some, the Apostle seems to have in view the saying that he quotes from Hosea later on in chapter 9:25: "I shall call them 'my people' who are not my people."

But since it is said absolutely, "He calls τὰ μὴ ὄντα [the things that are not]," it is more correctly asserted that the Apostle has in view the article of creation, in that God commands "light to shine out of darkness," and ἐκ τῶν μὴ ὄντων [from the things that are not] "He produced creatures" (2 Cor. 4:6), and thus he presented a noble specimen of His omnipotence.

v.18 Ὃς παρ' ἐλπίδα ἐπ' ἐλπίδι ἐπίστευσεν, εἰς τὸ γενέσθαι αὐτὸν πατέρα πολλῶν ἐθνῶν, κατὰ τὸ εἰρημένον: Οὕτως ἔσται τὸ σπέρμα σου.

v.18 Who against hope believed in hope, that he might become the father of many nations, according to that which was spoken, So shall thy seed be. (KJV)

The Apostle submits a description of that true and living faith through which we are justified before God, as he has been teaching thus far, namely, that it rests with firm confidence on the power and goodwill of God, as in the example of Abraham.

Παρ' ἐλπίδα [beyond hope]. The Syriac translates דְּלָא סַבְרָא, "apart from hope." Luther: "*Da nichts zu hoffen war* [Where there was nothing to hope]."

He believed "toward hope," "beyond hope" or "contrary to hope," since there didn't seem to be anything to hope for; he was hoping in hopeless things, despairing of himself, despairing of God.

The Vulgate translates "against hope toward hope." Against

hope in nature, toward hope in the divine promise; against the hope that he could conceive from a consideration of natural things, he believed on the basis of hope, namely, the hope he conceived from a consideration of divine power and the promise made to him.

Heb. 11:19 similarly praises the faith of Abraham, that he believed that God was able to bring Isaac back from death to life.

Εἰς τὸ γενέσθαι [in order to become], "it would be that he would become." Abraham did not believe for this goal or purpose, in order that he might become the father of many nations. Rather, he believed that what was being promised would certainly take place, namely, that he would be the father of many nations. Therefore, it is not the goal of faith that is being expressed with regard to intention, but the object of faith with regard to the promise, which is also how the Syriac translates: "He believed that he would be the father of a multitude of nations."

Οὕτως ἔσται τὸ σπέρμα σου [So shall be your seed]. Understand "as are the stars of the heaven." The passage is from Gen. 15:5.

v.19 Καὶ μὴ ἀσθενήσας τῇ πίστει, οὐ κατενόησε τὸ ἑαυτοῦ σῶμα ἤδη νενεκρωμένον, ἑκατονταέτης που ὑπάρχων, καὶ τὴν νέκρωσιν τῆς μήτρας Σάρρας,

v.19 And being not weak in faith, he considered not his own body now dead, when he was about an hundred years old, neither yet the deadness of Sara's womb: (KJV)

"He was not made weak in faith, nor did he consider his own body to be already dead." A hendiadys. "He was not weakened in faith by viewing or considering his body to be dead." Syriac: "Although he considered his body, etc."

The sterility both of Abraham and of Sarah is emphatically indicated. The body of Abraham is called νενεκρωμένον [dead], not absolutely and in a simple sense, but according to that which has to do with the ability to beget children. To Sarah likewise is attributed the νέκρωσις τῆς μήτρας, "the mortification of the womb," to mean the inability to conceive.

06

But how is Abraham's body called "dead," since he had barely reached
half his age? For he reached the age of 175 (Gen. 25:7).

Origen, writing on this passage, answers: "Abraham's body was
still naturally suitable for producing children, but spiritually dead
through the gift of abstinence." The text, however, is not talking
about spiritual mortification, but about the natural inability to beget children.

Augustine, therefore, answers more correctly in Bk. 1, *Questions
on Genesis*, Q. 35: "'A dead body' is not to be understood as if he had
absolutely no ability to produce children, even if he had a younger
wife; but it is dead for this reason, that by a woman of advanced
age he could not beget children. This is why he was able to beget a
child with Keturah, since he found her as a young woman." Nevertheless, he also adds in Bk. 16, *The City of God*, ch. 28: "In begetting
Isaac, Abraham received a special divine gift to be able to beget a
child, which he still retained later, after the death of Sarah."

From the verb κατενόησε [he considered], the papists wish to infer
that "Abraham's faith was not 'trust,' since trusting pertains to the
intellect, not to the will" (Bellarmine, Bk. 1 *On Justification*, ch. 6).

We reply: (1) These are coordinate things. Faith is knowledge
in the intellect, while confidence is in the will. Therefore from the
fact that faith is knowledge and assent, one cannot infer that it is
not trust.

(2) The object and bedrock of the faith of Abraham is said to
be the promise of the truthful and omnipotent God. Abraham embraced this not only with assent, but also with a firm trust, and
"against hope he believed toward hope, nor did he hesitate with
despair." Therefore, Abraham's faith was the immovable confidence of the heart, as is clear both from the object, namely, the
promise; and from the contrast, namely, despair; and from the ad-
jacent word, namely, πληροφορία [full persuasion].

v.20 εἰς δὲ τὴν ἐπαγγελίαν τοῦ Θεοῦ οὐ διεκρίθη τῇ ἀπιστίᾳ, ἀλλ᾽
ἐνεδυναμώθη τῇ πίστει, δοὺς δόξαν τῷ Θεῷ,

v.20 He staggered not at the promise of God through unbelief; but was strong in faith, giving glory to God; (KJV)

The noun τῇ ἀπιστίᾳ [by unbelief] is added either as a limit, if τὸ διακρίνεσθαι [to waver] is taken generally as an inquiry; or exegetically, if it is taken specifically as doubt.

Οὐ διεκρίθη τῇ ἀπιστίᾳ, "he did not hesitate," he did not dispute "by unbelief." For he is said to διακρίνεσθαι [waver] who is inclined in two directions, uncertain in his judgment about which he should choose.

The Syriac has the word אֶתְפַּלַּג, which is transferred to the soul by way of metaphor and means: "He was divided into diverse conclusions," even as the poet sings of a division of this kind:

The uncertain commoner is torn by contrary pursuits.

And so he divides the hasty soul, now here, now there.

In Mat. 14:31 and Mark 11:23, it corresponds to this Greek verb διστάζειν, "to keep turning in two different directions, to be in a state of suspense, to be driven now this way, now that," as ships are driven by the waves, and as meteors in the air turn, with a suspenseful and doubtful spirit, now this way, now that.

Observe: (1) Not every form of διάκρισις [wavering], that is, inquiry and debate in divine matters, is illicit, but only that which is of reason and not of faith—that which ends in doubt without seeking confirmation.

(2) Faith is confidence, since it is contrasted with that phrase, διάκρισις τῆς ἀπιστίας [wavering of unbelief]. Jam. 1:6: "Let him pray in faith μηδὲν διακρινόμενος [wavering nothing]."

"He gave glory to God," that is, the glory of truthfulness and divine omnipotence.

Observe: Faith gives glory to God. Unbelief brings dishonor upon Him. For "he who does not believe God has made Him a liar" (1 John 5:10).

v.21 καὶ πληροφορηθείς, ὅτι ὃ ἐπήγγελται, δυνατός ἐστι καὶ ποιῆσαι.

v.21 And being fully persuaded that, what he had promised, he was able also to perform. (KJV)

He is said to be πληροφορείσθαι [fully persuaded] who, as with full sails, is carried along by his confidence toward that thing in which he confides, as a metaphor taken from sailing ships.

The Vulgate translates, "knowing most fully," so that it is referred to the intellect. But it is more correctly translated, "being fully persuaded, a definite persuasion having been conceived," as Erasmus translates, so that it is referred to the will and the heart. Rom. 14:5, ἕκαστος ἰδίῳ νοῒ πληροφορείσθω, "Let each one be completely certain in his spirit." 2 Tim. 4:5, τὴν διακονίαν σου πληροφόρησον, "carry out your ministry with great confidence of spirit." Budaeus of Basil alleges a passage in which it means "to be rendered certain and secure."

In the Old Testament it occurs only once as מָלֵא, "he fulfilled." Ecc. 8:11, ἐπληροφορήθη καρδία υἱῶν τοῦ ἀνθρώπου [the heart of the sons of man was fully persuaded], where it is used of that preposterous and damnable confidence that men conceive from the postponement of the punishment for their sins.

Ships, which are carried along by full and inflated sails, endeavor on a straight course toward a predetermined place. They move quickly; they do not pause, nor do they look about for rocks. All of these things can be accommodated to faith as it clings firmly to the divine promises.

Basil, in *Ethical Definitions*. 8, Vol. 2, p.201: "One must not hesitate or doubt concerning those things that are said by the Lord. Rather, it must be considered as certain that every word of God is true and powerful, even if nature should cry out in protest. For this is the struggle of faith."

Observe that "faith" is "confidence," since πληροφορία [full persuasion] is a matter of confidence. Heb. 10:22, "Let us approach ἐν πληροφορίᾳ πίστεως [in full assurance of faith]." 1 The. 1:5, "ἐν πληροφορίᾳ πολλῇ [in much full assurance]," namely, πίστεως [of faith]. Col. 2:2, "πληροφορία τῆς συνέσεως, 'of a persuaded intelligence.'" Heb. 6:11, "πληροφορία ἐλπίδος [the full assurance of hope]."

The papists raise the following objection: "That phrase, 'he did not hesitate with distrust,' means that the faith of Abraham was notable, so that it also begat trust; and distrust, in this passage, is used for unbelief, since in Greek it is ἀπιστία [unbelief, distrust]. The Apostle has also recounted clearly enough what the faith of Abraham was, when he says, 'knowing full well,' since whatever God promised, He is capable of doing. Therefore, Abraham believed in the omnipotence of God. But that God is omnipotent, we hold by faith, not by trust." (Bellarmine, Bk. 1, *On Justification*, ch. 11).

We reply: (1) The Latin version that was made official at the Council of Trent translates ἀπιστίαν in this passage with "distrust." Therefore, by contrast, πίστις is "trust." (2) πληροφορία [full assurance], which the Apostle attributes to the faith of Abraham, not only denotes the certainty of knowledge or assent, but also a firmness of trust. (3) Abraham is said to have "believed toward hope, against hope." But hope is in the will. Therefore the faith of Abraham cannot only be defined as knowledge and assent. (4) Abraham's faith had not only the omnipotence of God in view, but also the word of promise on which the firm confidence of his soul relied. (5) If the faith of Abraham produced trust, then surely trust cannot be separated from faith.

But how does this praise for Abraham's faith fit with this, that in Gen. 17:17 Abraham is recalled as having said in his heart, "Will a son really be born to a man who is a hundred years old?"

Ambrose, Bk. 1, *On Abraham*, ch. 4, answers: "The fact that Abraham laughed at the promise of a son from Sarah was not an indication of unbelief, but of exultation." Augustine, Bk. 16, *The City of God*, ch. 26, likewise calls it the "exultation of gratitude, not the derision of distrust." Lyranus on Genesis ch. 17: "Abraham did not laugh from derision, or else he would have been rebuked by God as Sarah was. Rather, he laughed from exultation of heart. It says this, not because he was doubting, but because he was marveling at the divine benefit."

But Chrysostom offers a contrary opinion in Homily 6, *On Repentance*, and Jerome in Bk. 3, *Dialogue Against the Pelagians*. They think that Abraham suffered to some degree from human weakness in this area, and that this [laughter] was prompted by a wavering heart, and therefore they conclude that this sin of Abraham was punished in his posterity by their four hundred years of slavery. Johannes Arboreus answers: "Abraham certainly doubted in the beginning, since he was still weighing the divine promise by means of his reason. But he firmly believed when he directly heard the declaration and confirmation of the divine promise."

Cajetan thinks that "Abraham certainly doubted. But it wasn't the truthfulness of the divine promise that he doubted; it was concerning the understanding of the words, namely, whether He was speaking of carnal posterity, or of spiritual and mystical posterity."

v.22 Διὸ καὶ ἐλογίσθη αὐτῷ εἰς δικαιοσύνην.

v.22 And therefore it was imputed to him for righteousness. (KJV)

There is an understood τοῦτο [this], "this very thing," that he firmly believed the divine promise; or, "this faith" was imputed to him for righteousness.

v.23 Οὐκ ἐγράφη δὲ δι᾽ αὐτὸν μόνον, ὅτι ἐλογίσθη αὐτῷ.

v.23 Now it was not written for his sake alone, that it was imputed to him; (KJV)

v.24 ἀλλὰ καὶ δι᾽ ἡμᾶς, οἷς μέλλει λογίζεσθαι τοῖς πιστεύουσιν ἐπὶ τὸν ἐγείραντα Ἰησοῦν τὸν Κύριον ἡμῶν ἐκ νεκρῶν.

v.24 But for us also, to whom it shall be imputed, if we believe on him that raised up Jesus our Lord from the dead; (KJV)

The purpose for which Moses told the history of Abraham is chiefly this, that through it he might set forth for us the manner of justification, which is one and the same in the Old and New Testaments.

One asks, *Why is Christ's resurrection from the dead declared specifically to be the object of justifying faith?* We reply: (1) Because by raising His Son, our Bondsman[48], who was put to death for our sins, God made manifest by that very act that full satisfaction has been made to Him by Christ's death. (2) Consideration is given at the same time to the power of God which He exerted in the raising of Christ (Eph. 1:20). This is how that statement is applied to the example of Abraham, whose faith is commended in 4:20 for the fact that "he gave praise to God." (3) The summary of the entire Gospel is contained in this article of the resurrection of Christ, and this single article encompasses all the rest (1 Cor. 15:1 ff.). For it is understood from the fact that Christ rose from the dead that He truly died. And since He truly died, He was therefore also truly conceived and born, and truly suffered for our sins.

v.25 ὃς παρεδόθη διὰ τὰ παραπτώματα ἡμῶν, καὶ ἠγέρθη διὰ τὴν δικαίωσιν ἡμῶν.

v.25 *Who was delivered for our offences, and was raised again for our justification.* (KJV)

The papists conclude from this passage that our justification does not consist solely in the remission of sins, but also in inner renewal.

Pererius, Disputation 10 on Romans ch. 4, Th. 48: "Paul distinguishes in this passage between the remission of sins and justification, saying that 'Christ died for our sins and rose for our justification,' clearly indicating that our justification does not consist solely in the remission of sins, but that the principal part of justification is renewal of life and uprightness of mind. The resurrection of Christ was an example of this."

Bellarmine, Bk. 2, *On Justification*, ch. 6: "The Apostle attributes the word 'justification' to the inner renewal rather than to justification, etc. For neither can it be doubted that the Apostle meant that the death of Christ was a model for dying to sin, while resurrection is a model for the inner renewal and regeneration by which we walk in newness of life."

We reply: (1) Their argument depends on this hypothesis, that Paul does not attribute our justification to the death and resurrec-

48 Latin: *sponsorem*

tion of Christ for any other reason except that the death of Christ was a model for dying to sin, and the resurrection of Christ a model for inner renewal. But the following points show that this hypothesis is false.

(2) In this same chapter the Apostle expressly teaches that our justification before God consists in the gracious imputation of the righteousness of Christ and the non-imputation, or the remission, of sins; it does not consist in our works. He cannot be stating in the conclusion of this chapter the opposite of what is deduced from the things said above.

(3) The Apostle, in this chapter, is not yet dealing with the effects and fruits of justification, to which renewal also pertains. Rather, he is dealing both with the cause and with the merit of justification, as one gathers from the particle διὰ, "because of." He is, furthermore, discussing the form and method of justification, which consists in the remission of sins which have been atoned for through Christ. He is also dealing with the proper object of justifying faith, which is Christ, who died for our sins and was raised for our justification.

(4) Although we do not disapprove of the goal of treating the death and resurrection of Christ as a model when explained according to the analogy of faith, nevertheless the Apostle is not yet dealing with that in this passage, although later he does, in chapter six and following. Here, however, he explains the other, and indeed, the principal goal of the death and resurrection of Christ, which is the expiation of our sins and our justification before God— indeed, the merit of our righteousness and salvation.

(5) We grant that the resurrection of Christ is not only a model and a figure, but also the cause of our renewal, just as the death of Christ is not only the model of spiritual mortification, but is also the efficient cause of it (2 Cor. 4:12). But from that it cannot be inferred that our justification formally consists in that very renewal, because one must deal differently with different benefits. And it is proved in its place that renewal is not part of justification, but a consequence and fruit of it.

(6) The Apostle, neither in this passage nor ever, anywhere, attributes the word "justification" to renewal. Rather, he asserts that faith, which lays hold of Christ who died for our sins and was raised for our justification, is imputed to us for righteousness.

But if someone further inquires: *In what sense and respect, then, is our justification, which consists in the remission of sins, attributed to the resurrection of Christ?*

We reply: It should be taken in this way.

(1) With respect to *the manifestation, demonstration and confirmation,* because the resurrection of Christ is the clear testimony that full satisfaction has been made for our sins and that perfect righteousness has been procured. Jerome on this passage: "Christ rose in order that He might confirm righteousness to believers." Chrysostom, Homily 9 on Romans: "In the resurrection it is demonstrated that Christ died, not for His own sins, but for our sins. For how could He rise again if He were a sinner? But if He was not a sinner, then He was crucified for the sake of others."

(2) With respect to *the application.* If Christ had remained in death, He would not be the conqueror of death, nor could He apply to us the righteousness that was obtained at such a high price (Rom. 5:10, 8:34). But since He rose from the dead and ascended into heaven and sat down at the right hand of God, He thus also offers to the world, through the Word of the Gospel, the benefits obtained by His suffering and death, applies them to believers, and in this way justifies them. With respect to this application, Cardinal Toletus (in his commentary on this passage, and Suarez, Vol. 2, in part 3, *Thom. Disputation* 44, p.478) acknowledges that our justification is attributed to the resurrection of Christ, writing thus: "Christ, by His suffering, sufficiently destroyed sin. Nevertheless, in order that we might be justified and that sin might be effectively remitted to us, it was necessary for the suffering of Christ to be applied to us through a living faith." Christ arose, therefore, for the sake of our righteousness, that is, so that our faith might be confirmed, and in this way we might be effectively justified. The Apostle notably says that Christ died for our sins and was raised,

214

not for the sake of δικαιοσύνην [righteousness], which is contrasted with sins in general, but διὰ τὴν δικαίωσιν ἡμῶν, "for the sake of our justification," which consists in absolution from sins.

(3) With respect to *the actual absolution from sin.*[49] By delivering Christ into death for the sake of our sins, the heavenly Father condemned sin in His flesh through sin (Rom. 8:3). He condemned it because it had sinned against Christ by bringing about His death, even though He was innocent, and so He withdrew from sin its legal right against believers so that it cannot condemn them any longer. He also condemned it, in that He punished our sins in Christ, which were imposed on Him and imputed to Him as to a bondsman. So also, by the very act of raising Him from the dead, He absolved Him from our sins that were imputed to Him, and consequently also absolves us in Him, so that, in this way, the resurrection of Christ may be both the cause and the pledge and the complement of our justification. The following passages pertain to this: 1 Cor. 15:17, 2 Cor. 5:21, Eph. 2:5, Col. 2:12-13, Phi. 3:8-10, 1 Pet. 1:3.

Based on this foundation, one can easily respond to the question, *Does the resurrection of Christ pertain to the merit that has been provided for us?* We reply: The word "merit" is understood either generally as all that pertains to our justification; or specifically as that which Christ has provided for us and which we ourselves were obligated to provide. In the first sense, the resurrection of Christ pertains to merit, because the resurrection of Christ was required for our justification in the ways explained thus far. But with regard to the second sense, it does not pertain to merit, because, although Christ arose for our sake, He did not arise in our place, whereas He suffered and died, not only for our sake, but also in our place.[50]

---

49 Latin: *respectu actualis a peccato applicationis.* Given the content of this paragraph and Abraham Calov's later quotation of it in his *Biblia Illustrata* on this verse, it is suggested that the word *applicationis* is a typographical error and should rather be *absolutionis.* If the word *applicationis* is correct, then the translation would be: "*the actual placement under Christ's protection from sin.*" See *Lewis & Short: A Latin Dictionary* under *applicatio.*

50 Latin: *non solum propter nos, sed etiam pro nobis*

Notes on the Epistle to the Romans: Chapter 5

The chapter can be divided in three ways: (1) Exegetical, (2) apodictic, (3) elenctic.

v.1 Δικαιωθέντες οὖν ἐκ πίστεως, εἰρήνην ἔχομεν πρὸς τὸν Θεὸν διὰ τοῦ Κυρίου ἡμῶν Ἰησοῦ Χριστοῦ.

v.1 Therefore being justified by faith, we have peace with God through our Lord Jesus Christ: (KJV)

Some wish to assert that a new argument is being proposed here in which it is proved that justification is not by works. The argument could be fashioned in this way: We are justified before God by that which renders our conscience peaceful and calm. Yet neither the law nor the works of the law, but faith in Christ renders the conscience peaceful and calm. Therefore, we are not justified by the law or by the works of the law, but by faith in Christ. But the illative particle οὖν [therefore] shows that the Apostle is deducing the things that he submits in this chapter prismatically from the justification by faith that has been demonstrated.

With εἰρήνην [peace] is understood (1) reconciliation with God, for πρὸς τὸν θεὸν [with God] is added; (2) the quietness and tranquility of the conscience, which is the fruit of that reconciliation.

Observe: The Apostle does not say ἔχωμεν εἰρήνην [let us have peace], using an optative or hortative form; but ἔχομεν [we have], using an indicative form. "Having been justified, we have peace," he says. He is not encouraging them to have peace or to pursue peace. He wants to console, not exhort. The Syriac has the future נֶהֱוֵא, "there will be peace for us." While it certainly could be taken as a conjunctive, it is clear from the Greek text that it is to be taken as an indicative.

v.2 δι' οὗ καὶ τὴν προσαγωγὴν ἐσχήκαμεν τῇ πίστει εἰς τὴν χάριν ταύτην ἐν ᾗ ἑστήκαμεν, καὶ καυχώμεθα ἐπ' ἐλπίδι τῆς δόξης τοῦ Θεοῦ.

v.2 By whom also we have access by faith into this grace wherein we stand, and rejoice in hope of the glory of God. (KJV)

He had said in ch. 3:25 that "Christ was made by God to be for us a Propitiatorium through faith in His blood." Therefore, just as the Israelites would flee for refuge in danger and adversity to the Old Testament Propitiatorium as a type, so he asserts that there is open to us in the New Testament access to the true and only Propitiatorium.

Δι' οὗ [through whom], namely, χριστοῦ [Christ], καὶ τὴν προσαγωγὴν ἐσχήκαμεν, "we have had entrance," that is, we have been led by faith into that grace, that is, into the reconciliation with God that Christ obtained for us with His death (v.1). Some understand "grace" as "the grace of adoption and heirship." This explanation is coordinated with the first, since reconciliation with God consists in adoption, which also brings with it the grace of heirship.

Luther translates in the present tense. "*Wir haben einen Zugang* [We have an entrance]." Before we were reconciled to God through Christ, we were forced to flee from God, and to "hide ourselves from before His face" (Gen. 3:8). But now that we have been reconciled to God by faith in Christ, there is open to us a perpetual and free access to divine grace. Parallel passages are Eph. 2:18 and Heb. 4:16.

Ἐν ᾗ ἐστήκαμεν, "in which we stand," that is, we confide, we do not permit ourselves to be dislodged from it by any temptations or persecutions.

Στῆναι does not simply mean "to stand," but also "to continue in a stance, to remain in firm trust"—a metaphor drawn from the battle line, where active soldiers do not yield even a foot's breadth to the enemy.

Καυχώμεθα ἐπ' ἐλπίδι τῆς δόξης τοῦ Θεοῦ [We boast in hope of the glory of God]. "We boast in hope, from hope, because of the hope of the glory of God," based on this, that we certainly hope that we will be participants in the glory of heaven. This is called "the glory of God" (1) because it is given to believers by God for the sake of Christ; (2) because it consists in the beatific vision of God; (3) because it involves glory with God, not with men.

He does not say that they boast because of the promised glory of eternal life, but because of the hope of glory, and in this way he runs to meet the tacit objection: *The godly are exposed to many calamities in this life, and therefore they boast in vain of their happiness.* The Apostle replies: their happiness does not rest on the earth, but in heaven, under hope. And this hope is so certain and firm that they boast in that happiness no less than if they already possessed it.

Observe: The individual words are individual weights against papistic doubting. (1) "We are justified by faith." That faith is the confident laying hold of the merit of Christ. (2) "We have peace with God." Doubt is opposed to this reconciliation with God and peace of conscience. (3) "Through Christ we have access to that grace," that is, we can approach the Throne of Grace with confidence (Heb. 4:16). Doubt is opposed to this confident access. (4) "We stand in grace," namely, with a strong and fearless spirit. (5) "We boast because of the hope of heavenly glory." We are, therefore, firmly confident that we will receive it.

From the general faith that believes that Christ has suffered and died for the human race is born that special faith by which any believer says with the Apostle, "Christ loved me" (Gal. 2:20). Therefore, he does not doubt that the benefits of Christ pertain also to him and that they are offered to him in the word of the Gospel. He therefore applies them to himself in hope. From this special application of the benefits of Christ is born that προσαγωγὴ [entrance].

v.3 Οὐ μόνον δέ, ἀλλὰ καὶ καυχώμεθα ἐν ταῖς θλίψεσιν, εἰδότες ὅτι ἡ θλῖψις ὑπομονὴν κατεργάζεται.

v.3 And not only so, but we glory in tribulations also: knowing that tribulation worketh patience; (KJV)

The rhetoric builds. Not only do we boast in calamities because of the hope of heavenly glory, but we also boast in the calamities themselves, so that, far from rendering us miserable before God or robbing us of the promised happiness in heaven, the calamities themselves supply the substance of exultation.

218

Ἐν ταῖς θλίψεσιν [in tribulations], "about tribulations," or "on account of tribulations." Ἐν [in] is used for "on account of" in the Hebrew idiom.

But why do the godly boast in tribulations? (1) Because tribulations sustain them on account of Christ and His Word (Acts 5:41); (2) because they are like a kind of indication of υἱοθεσίας [sonship] and of the fatherly love of God (Heb. 12:6-7, Rev. 3:19); (3) because they serve to advance salvation (Acts 14:22). (4) The Apostle supplies a fourth reason in the next phrase.

Ἡ θλίψις κατεργάζεται ὑπομονὴν [the tribulation works patience], "affliction produces patience," not by itself, but by accident, in the godly, namely, in the truly believing. For they see in the cross the fatherly will of God, and the purpose of advancing our salvation through afflictions, conformity with Christ, and other useful purposes of calamities. Through the consideration of these things, the Holy Spirit works patience in their hearts.

Ἡ θλίψις κατεργάζεται ὑπομονήν [the affliction works patience]. From the verb κατεργάζεται [works] the papists understand the merits of works and sufferings. We reply: (1) The Apostle himself runs to meet this understanding (Rom. 8:18). (2) ὑπομονὴ [patience], properly speaking, is not the effect of θλίψεων [afflictions] insofar as they are afflictions, or else all who experience afflictions would be patient. Rather, it is the effect of afflictions insofar as the Holy Spirit is effectively working in afflictions and through afflictions. (3) Consequently, we are said to "enter the kingdom of heaven," not *because of* tribulations, but *through* afflictions (Acts 14:22). (4) Only the suffering of Christ is the λύτρον καὶ ἱλασμὸς [price and propitiation]. Our afflictions are either τιμωρίαι [chastisements] or δοκιμασίαι [tests] or μαρτύρια [testimonies].

v.4 ἡ δὲ ὑπομονὴ δοκιμήν, ἡ δὲ δοκιμὴ ἐλπίδα.

v.4 And patience, experience; and experience, hope: (KJV)

"Patience produces testing or experience," so that we actually experience that we are children of God, and that God will never leave us in any calamity (Psa. 91:15).

Outside the cross, we are mere observers; in the cross, the true and living practice of the article of free justification is set forth (Sir. 34:10).

Ἡ ὑπομονὴ κατεργάζεται δοκιμὴν [Patience produces testing]. Jam. 1:3 states the opposite, τὸ δοκίμιον τῆς πίστεως κατεργάζεται ὑπομονήν [the testing of faith produces patience].

Thomas, in his commentary, connects them in this way: "Testing is taken in two ways: in one way, insofar as it is in the one who is tested. In this sense it is not distinguished from the tribulation itself by which someone is tested. This is how it is taken in James, so that the sense is, 'testing produces patience,' that is, tribulation produces patience. In another way, testing is understood as 'to be tested and approved.' This is the sense in which Paul takes it. Patience produces testing, for from the fact that a man patiently bears up under tribulation, he is rendered approved, and his virtue is shown to be all the more outstanding."

With this connection in mind, a fitting conclusion is drawn by those who say that affliction, which is properly called θλίψις [tribulation] by Paul, is called τὸ δοκίμιον τῆς πίστεως [the testing of faith] by James by way of metonymy.

Paul uses the phrase "the testing of faith" to signify "the effect of patience," for patience in adversity renders men's faith approved, and Paul calls this δοκιμὴν [testing]. James uses the phrase to signify "the tribulation itself" by which faith is tested, which he therefore calls τὸ δοκίμιον τῆς πίστεως [the testing of faith]. Therefore, the same word can be used in each sense. James attributes it by metonymy to the testing that has been produced, that is, to the tribulation through which the testing of faith happens. Paul expressly attributes this to tribulation.

Paul proceeds from the front end. James, from the testing of faith, as from the back end, concludes that patience has gone before, having already been proved and tested from the faith of the believer, and it is assumed that he has patiently suffered and mightily overcome the adversities of this world.

Ἡ δοκιμὴ κατεργάζεται ἐλπίδα. "Experience or testing produces hope," namely, hope of the heavenly inheritance.

But how does testing produce that hope? We reply: Those who, in the cross and by the cross, are conformed to the image of the Son of God (Rom. 8:29) are rendered steadfast from the knowledge that they are eventually going to be conformed to Him in glory. Those who receive one part of the inheritance in this life, namely, the cross, will certainly not be robbed of the other part of the inheritance that is laid up for the children of God in heaven. Those who persevere on the path of tribulation will enter the kingdom of heaven, "since it is necessary that through many tribulations we enter the kingdom of heaven" (Acts 14:22).

With ἐλπίδα [hope], some understand "hope in God"—we believe that since He is now present with us in calamities, He will also be with us again in the future. But it comes down to the same thing. For through the tribulations that have come upon us for the sake of Christ and that have been borne patiently by the power of the Holy Spirit, we are rendered certain that God will always be with us in this life and will eventually glorify us in eternal life.

v.5 Ἡ δὲ ἐλπὶς οὐ καταισχύνει, ὅτι ἡ ἀγάπη τοῦ Θεοῦ ἐκκέχυται ἐν ταῖς καρδίαις ἡμῶν διὰ πνεύματος ἁγίου τοῦ δοθέντος ἡμῖν.

v.5 And hope maketh not ashamed; because the love of God is shed abroad in our hearts by the Holy Ghost which is given unto us. (KJV)

"Hope does not put to shame." This means that the godly are not disappointed in their hope. For those who are disappointed in their hope, that is, for whom the matter turns out differently than they had hoped—they tend to be covered in shame. In this way, then, the Apostle understands what goes before from the result that follows. He rightly draws from what comes later when he uses the word "shame" to mean "disappointment," namely, since shame usually follows disappointment.

The Latin interpreter has in view the disturbance of the soul that usually follows being covered with shame. For "to confound" is no different than "to disturb."

Observe: There is a great difference between earthly and heavenly hope. What the poet says is relevant here:

Good hope is often deceived by its prediction.[51]

But since hope rests on the divine promise, which is immovable truth, it is therefore never put to shame.

"The love of God has been poured out in our hearts by the Holy Spirit who has been given to us."

Augustine, in his book *On the Spirit and the Letter*, ch. 32, takes it concerning "the active love with which we love God. In order for God to be loved," he says, "the love of God is poured out in our hearts, not by a free will that arises from within us, but by the Holy spirit who has been given to us." Similar things are said in Bk. 2, *On the Merits and Forgiveness of Sins*, ch. 17; *On Nature and Grace*, ch. 64; Bk. 1, *On the Grace of Christ*, ch. 12; Bernhard, *Epistle 107*; Anselm, on this passage.

Pererius, Stapleton and other papists follow Augustine's exposition. They wish to prove from it that "the love with which we love God is the grace that makes us acceptable, that is, the grace that justifies us" (Bellarmine, Bk. 2, *On Justification*, ch. 3; Bk. 1, *On Grace and Free Will*, ch. 4).

A commentary that is ascribed to Ambrose takes it concerning "the passive love with which God loves us. We have," he says, "a pledge of love in us through the Holy Spirit who has been given to us." The usual interpretation embraces this explanation, and all the interpreters in common (Dominicus a Soto on this passage, Cajetan on this passage, Benedictus Justinianus, Toletus, etc.) likewise take it concerning "the love with which God loves us." This explanation is confirmed (1) from the context. The Apostle goes back to confirm this proposition, "that hope is not confounded." He proves it with this argument, that the love of God has the most ample testimony in our hearts through the Holy Spirit who has been given to us. But our love is not, nor can it be, that most firm and immovable foundation of our faith. Instead, our hope is founded on that love

---

51 Latin: *Fallitur augurio spes bona saepe suo.*

of God with which He loves us in the Beloved (Eph. 1:4). Only the love of God toward us, which we feel in our hearts by the testimony of the Holy Spirit, can seal that infallible hope that we have in God; (2) from v.8. "God commends His love toward us." Ch. 8, last verse, "no creature can separate us from the love of God that is in Christ Jesus." (3) From the verb ἐκκέχυται [has been poured out]. The love of God is said to have been "poured out in our hearts." But this cannot be said about the love with which we love God, for that is much fainter than the word "poured out" allows, since it signifies abundance. "For we have only received the firstfruits of the Spirit" (Rom. 8:23). Therefore, although we have certainly begun to love God, we do not love perfectly. (4) From the parallel passages. 1 John 4:13, "This is how we know that we remain in Him and He in us, for He gave us of His Spirit." V.16, "And we have known and believed the love that God has in us," that is, "toward us."

Chrysostom explicitly explains it concerning "the love ἣν περὶ ἡμᾶς ὁ θεὸς ἐπεδείξατο [which God showed concerning us]." And later: "After he said, 'That hope does not put us to shame,' he assigned everything, not to our merits, but to the love of God."

Theophylact: "He confirms that those things will come to us by the very love that God shows to us."

Oecumenius: "He says it is the Spirit who has come into us only from the love of God with which He has loved us."

Ambrose: "For we have the pledge of the love of God in us through the Holy Spirit who has been given to us."

Primasius: "From this we know how God loves us."

This explanation is not impeded by the fact that the love of God is said to have been poured out in our hearts—which doesn't seem to fit with the love of God with which God loves us. For it is said to have been "poured out" and "poured broadly in our hearts," not with regard to a subjective inhesion or inhering, but with regard to the effect, both because the Holy Spirit, who has been given to us, has been "poured out richly" from love (Tit. 3:5, Is. 44:3, Eze. 36:25, Joel 2:28, Zech. 12:10), and because the feeling of that love is poured out in our hearts, for we feel that we are loved by God, and we taste how good and pleasant the Lord is (Psa. 34:9).

Pererius, *Disputation 2* on Rom. 5:9: "Whether we read 'poured broadly' or 'poured out,' he means nothing else with that word but that the love of God has been openly and clearly declared through many and various gifts of the Holy Spirit which He has poured out on us, that is, which He has generously, copiously and abundantly conferred on us."

In this he follows Chrysostom, who makes the following comments on this passage: "When the Apostle said, 'Hope does not put to shame,' he also added the proof, saying that the love of God has been poured out in our hearts. He did not say, 'has been given,' but 'has been poured out,' showing generosity. For He has given the greatest gift He could possibly give: not heaven, not earth, not sea, but that which was more ancient and more precious than these things. He has made angels out of men and sons of God and brothers of Christ. But what is this? It is the Holy Spirit. But if He did not mean to bestow great crowns on us *after* our labors are finished, He would never have given so many and such great gifts *before* those labors are finished. But now He declares the fervor of His love from this, that He did not honor us little by little or gradually, but He poured out the fountain of gifts all at once and with a full hand— and that, He did before the trial itself takes place. He did this in order that you may neither count yourself too worthy nor despair, since you have a great Advocate on your side, the love of the Judge. It is for this reason that, with these words, 'Hope does not put to shame,' he referred the praise for the whole matter, not to our merits, but to the love of God and His charity toward us."

Origen, Chrysostom, Theodoret, Sedulius, Oecumenius, Thomas, and, among the more recent papists, Cornelius a Lapide, combine both explanations and take this passage to be as much about the love of God toward us as it is about our love toward God. Pererius, quoting Michael Ghislerius in his commentary, Cant. 3: "The Apostle understands the mutual love with which God pursues us and with which we love God, for both kinds of love are joined in our hearts by the Holy Spirit."

But even if we were to grant to the greatest extent possible that the apostolic passage can be understood secondarily concerning our love toward God, since the Holy Spirit who was given to us from the love of God toward us kindles a reciprocal love in us toward God, nonetheless, it does not aid the cause of the papists. For (1) by "the love of God spread out in our hearts," there is not understood a disposition or an infused quality, but rather a certain firm persuasion in our minds concerning the mercy, goodness and φιλανθρωπίᾳ [philanthropy] with which God embraces us in Christ. (2) Our love is not the foundation of that living hope that we have in God; instead, it is the testimony of the Holy Spirit who has been given to us out of the love of God. (3) Even if we grant that the love that is kindled in our hearts by the Holy Spirit is here understood, does that really mean that the grace by which we are justified must be that love? Does the Apostle say that we are justified "through and for the sake of that love?"

v.6 Ἔτι γὰρ Χριστός, ὄντων ἡμῶν ἀσθενῶν, κατὰ καιρὸν ὑπὲρ ἀσεβῶν ἀπέθανε.

v.6 *For when we were yet without strength, in due time Christ died for the ungodly. (KJV)*

The Latin interpreter must have either read something different, or he must have been hallucinating when he translated: "For as what Christ..." The Greek manuscripts consistently read: "For still Christ..." Only the Syriac interpreter seems to have read it altered as εἰ [if]: "For if Christ..."

The Apostle demonstrates (1) the most effective consolation that is to be set against any adversity. Christ loved us, and out of love He suffered and died for us when we were still weak, sinners, and ungodly. Therefore, having been justified and sanctified in Him, He will not desert us in any adversity, not even in death itself. (2) That the clearest testimony of divine love was set forth for us in the death of the Son, by which we can be absolutely certain that, now that our reconciliation with God has been made by the death of Christ, all things necessary for salvation will be kindly supplied to us.

This is the effect of that love of which he had spoken in the preceding verses. For when we were still weak, in His time Christ died for the ungodly. He illustrates this from the things that have been established. Theophylact on this passage: "He had said that the love of God had been proffered in the hearts through the Holy Spirit, whom He had conferred." He then expresses the magnitude of this divine love on account of which Christ subjected Himself to death for our sake, who are weak, that is, who fall short.

Ὄντων ἡμῶν ἀσθενῶν [we being weak]. "When we were still under the slavery of sin, under the captivity of Satan, under the power of death, and thus weak toward every good work." The Syriac translates: "on account of our infirmity."

Κατὰ καιρόν [at the time]. Luther refers this to the word ἀσθενῶν [weak], "at the time of our infirmity," so that the past status is thus distinguished from the present.

Ambrose and Theophylact refer it to the verb ἀπέθανε [he died], so that it signifies that "Christ died at the divinely established time" (Gal. 4:4-5).

Observe against the Photinians that Christ is said to have died ὑπὲρ ἀσεβῶν, "for the ungodly." But the preposition "for" is normally understood in the Scriptures in one of five ways: (1) It is occasionally the equivalent of the preposition "about," as in 1 Sam. 9:5, "he is worried for us," that is, "about us." Also Isa. 37:21, 1 Cor. 1:4, Phi. 1:7. (2) It is often used in place of something and in exchange for something else, or it indicates a certain kind of replacement. Gen. 4:25, "He gave another seed for Abel," that is, in place of Abel. Also Gen. 30:2, Exo. 7:1, Pro. 11:8. (3) It sometimes denotes advantage, as something that happens for someone, so that something is done for his benefit. Job 13:7, "Is it possible that you will utter iniquity for God?" that is, for the favor and advantage of God. Luke 9:5, "He who is not against us is for us." John 10:11, "The Good Shepherd lays down His soul for the sheep." (4) Not infrequently it indicates the efficient and motivating cause, so that it means the same thing as "because of." Gen. 21:11, "Abraham took this hard for his son," that is, because of his son. Also Gen. 27:41, 1 Chron.

16:21, Acts 12:23, Eph. 5:31. (5) It often includes merit, and signifies not only disadvantage, but also satisfaction. Thus sacrifices are said to be offered "for sin" (Lev. 4:3). In the same sense Christ is said to have suffered "for the life of the world" (John 6:51), "for the sins of the world" (1 John 2:2), "for all" (Rom. 8:32).

But when Christ is said to have died "for us," it is clear that not only benefit and advantage are signified (as the Photinians desire), but also satisfaction. This is made clear from the fact that Christ is called "our Redeemer" and "our redemption" (Luke 1:68, Rom. 3:24, 1 Cor. 1:30, etc.); our ἱλασμὸς [propitiation] (1 John 2:2, 4:10); ἱλαστήριον [Propitiatorium] (Rom. 3:24); and is said to have given Himself and His life λύτρον καὶ ἀντίλυτρον [as the price and redemption] for us (Mat. 20:28, Mark 10:45, 1 Tim. 2:6); and even made sin for us (2 Cor. 5:21) and a curse (Gal. 3:13); namely, because of our sins that were laid upon Him (Is 53:6) and taken back upon Him (Psa. 69:5, John 1:29, 1 Pet. 2:24). For this reason the Syriac translated it with חֲלָף, which signifies a certain exchange.

v.7 Μόλις γὰρ ὑπὲρ δικαίου τις ἀποθανεῖται, ὑπὲρ γὰρ τοῦ ἀγαθοῦ τάχα τις καὶ τολμᾷ ἀποθανεῖν.

v.7 *For scarcely for a righteous man will one die: yet peradventure for a good man some would even dare to die. (KJV)*

He illustrates what he had just said, "Christ died for us when we were still ungodly."

Ὑπὲρ δικαίου [for a righteous man]. Jerome in *Epistle to Algasia*, q. 7, states: "'The righteous' here does not refer to a certain person, but to the thing itself, namely, righteousness and goodness." For this reason, some interpreters—among them also Blessed Luther—translated in the abstract. Luther: "*Umb des rechts willen* [For the sake of what is right]." Likewise: "*Umb etwas gutes willen* [For the sake of something good]."

But others take "righteous" as used concretely for a person. This explanation is proved by (1) the contrast in the apostolic text. "Christ died ὑπὲρ ἀσεβῶν [for ungodly men]," (v.6), ὑπὲρ δικαίου τὶς ἀποθανεῖται [someone may die for an unrighteous man]. (2) By the

Syriac translation: "For hardly anyone רִשִׁיעֵא חלָף will die for the wicked."

With τὸν ἀγαθὸν [the good one], some understand him who is useful to someone, so that it is the same as ὁ χρηστός [the useful one]. But the sequence of thought in the text demonstrates that it is equivalent in this passage with τῷ δικαίῳ [the righteous one].

Τάχα τὶς καὶ τολμᾷ [Perhaps someone would even dare], etc. By way of a sort of correction he submits that it certainly happens, though rarely, that someone dies for a righteous man. Τολμᾷ [he dares], someone not only puts up with the most bitter things, but even with death itself. The customary meaning of the verb τολμᾶν [to be bold] can also be retained, for it is a kind of "boldness," to go to one's death in place of someone else. Syriac: אֲמְרַח, "he dared."

v.8 Συνίστησε δὲ τὴν ἑαυτοῦ ἀγάπην εἰς ἡμᾶς ὁ Θεός, ὅτι ἔτι ἁμαρτωλῶν ὄντων ἡμῶν Χριστὸς ὑπὲρ ἡμῶν ἀπέθανε.

v.8 But God commendeth his love toward us, in that, while we were yet sinners, Christ died for us. (KJV)

In the two preceding verses he had commended the love of Christ from the fact that He died for us, the ungodly. Now he illustrates the love of God from the fact that He delivered Christ over to death for us while we were still sinners, teaching that not only the love of Christ, but also the love of God Himself is manifest from the death of Christ.

Συνίστησε [He commended] does not only mean "He commended," but also "He made noble and notable, He illustrated most clearly, He rendered commendable, and He demonstrated" that His love is exceedingly great. For since it is something noble and grand to do good to one's enemies—and indeed, to do good in this way, that He expends for them that which is most precious of all—for this reason God is deservedly said to have demonstrated His noble and grand love when He delivered His most beloved Son over to death for His enemies.

Ἔτι ἁμαρτωλῶν ὄντων [while we were yet sinners]. Those

whom he had earlier called ἀσεβείς [ungodly] (v.6), he here calls ἁμαρτωλοὺς [sinners].

But even after the reconciliation made through Christ and the application of the benefits obtained by the death of Christ, are we not still sinners in this life? (1 John 1:7) We reply: With ἁμαρτωλοὺς [sinners] in this passage are understood the men who are given over to sins—dead in sins and enemies of God (v.10).

v.9 Πολλῷ οὖν μᾶλλον δικαιωθέντες νῦν ἐν τῷ αἵματι αὐτοῦ, σωθησόμεθα δι᾽ αὐτοῦ ἀπὸ τῆς ὀργῆς.

v.9 Much more then, being now justified by his blood, we shall be saved from wrath through him. (KJV)

He contrasts τοῖς ἀσεβεῖσι καὶ τοῖς ἁμαρτωλοῖς [the ungodly and the sinners] with δικαιωθέντες [having been justified], "those who have been justified," that is, absolved from sins and cleansed in the blood of Christ. This sequence of events is exceedingly sweet. Christ died for us when we were still sinners and enemies. Therefore, much more will He save us from the wrath of God, now that we have been justified and absolved from sins.

Σωθησόμεθα, "we will be saved," we will be protected from wrath. Luther: "*Wir werden behalten werden* [We will be kept safe]." The Syriac translates: "How much more will we now be justified in His blood and be rescued from wrath through Him." But the Greek δικαιωθέντες [having been justified] has the perfect-tense meaning, and the Apostle is speaking with the reborn and about the reborn.

The Syriac expresses the verb σωθησόμεθα [we will be saved] with the verb אֶצְטְנָא, "he was freed, he was released," for he who frees someone releases his bonds.

Ἀπὸ τῆς ὀργῆς, "from that wrath" that is coming, namely, of the final judgment of condemnation and hell. For he uses the verb in the future tense. 1 The. 1:10, "Christ has freed us ἀπὸ τῆς ὀργῆς τῆς ἐρχομένης [from the wrath that is coming]."

Some, however, take it generally of the temporal and eternal punishments that proceed from the wrath of God.

v.10 Εἰ γὰρ ἐχθροὶ ὄντες κατηλλάγημεν τῷ Θεῷ διὰ τοῦ θανάτου τοῦ Υἱοῦ αὐτοῦ, πολλῷ μᾶλλον καταλλαγέντες σωθησόμεθα ἐν τῇ ζωῇ αὐτοῦ.

v.10 *For if, when we were enemies, we were reconciled to God by the death of his Son, much more, being reconciled, we shall be saved by his life. (KJV)*

There is a very beautiful epimone here. Just as earlier he had contrasted ἀσεβεῖς [ungodly] and δικαιωθέντες [having been justified], so now he contrasts the death and the life of Christ, arguing likewise from the lesser to the greater in this way: If the death of Christ was so efficacious that it reconciled us to God, even more will His life be so efficacious that it will save us who have now been justified.

Ἐν τῇ ζωῇ αὐτοῦ. "In His life," through Him who lives and reigns in heaven and who communicates spiritual and heavenly life to believers. The Syriac has the prefix ב, which can also mean "through His life." Luther: *"durch sein Leben* [through His life]."

v.11 Οὐ μόνον δέ, ἀλλὰ καὶ καυχώμενοι ἐν τῷ Θεῷ διὰ τοῦ Κυρίου ἡμῶν Ἰησοῦ Χριστοῦ, δι' οὗ νῦν τὴν καταλλαγὴν ἐλάβομεν.

v.11 *And not only so, but we also joy in God through our Lord Jesus Christ, by whom we have now received the atonement. (KJV)*

He has in view vv. 2 & 3. Not only do we boast in the hope of glory, and in afflictions, but also in God Himself, namely, that He is our God, that He loves us as a Father, cherishes and keeps us, and that we are His children. Not only do we boast about future glory and blessedness, but we also boast about our present status, that God has been reconciled to us through Christ and embraces us with fatherly love. This explanation is deduced from the particle νῦν [now].

"To boast in the Lord" is taken differently in the last verse of 1 Cor. 1 than it is in this passage. There it means to attribute all things to the working of God with praise and thanks.

v.12 Διὰ τοῦτο, ὥσπερ δι' ἑνὸς ἀνθρώπου ἡ ἁμαρτία εἰς τὸν

κόσμον εἰσῆλθε, καὶ διὰ τῆς ἁμαρτίας ὁ θάνατος, καὶ οὕτως εἰς πάντας ἀνθρώπους ὁ θάνατος διῆλθεν, ἐφ᾽ ᾧ πάντες ἥμαρτον.

v.12 Wherefore, as by one man sin entered into the world, and death by sin; and so death passed upon all men, for that all have sinned: (KJV)

Some want this to be understood prismatically, as a consequence, from the immediately preceding verses. Since we received reconciliation through Christ, the consequence is that Christ, as a Second Adam, is contrasted with the first Adam. The illative particle διὰ τοῦτο [on account of this] favors this interpretation.

The application, or the apodosis, is omitted by the Apostle, and should be supplied in this way: "...so through one Man, namely, Christ, righteousness came into the world, and through righteousness, eternal life."

Δι᾽ ἑνὸς ἀνθρώπου [Through one man]. Paul does not understand here the unity of sex, but of species.

Ἡ ἁμαρτία εἰς τὸν κόσμον εἰσῆλθε [Sin came into the world]. Augustine in *Enchiridion*, ch. 26: "Here the Apostle named the entire human race with the word 'world.'"

Therefore: (1) Mary is not exempt from sharing in original sin. (2) Sin spread into the world, not by imitation, but by propagation.

In the verbs εἰσῆλθε καὶ διῆλθε [it came into and spread] there is an elegant paronomasia. For διῆλθε [it spread] properly means "it went throughout," namely, in this way, like a pestilence that spreads throughout an entire gathering and so infects them. Augustine, Sermon 4, *On the Words of the Apostle*: "It spread thoroughly. Pay attention to the word that you have heard; consider and see. What was it that spread thoroughly? This is why a small child is guilty. He did not commit sin; he contracted it. Indeed, sin did not remain in its source, but spread thoroughly. It spread thoroughly, not to this one or to that one, but to all men." Sermon 7, *On the Words of the Apostle*, skillfully deduces from the same verb that "sin and death did not stop with Adam, but thoroughly spread from him and out of him to all his posterity."

Ἐφ᾿ ᾧ πάντες ἥμαρτον [upon which all people sinned]. Most of the ancients explain: "In whom, namely, Adam, all sinned. Namely, all men were in his loins, just as Levi is said to have tithed in Abraham, in whose loins he was (Heb. 7:9). Likewise in Adam all men are said to have died, that is, they became subject to death (1 Cor. 15:22). Therefore, all sinned in Adam as in a common tree from which all men proceed as branches."

But since ἐπὶ [upon] is hardly ever known to be used in this sense for ἐν [in], and since this interpretation depends on the nearest preceding words, in which there is no mention of Adam (for it seems too difficult to refer the relative pronoun to the name of the "one man" who was mentioned in the beginning of the verse), therefore it is simpler to explain it causally, "because all sinned."

There is an example of this meaning in Rom. 8:3, ἐν ᾧ [in which], that is ἐφ᾿ ᾧ [upon which], "because it was weakened by the flesh." 2 Cor. 5:4, ἐφ᾿ ᾧ οὐ θέλομεν [upon which we do not want], "because of which we do not want to be unclothed." The Syriac likewise translates בְּהָי, "because." Luther: "*dieweil* [since]." It is, nevertheless, to be understood with the verb ἥμαρτον [they sinned] that all sinned in Adam, that is, that from Adam all contract sin, namely, through carnal generation. For what he says in this passage, that "all sinned," he explains in verse 19, "they were made sinners," for it is an idiom of the Hebrew language to express a condition with an action verb.

"Death spread thoroughly to all, because all sinned," that is, because Adam sinned, being the father of the human race, representing the person of all his posterity who descend from him by carnal generation. He who was made in the divine image had received those gifts not only for himself, but also for all of his posterity.

Observe: This is the proper *sedes doctrinae* of original sin, which entered into the world, not by imitation, but by propagation, οὐ μιμήσει ἀλλὰ φύσει [not by imitation but by nature]. (1) For if the apostolic purpose were to deal with the imitation of sin, then he would have said rather, according to the example of Christ in John 8:41, that sin entered into the world through the angel, for he sinned first. This is the observation of Augustine in Bk. 1, *On the Merits and Forgiveness of Sins*, ch. 9. (2) And since many actually sin who are ignorant of Adam's sin, it cannot be said of them that the sin of Adam injures them by example. This is also the observation of Augustine, Bk. 6, *Against Julian*, ch. 12.

(3) The particle διὰ [through] with the genitive expresses the true and proper cause of a thing. But those who sin do not sin in order to imitate Adam. Consequently, if the Apostle were speaking only about imitation, he couldn't have said that "through one man sin entered into the world."

Schmaltzius objects to this in his refutation of Dr. Frantzius' second disputation, *On Original Sin*, p.45. "The Apostle affirms that not an inherent corruption of nature, but death spread thoroughly to all; not because men are participants in the first guilt, but because they themselves sin. Nonetheless, we do not deny that, due to the propagation itself that all men have from Adam, they, too, are subject to eternal death, even if they do not sin. Just as also all who believe in Christ will obtain eternal life, even if they are not as obedient as Christ was, on account of the propagation that they have from Christ, which is nothing other than faith in Christ."

We reply: Schmaltzius advances points that cannot be defended.[52] For (1) if all men, due to the propagation that they have from Adam, are subject to eternal death, then certainly sin is also propagated to them by Adam. For it is not the propagation of nature, as such, that makes a man subject to eternal death, but insofar as it is a propagation of a nature that has been corrupted by sin. (2) The Apostle does not only say that death spread to all men, but also that sin entered the world through one man. This sin is nothing other than the inherent corruption of nature. (3) As through sin, death entered the world, so through one man, sin entered the world. But sin is the proper cause of death, not the improper cause as if death came either by chance or by accident. Therefore that one sinful man is also the proper cause of the sin that is propagated to his posterity. If he only did injury by example, only by accident,

---

52 ἀσύστατα

then he would also be the cause of sin by chance. (4) The Apostle teaches that the righteousness of Christ is not communicated to us by propagation, but by imputation (Rom. 4:6).

v.13 Ἄχρι γὰρ νόμου ἁμαρτία ἦν ἐν κόσμῳ, ἁμαρτία δὲ οὐκ ἐλλογεῖται, μὴ ὄντος νόμου.

v.13 *For until the law sin was in the world: but sin is not imputed when there is no law. (KJV)*

Vulgate: "Sin was not imputed, since there was no law." But the Greek has a different sense: "Sin is not imputed when there is no law." For Paul would seem to be affirming that there was no law, which is not true. Rather, he is speaking hypothetically, that sin would not be imputed if there were no law.

From the fact that men died even before the law, he proves that the guilt of sin did not take hold only after the law was given by Moses and violated. For if death took place before the law, then certainly also sin took place before the law, since sin is the cause of death. Then, in turn, since sin existed at that time, he concludes from that that there was also a certain law at that time, since apart from law sin is not imputed. The sense, then, is this: Although sin was not reckoned before Moses, it was in the world, since at the time when the law was not yet solemnly pronounced, sin was already in the world, and indeed, already from the time of Adam onward. He proves this in the following verse from the effect of sin, namely, death.

But the Syriac clearly renders it the opposite way and inverts the genuine sense. "For until the law, sin, although it was in the world, was not reckoned as sin, because there was no law." But (1) although the law had not yet at that time been pronounced, it was still written in the hearts of all. (2) How was sin not imputed at that time, since all people died on account of sin? Those words ἄχρι νόμου [until law] are to be taken exclusively, that is, "until the end of the law and the advent of Christ," as Origen concludes.

Οὐκ ἐλλογεῖται [It is not reckoned], that is, ἐν λόγῳ οὐκ ἔστι [it is not in thought], "its reckoning is not counted." Therefore, when

234

it says that sin is not imputed when there is no law, it means that
its force and fury is not easily noticed apart from the law. Luther:
"*da achtet man der Sünde nicht* [there one does not pay attention to
sin]." But we demonstrated above that it is more correctly understood concerning the divine imputation. The word is used with
this meaning in Rom. 4:3-6.

v.14 Ἀλλ᾽ ἐβασίλευσεν ὁ θάνατος ἀπὸ Ἀδὰμ μέχρι Μωϋσέως καὶ
ἐπὶ τοὺς μὴ ἁμαρτήσαντας ἐπὶ τῷ ὁμοιώματι τῆς παραβάσεως Ἀδάμ,
ὅς ἐστι τύπος τοῦ μέλλοντος.

v.14 *Nevertheless death reigned from Adam to Moses, even over them
that had not sinned after the similitude of Adam's transgression, who is
the figure of him that was to come.* (KJV)

That the death that ruled in the world even before Moses, that
is, before the Mosaic pronouncement of the law, was not brought
about by a certain sin on the part of individuals, but was the wages
of original sin propagated by Adam, he proves from the fact that
even infants died, who did not transgress the natural law actually
and voluntarily in the same way as Adam. The sense, then, is this:
Whatever there may be to that objection that before Moses there
was no law and, therefore, no sin, the effect itself, that is, death,
testifies that there was also sin in the world before the law was
pronounced by Moses.

Ἐβασίλευσεν ὁ θάνατος [Death reigned]. Death, like a king who
has conquered his enemies, raged against men. But since the devil
has the power of death (Heb. 2:14), therefore it is understood that
the devil reigned through death.

Καὶ ἐπὶ τοὺς μὴ ἁμαρτήσαντας ἐπὶ τῷ ὁμοιώματι τῆς παραβάσεως
Ἀδάμ [Even upon those who did not sin according to the likeness
of the transgression of Adam]. Marloratus says that this is to be
understood concerning those who sinned without the law (Rom.
2:12). But the conjunction καὶ [and], which in this passage should
be translated "even," is opposed to that explanation, since it infers
some distinction between men. Moreover, if this were the sense of
Paul's words, that death reigned even in those who did not have

the will of God unquestionably revealed by the oracle of God as Adam did, but only the testimony of conscience, then the conjunction καὶ [and] would be superfluous. For there would be no need here of a distinction, since the phrase, "they sinned without the law," applies to each and every man from the fall of Adam until the giving of the law. In other words, they had no knowledge of the law of Moses, and they did not violate it as it was publicly handed down inscribed on tablets.

Joh. Driedo contends that "the Greek text in this passage is corrupt, since Ambrose contends that it should rather be read with the negation removed, "to those who sinned in the likeness of the transgression of Adam." Indeed, this is how Tertullian, Victorinus and Cyprian read it long ago, even if the corrupted Greek manuscripts disagree now that they have been translated into Latin, since the manuscripts of the translation remained purer due to the simplicity of the times."

We reply: (1) All the Latin manuscripts today read with the negation added. Therefore, they would all have to be corrupt.

(2) The Syriac likewise has the negation added.

(3) The context favors this reading. The Apostle is teaching on the basis of the result, that all men are guilty of sin, even infants who do not sin like Adam, that is, intentionally. For that is what Paul is teaching, that the guilt of sin results in the penalty of death, which it would not do if death were not said to have reigned over all who sinned according to the likeness of Adam, since infants, over whom the same death reigned even though they did not share in the likeness of sin, could be exempted.

But how can it be said of infants that they did not sin according to the likeness of the transgression of Adam, since original sin also produces actual sins in infants? We reply: Some actual sins are committed intentionally; others unintentionally. The Apostle is properly speaking of the former when he denies that infants sin according to the likeness of Adam, that is, intentionally.

Ὅς ἐστι τύπος τοῦ μέλλοντος [Who is a type of the coming One], that is, of Christ. Syriac: "of Him who was to come." The Apostle later declares this very thing more extensively in this way: As Adam communicates sin and death to all who are born from him, so Christ communicates righteousness and life to all who are grafted into Him by faith.

Τύπος [type] in this passage is not used in the same way that figures in the Old Testament are sometimes called "types." For there is only a comparison being set up here between Adam and Christ, and indeed, more of a comparison of dissimilar than of similar things. The protasis of this likeness is set forth in v.12; the apodosis is not added with expressed words, but is only insinuated.

Τύπος [type], therefore, here means only "likeness," which is also how the Syriac renders it, רְמוּתָא.

v.15 Ἀλλ' οὐχ ὡς τὸ παράπτωμα, οὕτω καὶ τὸ χάρισμα. Εἰ γὰρ τῷ τοῦ ἑνὸς παραπτώματι οἱ πολλοὶ ἀπέθανον, πολλῷ μᾶλλον ἡ χάρις τοῦ Θεοῦ, καὶ ἡ δωρεὰ ἐν χάριτι τῇ τοῦ ἑνὸς ἀνθρώπου Ἰησοῦ Χριστοῦ εἰς τοὺς πολλοὺς ἐπερίσσευσε.

v.15 But not as the offence, so also is the free gift. For if through the offence of one many be dead, much more the grace of God, and the gift by grace, which is by one man, Jesus Christ, hath abounded unto many. (KJV)

He had said that Adam is similar to Christ. Now he submits how they are different. The similarity consists in the fact that each of them propagates to his own that which belongs to him. The difference consists, first of all, in that Adam propagates guilt by nature for the destruction of his posterity, whereas Christ communicates righteousness by grace for the salvation of His own. For the word χάρισμα [free gift] demonstrates that this is the force of the comparison. Secondly, they are different in that the power for justifying and saving that passes down from Christ to believers is more efficacious than the power of sin and death that is propagated by Adam to his posterity. For the particles πολλῷ μᾶλλον [much more] and ἐπερίσσευσε [it abounded] demonstrate that this is the force of the comparison.

Τὸ χάρισμα [The free gift] is that which passes down from the grace of God, the kindness that God shows to man. Luther has *"Gabe* [gift]." In the next verse Paul calls it τὸ δώρημα, "the benefit." With both nouns he understands the righteousness obtained by the death of Christ that is communicated by grace, through imputation, to those who believe in Him. The Syriac has the noun מַוהַבתָא, "gift," for both words.

From the fact that many are said to have died by the transgression of one, the Pelagians deduced long ago—as the Photinians do today—that "the sin of Adam only harms his posterity by example and imitation. For if it did harm by propagation, then it would certainly harm all, not just many." We reply: (1) The Apostle himself explains the word πολλοὶ [many] universally in verse 12: "Sin entered into the world, and death through sin, and in this way it spread to all men, because all sinned." Verse 18: "Through one transgression, guilt came to all men." (2) Therefore, the word "many" is being used indefinitely; it is not meant in this passage to restrict, but to broaden. "Many were made sinners," that is, "all," which is certainly also "many." Augustine, Bk. 6, *Against Julian*, ch. 12, brings together these two propositions. "I have made you the father of many nations. And in your Seed all nations will be blessed." Later he adds: "The sound meaning is that the Scripture has spoken in this way because sometimes 'all' can mean things that are not 'many,' and again, sometimes 'many' can mean things that are not 'all.'"

Ἀπέθανον [They died]. By the fall of one, many died, that is, because of the fall of one, namely, Adam, all men are bound to die. The Hebrew words often signify, not the act, but what the outcome is supposed to be. In Psa. 32:9, "the way in which you go," means "the way in which you ought to go." In Heb. 5:4, "no one will take," means that "no one ought to take." The Apostle, then, has in mind the primeval threat (Gen. 2:17).

Ἡ χάρις τοῦ θεοῦ καὶ ἡ δωρεὰ [The grace and the gift of God] is "the gift that passes down from the grace of God," namely, the righteousness obtained by the death of Christ which God gives by grace to believers.

Ἐν χάριτι τῇ τοῦ ἑνὸς ἀνθρώπου Ἰησοῦ Χριστοῦ [In the grace that is of the one Man Jesus Christ]. Luther translates: "*Durch Jesum Christum / der der einige Mensch in Gnaden war* [Through Jesus Christ, who was the only man in grace]." The Syriac translates in practically the same way: "Because of the one Son of Man, Jesus Christ." In other manuscripts it reads: "*Durch die einige Gnade des Menschen Jesu Christi* [Through the singular grace of the man Jesus Christ]," that is, through the merit of Christ, which is imputed to us by grace.

Ἐπερίσσευσε, "abounded, was poured out abundantly," so that it is a metaphor taken from overflowing rivers. The Syriac has the verb יָתַר, which is used of both quantity and quality, "abounded, excelled."

v.16 Καὶ οὐχ ὡς δι᾽ ἑνὸς ἁμαρτήσαντος, τὸ δώρημα· τὸ μὲν γὰρ κρίμα ἐξ ἑνὸς εἰς κατάκριμα, τὸ δὲ χάρισμα ἐκ πολλῶν παραπτωμάτων εἰς δικαίωμα.

v.16 *And not as it was by one that sinned, so is the gift: for the judgment was by one to condemnation, but the free gift is of many offences unto justification.* (KJV)

He explains the third difference, namely, that guilt went forth from Adam to all of his posterity; but the righteousness of Christ that has been freely given by imputation not only absolves believers from the guilt of original sin, but also from all other guilt of actual sins.

There are numerous ellipses in this verse. Καὶ οὐχ ὡς δι᾽ ἑνὸς ἁμαρτήσαντος, τὸ δώρημα [But not as through the one who sinned]. "Nor as that which entered through one who sinned is the gift," that is, it does not take place with the gift as it did when, through one who sinned, namely, Adam, it entered into the world, that is, as with the sin and death that were propagated from Adam to us all. Καὶ [and/even/but] in this passage is adversative, according to the Hebrew usage.

Τὸ μὲν γὰρ κρίμα ἐξ ἑνὸς εἰς κατάκριμα [For the judgment from one for condemnation]. *For the judgment*, that is, the charge of the guilt in the judgment, *is from one*, namely, from the fall, from one offense, *for condemnation*; τὸ δὲ χάρισμα, *but grace*, or the gift through grace, that God shows kindness to man, *from many falls*, that is, not only from the fall of Adam, but also from each man's own fall, *for justification*, namely, is given. The Syriac adds הָיָה, "was for righteousness."

Aristotle defines τὸ δικαίωμα [righteousness] as τὸ ἐπανόρθωμα τοῦ ἀδικήματος [the amendment of wrong] (5. *Nicomachean Ethics*, ch. 7). But that "amendment" or correction of wrong is either active or passive. *Active* is that which happens through legal action and through the execution of the judicial sentence. It is *passive* when the defendant who committed the wrong pays the due penalties and then is constrained to obedience. Michael of Ephesus, ch. 9, *Ethics*: "Δικαιοῦσθαι [to be justified] means 'to receive justice;' it refers both to the one who receives that which was stolen from him by the criminal, and also to the one who is punished by the law."

In this passage, δικαίωμα [righteousness] is that on account of which a man is absolved from transgression, or the ἀδικία [unrighteousness] that results from transgression, namely, the righteousness of Christ imputed through faith. It is also the actual absolution from that unrighteousness on account of the righteousness of Christ imputed by faith, which is properly δικαίωσις [justification].

v.17 Εἰ γὰρ τῷ τοῦ ἑνὸς παραπτώματι ὁ θάνατος ἐβασίλευσε διὰ τοῦ ἑνός, πολλῷ μᾶλλον οἱ τὴν περισσείαν τῆς χάριτος καὶ τῆς δωρεᾶς τῆς δικαιοσύνης λαμβάνοντες, ἐν ζωῇ βασιλεύσουσι διὰ τοῦ ἑνὸς Ἰησοῦ Χριστοῦ.

v.17 For if by one man's offence death reigned by one; much more they which receive abundance of grace and of the gift of righteousness shall reign in life by one, Jesus Christ. (KJV)

He concludes from the points of dissimilarity that have been demonstrated thus far that the righteousness of Christ, imputed by faith, is more efficacious for conveying life to believers than was the unrighteousness of Adam, propagated to them by carnal generation, for conferring death on them.

Τῷ τοῦ ἑνὸς παραπτώματι [By the trespass of the one]. Through and because of that transgression "of the one," namely, of the first man, death reigned.

With τὴν περισσείαν τῆς χάριτος καὶ τῆς δωρεᾶς τῆς δικαιοσύνης [the abundance of grace and of the gift of righteousness], he understands the righteousness obtained by the death of Christ which is given by grace to believers and abounds more than sin.

The papists understand "grace" as inherent righteousness, a gift inhering in the soul, since the Apostle adds the word δωρεᾶς [gift]. Therefore, Bellarmine: "He changes the abundance of giving into the abundance of gifts."

We reply: (1) The Apostle himself explains sufficiently clearly what he means with that "abundance of grace and the giving of righteousness," or "the gifts of grace," namely, the gracious reconciliation with God, made through Christ (v.10), "justification through His blood" (v.9), "the fullness of grace for righteousness" (v.15), "justification of life through the obedience and righteousness of Christ" (v.15). (2) In Eph. 2:7 he calls this περισσείαν τῆς χάριτος καὶ τῆς δωρεᾶς τῆς δικαιοσύνης [abundance of grace and of the gift of righteousness] the "ὑπερβάλλοντα πλοῦτον τῆς χάριτος [abundant riches of grace]." But this περισσεία [abundance], this πλοῦτος χάριτος [riches of grace] cannot be taken to refer to infused qualities or inherent righteousness, since the περισσεία [abundance] of spiritual gifts in the saints is not such, since they only receive the firstfruits of the Spirit (Rom. 8:23). (3) In v.20 he adds, "Where sin abounded, there grace ὑπερεπερίσσευσεν [superabounded]," where the same word περισσείας [abundance] is used. But that abundance of grace cannot be taken to refer to infused gifts except in an extremely absurd way. (4) The word δωρεᾶς [gift] does not directly infer a gift of inherent righteousness, since Christ is also the gift of God, and the righteousness of Christ is also the gift of God, and yet neither Christ nor the righteousness of Christ formally inhere in us. (5) That which resulted from many offenses is the same thing that resulted from all offenses. For if not all were condemned, then there would be no salvation, since he who sins in one thing is charged with all. But the infusion of righteousness is not being contrasted with all sins. "For if we say that we have no sin..." Therefore, this abundance of righteousness that is contrasted with all sins is not the infusion of righteousness.

v.18 Ἄρα οὖν ὡς δι᾿ ἑνὸς παραπτώματος εἰς πάντας ἀνθρώπους, εἰς κατάκριμα, οὕτω καὶ δι᾿ ἑνὸς δικαιώματος εἰς πάντας ἀνθρώπους εἰς δικαίωσιν ζωῆς.

v.18 Therefore as by the offence of one judgment came upon all men to condemnation; even so by the righteousness of one the free gift came upon all men unto justification of life. (KJV)

This verse is a summary of everything that came before. That I may briefly summarize, Paul says, what I have said thus far concerning the comparison between Adam and Christ, the matter comes down to this: Just as the guilt that was contracted from one transgression of Adam sentences all men to death, so the righteousness of Christ that is imputed to believers by faith justifies them, so that they are again made participants in the eternal life that had been lost in Adam and through Adam.

ὡς δι᾿ ἑνὸς παραπτώματος, εἰς πάντας ἀνθρώπους, εἰς κατάκριμα [As through one trespass, upon all men, unto condemnation]. *Just as through one offense*, namely, guilt came *upon all men for condemnation*. The Syriac translates: "Just as through sin, condemnation was to all the children of men." The Apostle contrasts τὸ παράπτωμα [the trespass] of Adam and τὸ δικαίωμα [the righteousness] of Christ. Likewise, he contrasts the κατάκριμα [condemnation] that was propagated to all from Adam's transgression with the δικαίωσιν ζωῆς [justification of life] that traces its origin from the δικαιώματι [righteousness] of Christ and flows down to all.

Οὕτω καὶ δι᾿ ἑνὸς δικαιώματος εἰς πάντας ἀνθρώπους, εἰς δικαίωσιν ζωῆς [So also through the righteousness of one, upon all men, unto justification of life]. *So through one Man's righteousness*, namely, the benefit overflowed *to all men for justification of life*, that is, salvific justification. For it is called "justification of life" because the goal and consequence of it is life and eternal salvation.

But how did the righteousness of Christ overflow to all men for justi-

fication, since not all men are justified? We reply: The Apostle is not talking about the application of the benefit, but about the acquisition of the benefit. If we want to descend to the application, that universality must be restricted to those who are grafted into Christ by faith. For as the unrighteousness of Adam is communicated to all those who are descended from him by carnal generation, so the righteousness of Christ is communicated to all those who are grafted into Him through faith and spiritual regeneration.

v.19 Ὥσπερ γὰρ διὰ τῆς παρακοῆς τοῦ ἑνὸς ἀνθρώπου, ἁμαρτωλοὶ κατεστάθησαν οἱ πολλοί, οὕτω καὶ διὰ τῆς ὑπακοῆς τοῦ ἑνὸς δίκαιοι κατασταθήσονται οἱ πολλοί.

v.19 For as by one man's disobedience many were made sinners, so by the obedience of one shall many be made righteous. (KJV)

He demonstrates the basis for the preceding comparison, which consists in this: These two men have been set up as two stocks from which righteousness and life are propagated to others. For Adam was set up in the first creation as the stock from which righteousness and life should be propagated to all his posterity. But since he turned away from God through sin, unrighteousness and death are propagated from him to all his posterity. Therefore, God, out of grace, took pity on the human race and opened up to us another source of righteousness and life. He sent Christ the Mediator, from whom, as a stock and a tree of life, righteousness and life should be communicated to all who are grafted into Him by faith. What he had earlier called παράπτωμα [trespass] he now calls παρακοήν [disobedience], since the origin and source of transgression was disobedience. And what he had earlier called δικαίωμα [righteousness], he now calls ὑπακοήν [obedience], since Christ, by obeying His heavenly Father unto death, even death on a cross (Phil. 2:9), acquired that righteousness for us. Then, in turn, what he had said earlier—that by one transgression, κατάκριμα [condemnation] came upon all—he now brings out in this passage, saying that "many were made sinners," since that propagation of sin and contraction of guilt is the cause of condemnation. And what he had said earlier—through one Man's righteousness the benefit overflowed to all εἰς δικαίωσιν [unto justification]—he now brings out here, saying that "through one Man's obedience many were made righteous." But he uses a verb in the future tense on account of τοὺς μέλλοντας πιστεύειν [those who are going to believe].

Godly men of old have this to say about this contrast between Adam and Christ:

Irenaeus, Book 5, ch. 18, p. 342: "Just as through one conquered man our race descended into death, so again through one conquering Man we have ascended into life. And just as death won the victory over us through a man, so again we have won the victory over death through a Man."

Augustine, Epistle 57 *To Dardan*, q. 2: "In the case of Adam, it became clear how the choice of a man availed for death; in the case of Christ, how the assistance of God availed for life." He says the same thing in Bk. 2, *On Original Sin*, ch. 24: "The Christian faith properly consists in the case of these two men. Through one of them we were sold under sin; through the other we are redeemed from sins. One of these men brought us to ruin in himself by doing his own will rather than the will of Him by whom he was made; the other Man saved us in Himself by not doing His own will, but the will of Him by whom He was sent."

Lyranus on this passage: "Just as through the disobedience of Adam his posterity were made unrighteous, so through the obedience of Christ many have been justified in the tree of the cross."

The Papists try to wrest out of this passage that "we are justified through an infused and inherent righteousness."

Pererius on this passage: "Paul did not say that they were made sinners 'by the disobedience of Adam,'[53] lest anyone should imagine that they were made sinners through imputed disobedience. Rather, he said 'through disobedience,'[54] namely, the disobedience brought about by the sin that dwells intrinsically in them from Adam's disobedience. Similarly, then, it is not that the obedience

53 Latin: *inobaedientia Adami*
54 Latin: *per inobaedientiam*

of Christ makes them righteous, as if men became righteous, not through an inherent righteousness, but through an imputed righteousness. Rather, they are made righteous through the obedience of Christ, because this was the meritorious cause."

We reply: This presupposes that the phrases "to become righteous by righteousness" and "to become unrighteous by unrighteousness" are meant only formally; while the other phrases, "to become righteous through righteousness" and "to become unrighteous through unrighteousness," are meant only meritoriously. And yet Pererius himself is forced to deny this hypothesis when τὸ διὰ πίστεως [the phrase "through faith"] (Rom. 3:22,30) is interpreted formally. Thus in 2 Tim. 3:15, faith is not the cause because of which a person merits becoming wise for salvation, but is rather itself the essence[55] of that wisdom. Thus when, in Gal. 5:6, "faith" is said to work "through love," love cannot be understood as the meritorious cause because of which faith works.

Bellarmine himself, Bk. 2, *On Justification*, ch. 3, says: "We are justified through His grace, that is, through the righteousness given and infused by Him. This is the formal cause." Bellarmine, Bk. 2, *On Justification*, ch. 3: "Through the unrighteousness of Adam we were made unrighteous, by an unrighteousness that truly and really inheres in us, not by imputed unrighteousness. Therefore, in the same way we are made righteous through the obedience of Christ, by a righteousness that inheres in us."

Becanus, part 1, *On Justification*, ch. 2, sect. 14: "Just as we were made unrighteous through the disobedience of Adam, so through the obedience of Christ we are made righteous. Yet we are made unrighteous through Adam's disobedience, not formally, but only efficiently and meritoriously. Therefore we are also made righteous through the obedience of Christ, not formally, but only efficiently and meritoriously."

We reply: (1) The comparison between the disobedience of Adam and the obedience of Christ is not being set up in a simple and absolute manner, but according to something in particular.

---

55 Latin: *forma*

For the Apostle is considering (a) the causes of our salvation and condemnation—that just as the condemnation derives its origin from Adam's disobedience, so our salvation draws its origin from Christ's obedience; and (b) the propagation and effects of Christ's obedience and of Adam's disobedience—that just as through the disobedience of one man, many were made sinners, so through the obedience of Christ they are made righteous.

(2) But by no means is this comparison to be extended to the mode of propagation and communication, which the Apostle is obviously not treating in this passage; he dealt with that in the preceding verses, teaching that the righteousness of Christ is imputed to us by faith, while Adam's sin is propagated to us by carnal generation.

(3) Now, if we wanted to go beyond the limits of the apostolic comparison, someone could infer from the same that the righteousness of Christ is propagated to us through carnal generation, since the unrighteousness of Adam is communicated to us in that manner. Likewise, one could infer that the righteousness of Christ is propagated to all men at once, without any regard for faith or unbelief, since the sin of Adam is propagated to all through carnal generation.

(4) But since that is absurd, a distinction must definitely be made between the acquisition and the application of the merit of Christ, that is, between the benefit itself and participation in the benefit. *The acquisition of the merit*, that is, the benefit itself obtained by the death of Christ, is general. For as Adam, by his disobedience, enveloped all of his posterity in the guilt of sin, so Christ, who suffered and died for the sins of all, also merited and acquired liberation from this guilt and righteousness for all. But this benefit is only applied to those who are grafted into Christ by faith, and only they become participants in this benefit.

(5) The contrast in this apostolic text between justification and condemnation is clear (v. 16 and v. 18). But since they are contrasted under the same genre, and condemnation is, to be sure, a judicial act, from that it follows that justification is also a judicial act,

and therefore it consists, not in the infusion of righteousness, but in the absolution from sins. Indeed, as through the sin of Adam, sin is propagated to all men, which results in condemnation for them—in other words, because of this propagation all men are damned by the righteous judgment of God unless reconciliation and remission take place—so through the merit of Christ, righteousness and salvation have been obtained for all, so that they may be justified by faith—that is, pronounced righteous, absolved from sins and freed from condemnation.

(6) "To be made righteous" and "to be justified" are considered by the Apostle to be equivalent expressions.[56] Therefore, "to be made righteous" (and "to be justified" in v. 18) is contrasted with "condemnation" in v.19. Each, therefore, has a forensic meaning. The verb κατασταθήσονται [they will be made] indicates that these things are carried out before the tribunal of God, the righteous Judge, who condemns Adam's posterity on account of sin, but absolves believers in Christ from that damnation and makes them righteous (Rom. 10:3, 2 Cor. 5:21).

(7) By no semblance of truth can it be denied that the sin of Adam is imputed to his posterity. For although the corruption of nature that arises from Adam's sin inheres in his posterity, nevertheless it cannot be denied that Adam's sin, from which the corruption of nature arises, is imputed to them (Exo. 20:5, Rom. 5:13). For as soon as our first parents sinned, in whose loins was the entire human race, and who received gifts not only for themselves, but also for their posterity, their transgression was reckoned as the transgression of the entire human race, and therefore was imputed to all of them, so that they were damned before they were born. Thus Bellarmine himself, Bk. 4, *On the Loss of Grace*, ch. 10, writes: "The sin of Adam is imputed to all his posterity in such a way as if all had committed the same sin." He also cites the saying of Bernhard: "Adam's guilt is ours, for although it was in another, nevertheless we sinned; and it was imputed to us by God's righteous (but hidden) judgment."

Stapletonus in his *Antidote* on this passage presses the verb

---

56 ἰσοδυναμοῦσι

κατασταθήσονται [they will be made]. "This vocable," he says, "is most suitable for explaining inherent righteousness, for its usage in Scripture teaches that it does not mean imputation, but the true and inherent acquisition and possession (Luke 12). Psalm 8 and Hebrews 2 place Him over all things. 'You placed Him over all the works of Your hands.' James 2, 'He is made an enemy of God.'"

We reply: (1) Some maintain that the verb "to be made" applies to the status of believers in the future age, in which they will be made righteous by inherent righteousness—and that, a most perfect righteousness. The benefits of Christ are not limited to this life; they extend also into the future life. Therefore, in this way this phrase would designate the effect of justification. The words of the Apostle amount to this: Those who receive the abundance of grace and of the gift of righteousness will reign in life. For they seem to be distinct times. They receive the abundance of the gift, already given in this life; yet they do not "reign" in life, but "will reign," namely, someday and in the age to come.

(2) In justification, believers are truly made righteous through the imputed righteousness of Christ—much like when a servant is at some time placed by his lord over all his goods, or when man is placed by God over all the works of His hands. But it does not follow if someone wishes to infer from this truth an inherence of righteousness. Nor in the examples cited is inherence necessarily established. A man is made lord of creation, not by inherence, but by relationship. A man is not made a friend of God by some affection inhering in the man himself, since God loved those who did not exist.

v.20 Νόμος δὲ παρεισῆλθεν, ἵνα πλεονάσῃ τὸ παράπτωμα. Οὗ δὲ ἐπλεόνασεν ἡ ἁμαρτία, ὑπερεπερίσσευσεν ἡ χάρις.

v.20 *Moreover the law entered, that the offence might abound. But where sin abounded, grace did much more abound: (KJV)*

The Apostle runs to meet the objection that could have been raised against the things he has said up till now. *If, then, sin was already in the world from Adam, and death ruled over all those who were descended from Adam so that no one can stand before God with his own righteousness, why was the law pronounced after the fall of Adam?* We reply: The Apostle answers that the law was pronounced, not in order to abolish sin, but in order to show sin, and so that, in this way, grace may be commended all the more. For where sin is perceived more strongly, there the benefit furnished for us in Christ is perceived more clearly.

Νόμος παρεισῆλθε [The Law entered alongside], that is, παρὰ τὴν ἐπαγγελίαν εἰσῆλθε [it entered alongside the promise], "it entered for the sake of the promise of grace." Some refer here to Adam and Christ, so that the sense is: It entered between Adam and Christ.

The Syriac translates it simply. מֶעֲלָנָא, εἴσοδος [entrance], namely, "the entrance that was to the law." In other words, entrance was given to the law in order that sin might increase. The root is עלל, which to the Syrians means "it went in." Luther: "*das Gesetz ist neben einkommen* [the Law came in beside]."

With νόμον [Law], Origen understands "the law of the members," that is, the law of sin inhering in the members (Rom. 7:23). But Chrysostom and Ambrose understand it more correctly as the law pronounced through Moses. The Apostle had said of this in Rom. 3:20 that through it is the recognition of sin.

Ἵνα πλεοάσῃ τὸ παράπτωμα [In order that the transgression may abound], "that sin may abound," that is, so that by it, sin may be better recognized and its power more greatly felt. For where there is no law, there sin is not recognized or esteemed. The pertinent rule is this: Active verbs in Hebrew are often taken declaratively. Lev. 13:14: טִמֵא, "he made unclean," that is, "he declared." 2 Sam. 15:4, Pro. 17:15: הִצְדִּיק, "he made righteous," that is, "he declared." Job 10:2, Pro. 17:15: הִרְשִׁיעַ, "he made wicked," that is, "he pronounced wicked."

Chrysostom advises that the particle ἵνα [so that] is not introducing a purpose clause, but a result clause; it is not giving the cause, but rather denotes the outcome. But it can easily be taken causally, since after the Fall, the chief purpose for which the law has been given is to show and to charge with sin (Rom. 3:20, 7:7; Gal. 3:22, etc.).

Jerome, q. 8 *To Algasia:* "The law was given to show the poison of sin."

Ambrose on Rom. 7: "The law is an index of sin, not a genitrix of it, causing sinners to be guilty."

Augustine, *De Medic. Poenit.*, ch. 1: "The law was given for this purpose, that it may expose the wounds of sins, which it heals by the benediction of grace."

Οὗ δὲ ἐπλεόνασεν ἡ ἁμαρτία, ὑπερεπερίσσευσεν ἡ χάρις [But where sin increased, grace abounded exceedingly]. The verb ὑπερεπερίσσευσεν [abounded exceedingly] is emphatic, "superabounded." This is not the same as saying that liquid abounds in such a way that what is superfluous is poured out, but it is like saying that it abounds exceedingly and beyond measure. For in Greek, ὑπὲρ [over] intensifies the meaning. Rom. 8:37, ὑπερνικοῦμεν [we conquer exceedingly]. 2 Cor. 12:7, ὑπεραίρομαι [I am exalted beyond measure]. 2 The. 1:3, ὑπεραυξάνω [to grow exceedingly]. Besides this, there is in the verb περισσεύειν [to abound] a clear sense of abundance, using the metaphor drawn from overflowing rivers. This is intensified with the particle ὑπὲρ [over]. 2 Cor. 7:4, ὑπερπερισσεύομαι τῇ χαρᾷ [I abound exceedingly in joy]. Mark 7:37, ὑπερπερισσῶς ἐξεπλήσσοντο [they were superabundantly amazed].

Lexicographers say that this is a rarer usage of these expressions. The result is that this abundance of grace itself is thus commended by means of the rarity of the word.

The grace of Christ, he says, is more efficacious and more abundant than the fall of Adam (1) because it not only takes away original sin, but also all the actual sins of those who believe in Christ; (2) because the unrighteousness of Adam is infinite evil only with regard to the object (since it was committed against infinite Good) and with regard to the effect (since it merits infinite and eternal penalties). But the righteousness of Christ is infinite, not only with regard to the object (since it was furnished to the heavenly Father who is infinite Good); not only with regard to the effect (since it merited eternal life, which is infinite good); but also with regard to the subject (since it proceeds from an infinite Person, for which reason it acquires the value and force of an infinite price).

The abundance of the grace of Christ compared with the fall of Adam (1) is not considered with regard to the object, but with regard to the material and the effect, that is, not with regard to men, but with regard to the things that are conferred on each side, where there is a much more abundant treasure in the restoration made through Christ than there is an abyss of evil deeds in the corruption introduced through Adam. (2) Nor is it considered with regard to the act, but with regard to its potency or sufficiency. For even though all people do not actually benefit from the merit of Christ, nevertheless it has been furnished for all, it is sufficient for the redemption of all, and it is offered to all in the Word of the Gospel.

Observe: As the grace of Christ superabounds more than the fall of Adam and original sin, so also it abounds more than all actual sins.

Sin is the work of the devil and of man, but grace is the work of the immense and infinite divine majesty. How, then, could that which is from the devil and man be greater than that which is in God and from God?

Chrysostom, Homily 19 on Genesis, Vol. 1, f. 132: οὐδὲν ἔστιν ἁμάρτημα, κἂν σφόδρα μέγα, ᾗ νικῶν αὐτοῦ τὴν φιλανθρωπίαν, ἐὰν ἡμεῖς ἐν καιρῷ τῷ δέοντι τὴν μετάνοιαν ἐπιδειξώμεθα, καὶ τὴν συγγεώμην αἰτῶμεν. "There is no sin that is so serious as to overcome His mercy, if only in due time we repent and seek forgiveness."

Homily 2 on Psalm 51, f. 706: τὶ ἐστιν ἁμαρτία πρὸς τὴν τοῦ δεσπότου φιλανθρωπῖαν, ἀράχνη. ἄνεμος φυσᾷ καὶ διασπᾶται ἀράχνη. θεὸς βούλεται καὶ οὐ παραλύεται ἁμαρτία; "What is sin compared to the mercy of the Lord? It is a spider web. The wind blows, and the web dissipates. God wills. Should not sin melt away?" Homily 3, *On Repentance*: "As small as a drop compared to the ocean, so little is the wickedness of man compared to the mercy of God. The sea, though great, can be measured. But the mercy of God knows no boundary."

Bernhard, Sermon 3 *On St. Andrew*, f. 332: "The mercy of the Lord is greater than any iniquity of men."

Cassiodorus on Psalm 61: "The magnitude of divine indulgence exceeds any multitude of sins."

v.21 ἵνα ὥσπερ ἐβασίλευσεν ἡ ἁμαρτία ἐν τῷ θανάτῳ, οὕτω καὶ ἡ χάρις βασιλεύσῃ διὰ δικαιοσύνης εἰς ζωὴν αἰώνιον, διὰ Ἰησοῦ Χριστοῦ τοῦ Κυρίου ἡμῶν.

v.21 *That as sin hath reigned unto death, even so might grace reign through righteousness unto eternal life by Jesus Christ our Lord. (KJV)*

He had said in v.14 that death reigned because of sin. In this passage he says that sin reigned into death and through death, since sin is the cause and the sting of death (1 Cor. 15:56). But he contrasts this sin and dominion of death with the dominion of grace through righteousness into eternal life. This benefit of grace and life descends to us from Christ, just as the poison[57] of sin and death flowed down to us from Adam. The Syriac says emphatically, "by the hand of our Lord Jesus Christ."

Ἐν θανάτῳ [in death]. That this should be translated "into death" is clear from the proposed antithesis εἰς ζωήν, "into life."

---

57 Latin: *veneficium*, in contrast to the *beneficium* ("benefit") in the protasis.

Notes on the Epistle to the Romans: Chapter 6

v.1 Τί οὖν ἐροῦμεν; ἐπιμενοῦμεν τῇ ἁμαρτίᾳ, ἵνα ἡ χάρις πλεονάσῃ;

v.1 What shall we say then? Shall we continue in sin, that grace may abound? (KJV)

Since regeneration and renewal, justification and sanctification are joined together in believers by an indivisible connection, therefore, after dealing thus far with the first benefit of Christ, he now proceeds to His second benefit.

He uses an elegant transition. He had said in v.20 of the preceding chapter that grace abounds more than sin. He therefore submits by way of anticipation: *If grace abounds more than sin, well, then, let us remain in sin, as the ungodly say, so that grace may abound even more.*

Oecumenius on this passage: "Since he had said above that, where sin abounded, grace abounded, lest this seem to some people of unsound mind to be an exhortation to sin, he refutes this notion, saying: Far be it!—which is an expression normally used about those things that are obviously absurd."

Ἐπιμενεῖν τῇ ἁμαρτίᾳ [to continue in sin] means "to indulge and to persevere in sin, to loosen the reins for sin, to remain in slavery to sin, to indulge in sin based on the pretext of gracious forgiveness without repentance." Luther: *"in der Sünde beharren* [to persist in sin]."

v.2 Μὴ γένοιτο. Οἵτινες ἀπεθάνομεν τῇ ἁμαρτίᾳ, πῶς ἔτι ζήσομεν ἐν αὐτῇ;

v.2 God forbid. How shall we, that are dead to sin, live any longer therein? (KJV)

The Apostle replies to the proposed objection with a simple repudiation. Those who have died to sin should not live in sin and indulge in it. Believers in Christ have died to sin. Therefore...

Ἀπεθάνομεν τῇ ἁμαρτίᾳ [We died to sin]. The Greek notes explain it this way: οὐκέτι ἐνεργοὶ ἔσμεν, οἱ γὰρ ἀποθάνοντες οὐδὲν ἐνεργοῦσι [we are no longer active, for those who have died do no work].

"To die to sin" in this passage means "to be liberated from sin, to say farewell to sin, etc." "To live to sin" means "to delight in it," and to enjoy it with daily actions.

But how are believers dead to sin?

We reply: In justification and regeneration they receive the Holy Spirit, who begins to renew the nature corrupted by sin and to mortify sin in their flesh, for which reason they are said to be dead to sin. Therefore, the phrases are different—"to be dead to sin" in the dative, and "to be dead by sin" in the ablative (Eph. 2:1), or the equivalent phrase, "to be dead in sin" (Col. 2:13). The first denotes that blessed death in which sin dies in us, that is, it is mortified, which is the beginning of true life. The second denotes that unhappy death in which sin lives in us and mortifies us, which is the beginning of eternal death.

v.3 ῍Η ἀγνοεῖτε, ὅτι ὅσοι ἐβαπτίσθημεν εἰς Χριστὸν ᾿Ιησοῦν, εἰς τὸν θάνατον αὐτοῦ ἐβαπτίσθημεν;

v.3 Know ye not, that so many of us as were baptized into Jesus Christ were baptized into his death? (KJV)

The Apostle demonstrates that the salutary medium through which sanctification—that is, the renewal of our corrupt nature, obtained by the death of Christ—is conferred on us: Baptism, which is, of course, a washing, not only of regeneration, but also of renewal (Tit. 3:5).

"To be baptized into the death of Christ" does not only mean "to utter a profession of faith concerning the death and burial of Christ," which used to be required of catechumens long ago before receiving Baptism. Nor does it only mean "to promise the mortification of sin to God"—a promise that likewise used to be demanded of the baptized. But it also and even especially means "to become a participant in the benefits obtained by the suffering and death of Christ through Baptism," which is the New Testament Sacrament that offers the benefits of Christ to men and confers, seals and confirms them to believers.

Therefore, this phrase involves both of these benefits obtained for us by the death of Christ and conferred on us through Baptism, namely, both regeneration—that is, remission of sins, and renewal—that is, the mortification of sin, which begins in Baptism and afterwards should continue and increase daily. For in Baptism we gain the efficacy of the death of Christ, not only because the remission of sins obtained by the death of Christ happens to us by faith, but also because we are made sharers of the Holy Spirit, whom Christ likewise merited for us by His suffering and death. The Spirit begins to renew the nature corrupted by sin and to mortify sin in the flesh.

v.4 Συνετάφημεν οὖν αὐτῷ διὰ τοῦ βαπτίσματος εἰς τὸν θάνατον, ἵνα ὥσπερ ἠγέρθη Χριστὸς ἐκ νεκρῶν διὰ τῆς δόξης τοῦ Πατρός, οὕτο καὶ ἡμεῖς ἐν καινότητι ζωῆς περιπατήσωμεν.

v.4 Therefore we are buried with him by baptism into death: that like as Christ was raised up from the dead by the glory of the Father, even so we also should walk in newness of life. (KJV)

The burial of Christ was connected with His death and followed immediately after it. Therefore, after stating that we have been baptized into the death of Christ and thus are spiritually dead to sin, the Apostle then adds that we were also buried together with Christ through Baptism into death. For long ago the baptized were immersed in water with their whole body, and thus it is as if they were being buried. Then they were drawn out of the water again as out of the grave. This, explains the Apostle, is what this rite of Baptism calls to mind for us, that in and through Baptism we spiritually die with Christ, are buried with Christ and rise with Christ, that is, we are made participants of the benefits obtained for us by the suffering, death, burial and resurrection of Christ, among which is also the giving of the Holy Spirit, through whom sin is mortified in us so that we die with Christ with regard to the Old Man and rise with Him with regard to the New Man.

Observe (1) that the death of Christ effects renewal in us, both with regard to merit, because by His death He merited for us the Holy Spirit who renews our nature, and as a type and model, because there is set forth for us in the death of Christ a model of the mortification of the flesh, while in His resurrection there is a model of the renewal of the Spirit.

(2) That Christ is said to be raised again διὰ δόξης τοῦ πατρὸς [through glory of the Father], both because He was raised again εἰς δόξαν καὶ πρὸς δόξαν τοῦ Πατρὸς [unto glory and for the glory of the Father] (2 Pet. 1:3), and because He was raised again by the glorious power of God.

(3) That Christ is said to have been raised by the glory of the Father, not exclusively (since He also raised Himself from death— John 2:19, 10:18), but inclusively, since the Son and the Holy Spirit are not at all excluded from this raising. But the resurrection of Christ is attributed to the Father, (a) because the Father is the source of the divinity which, from eternity, He communicated to the Son by generation, and to the Holy Spirit by spiration. (b) Because the mission of the Son, and the confirmation of His office made by the divine voice from heaven, and the miracles performed by Christ during the days of the flesh, are normally attributed to God the Father. The whole obedience of Christ is said to be furnished to God the Father. (c) In order to signify that the Father is fully appeased by the satisfaction of Christ.

(4) That in Baptism there is set forth for us a perpetual reminder of the mortification of the flesh and of the renewal of the Spirit. Origen, Bk. 4 on the Epistle to the Romans, ch. 4: "If we have arisen with Christ, who is righteousness, and if we walk in newness of life and live according to righteousness, then Christ has arisen for us for our justification. But if we have not yet put off the Old Man with his acts, but rather live in unrighteousness, then I dare say that Christ has not yet arisen for us for justification, nor was He delivered over for our sins. For He justifies those who have taken up a new life by the example of His resurrection and who cast off the old life of unrighteousness, along with the garments of iniquity as the cause of death."

v.5 Εἰ γὰρ σύμφυτοι γεγόναμεν τῷ ὁμοιώματι τοῦ θανάτου αὐτοῦ, ἀλλὰ καὶ τῆς ἀναστάσεως ἐσόμεθα·

v.5 For if we have been planted together in the likeness of his death, we shall be also in the likeness of his resurrection: (KJV)

Just as death and resurrection were joined together in Christ, so He requires that in us, too, the death of sin and the life of the Spirit should likewise be joined together with Christ—in death and in life. If we have been implanted in Him so that we are like Him in death, we will also be—or rather, we should be—implanted in Him and like Him in resurrection.

Σύμφυτοι [Planted together], "to be grafted in and made participants." He alludes to the grafting of a plant, which corresponds to our spiritual communion with Christ. For just as a shoot that is cut out of its native tree and grafted into another becomes a participant in the moisture of that tree into which it is grafted, so also those who are grafted into the body of Christ through Baptism become participants in the benefits obtained by His suffering and death. And yet the grafting into Christ seems rather to occur in the opposite direction than the grafting of a shoot into a tree. For a shoot takes the sap of the tree in which it is grafted and converts it into itself, while Christ, in whom we are grafted, transforms us into Himself.

v.6 τοῦτο γινώσκοντες, ὅτι ὁ παλαιὸς ἡμῶν ἄνθρωπος συνεσταυρώθη, ἵνα καταργηθῇ τὸ σῶμα τῆς ἁμαρτίας, τοῦ μηκέτι δουλεύειν ἡμᾶς τῇ ἁμαρτίᾳ.

v.6 Knowing this, that our old man is crucified with him, that the body of sin might be destroyed, that henceforth we should not serve sin. (KJV)

"Our Old Man was crucified together," namely, with Christ, since Christ, by His crucifixion, obtained for us not only the remission of sins, but also the giving of the Holy Spirit, by whose power our Old Man, that is, the sin that still dwells in the flesh, is mortified and deprived of its vigor.

Τὸ σῶμα τῆς ἁμαρτίας [The body of sin], that is, sin itself, which is called "the body" (1) because of the *subject*, since it is the bilge water and filth of many sins in a man that have occupied and infected all the powers of the soul and the whole body of a man like a sort of spiritual leprosy, so that in the whole body of man there is no soundness from the top of his head down to the sole of his feet (Isa. 1:6). (2) Because of the *effect*, since it exercises such great powers in us as if it were a body, as if it were the sort of thing that subsists of itself. (3) Because of the *particular qualities*. For as a body has its members, so sin has its particular qualities. Therefore it is called a body of sin, since original sin, which dwells in the body, is fertile and abounding in every kind of sin. For the Apostle teaches in Col. 3:4 that this variety of sins ought to be understood with the phrase "body of sin." "Mortify your members that are upon the earth: fornication, impurity, errant lust, evil desire and greed."

Some, with the phrase "body of sin," understand the law, that is, the impetus of sin dwelling in the members (Rom. 7:23). This does not contradict the other explanation; it can be reduced to the second class of denomination.

Flacius wanted to conclude from this that original sin is the very essence of man. We reply: (1) If anything that is ever described with essential words is *essence*, then it would have to be concluded that original sin is at the same time *essence and accident*, since in the Scripture, it is described not only with essential words, but also with accidental words. (2) Therefore, the major premise—*Anything that is properly and formally expressed with essential words is essence*—must be limited. For even Christ is described with accidental words when He is called the Way, the Resurrection, etc., and yet not as accident. (3) Sin, in the concrete, because of the subject in which it exists, is described with essential words due to the close—and, in this life, indissoluble—connection between sin and human nature. But in the abstract and in its nature it is described with accidental words when it is called κακὸν παρακείμενον καὶ εὐπερίστατον [an evil that is ready at hand and easily ensnares].[58]

---

58 cf. Rom. 7:21, Heb. 12:1

Since the Old Man is not so called because of essence, but because of his vicious qualities, therefore the destruction of the body of sin is not of something essential, but of something accidental, namely, of the depraved concupiscence dwelling in the members.

v.7 Ὁ γὰρ ἀποθανὼν δεδικαίωται ἀπὸ τῆς ἁμαρτίας.

v.7 *For he that is dead is freed from sin. (KJV)*

Some understand this to be talking about spiritual death: He who has died, namely, to sin, has been justified, that is, liberated and absolved from sin. Verse 2 agrees with this. "We who have died to sin—how shall we live in it any longer?"

Others understand it to be talking about civil death, in this sense: Those who have died civilly are not bound to any servitude. But those who have been justified by the crucifixion of Christ have died to sin. Therefore, they are no longer bound to any servitude.

Some think that the Apostle is alluding to the sentence of capital punishment which those who have been condemned to death are no longer obliged to serve. For just as they can no longer carry out the kinds of crimes for which they are sentenced to death, so the one who has died to sin has been freed from sin, so that he neither can nor should sin any longer.

It is most simply taken concerning natural death. For in it, the soul is separated from the body, and thus the dead cease from the actions of this life—and consequently, from sin. In death there is also a liberation from all servitude. Therefore, since we died to sin through the crucifixion of Christ, we should cease from sin and from the servitude of sin.

Δεδικαίωται [has been justified]. He uses a Hebrew phrase for ἠλευθέρωται [has been freed], for he who is justified, that is, absolved in the judgment, is liberated from punishment. Luther: "*der ist gerechtfertiget* [he is justified]."

Basil in *Discourse on the Baptism of Christ*, Vol. 1, p. 460: "He has been justified from sin, that is, he has been absolved, liberated, purged from sin—not only from the sin that has been committed in works and words, but also from the sin that has been committed in the thoughts themselves."

The Syriac has the verb אֶתְחֲרַר, "he has been liberated, emancipated."

v.8 Εἰ δὲ ἀπεθάνομεν σὺν Χριστῷ, πιστεύομεν, ὅτι καὶ συζήσομεν αὐτῷ.

v.8 Now if we be dead with Christ, we believe that we shall also live with him: (KJV)

"If we died with Christ," that is, if through the Spirit of Christ, into whose death we have been baptized and in whom we have been implanted by faith, we have received the power to die to sin, then also through the same Spirit we will receive the power to be raised again to newness of life. For as the death and resurrection of Christ were joined together, so also "to die to sin" and "to rise again to newness of life" should be joined together in us.

v.9 εἰδότες, ὅτι Χριστὸς ἐγερθεὶς ἐκ νεκρῶν οὐκέτι ἀποθνήσκει, θάνατος αὐτῷ οὐκέτι κυριεύει.

v.9 Knowing that Christ being raised from the dead dieth no more; death hath no more dominion over him. (KJV)

Just as Christ, now risen from the dead, dies no longer, so also, after we have risen with Christ spiritually from the death of sin, we should no longer indulge in sin, since sin is the spiritual death of the soul.

Θάνατος αὐτῷ οὐκέτι κυριεύει [Death no longer has dominion over Him]. What, then? Did death at one time have dominion over Christ? So asks the Calvinist Urbanus Pierius in his disputation *Contra Collationem Augustanae Confessionis Mentzerianam*. But we reply: (1) By His death, Christ destroyed him who had the power of death (Heb. 2:14). Therefore, He was not under the power of death. (2) It was impossible that He should be κρατεῖσθαι [held] by death (Acts 2:14). Therefore, death did not have dominion over Him. (3) Even in the midst of death He was and remained the ἀρχηγὸς ζωῆς [author of life] (Acts 3:15) and although the prince of this world has the power of death, he did not have any power over Him (John 14:30). Therefore death did not have dominion over Him. (4) Death does not even have dominion over the godly believers in Christ, simply speaking. Rather, they are kings and live to God (Rev. 1:6). (5) Christ approached death willingly, and it was His own will, not a foreign power, that caused Him to die.

Why, then, does the Apostle speak this way, saying that death no longer has dominion over Him? We reply: Some want to say that the Apostle has in view only the external appearance—that it seemed that way outwardly, as if death had dominion over Him. For the Scripture sometimes speaks about things, not as they are, but as they appear.

One can reply more simply that the subsequent time is excluded so as not to include the antecedent. Therefore what is denied, that death would have dominion over Christ in His posterity, cannot be inferred from the fact that it previously had dominion over Him. The clearest example of this matter is found in Acts 13:34, ὅτι δὲ ἀνέστησεν αὐτὸν ἐκ νεκρῶν, μηκέτι μέλλοντα ὑποστρέφειν εἰς διαφθοράν [and that He raised Him up from the dead, no longer to return to corruption]. But it still cannot be inferred from this that He would at some time see corruption.

v.10 Ὁ γὰρ ἀπέθανε, τῇ ἁμαρτίᾳ ἀπέθανεν, ἐφάπαξ· ὃ δὲ ζῇ, ζῇ τῷ Θεῷ.

v.10 For in that he died, he died unto sin once: but in that he liveth, he liveth unto God. (KJV)

In these words the Apostle sets forth both the rationale of the preceding verse—why Christ will no longer die—and the antecedent of the conclusion that is submitted in the following verse. For otherwise, the protasis of the comparison would have to be repeated. So then, just as Christ Himself died to sin but lives to God, so you also, count yourselves as those who are dead to sin but who live to Christ.

"He died to sin," that is, because of sin, that is, our sin (Rom. 4:25), namely, in order to make satisfaction for it and to put an end to it (Heb. 9:26). Therefore, it is one thing to say that Christ "died to sin" and another thing when we are said to "die to sin." (1) Christ died to sin by expiating it by His death and by furnishing perfect satisfaction for it; we die to sin by mortifying it in the flesh and by crucifying it. (2) Christ died to someone else's sin; we die to our own sin. (3) Christ died to the sin that was imputed to Him; we die to the sin that inheres in us.

"He lives to God," (1) having been raised from the dead for the glory of God the Father; (2) in order that He, as the Head of the Church, may reign with God the Father in perpetual blessedness and glory. (3) He no longer lives an earthly life, as He did on this earth before His death, but now He lives a heavenly and purely divine life.

v.11 Οὕτω καὶ ὑμεῖς λογίζεσθε ἑαυτοὺς νεκροὺς μὲν εἶναι τῇ ἁμαρτίᾳ, ζῶντας δὲ τῷ Θεῷ ἐν Χριστῷ Ἰησοῦ τῷ Κυρίῳ ἡμῶν.

v.11 *Likewise reckon ye also yourselves to be dead indeed unto sin, but alive unto God through Jesus Christ our Lord. (KJV)*

We are dead to sin when, by the power of the Holy Spirit who has been given to us by Christ and for the sake of Christ, sin is mortified in us.

v.12 Μὴ οὖν βασιλευέτω ἡ ἁμαρτία ἐν τῷ θνητῷ ὑμῶν σώματι, εἰς τὸ ὑπακούειν αὐτῇ ἐν ταῖς ἐπιθυμίαις αὐτοῦ,

v.12 *Let not sin therefore reign in your mortal body, that ye should obey it in the lusts thereof. (KJV)*

He infers an exhortation from the preceding words. Since you are dead to sin, therefore you should not permit sin to have dominion. Just as natural death does not have dominion over Christ, so also the spiritual death of sin should not have dominion over you.

Μὴ βασιλευέτω ἡ ἁμαρτία [Let not sin reign]. Later, in verse 14, he says, οὐ κυριεύσει, "it shall not have dominion," namely, in such a way that you want to serve it. With the word "sin" he understands the remnants of sin that still dwell in the flesh after regeneration. One should always be occupied with mortifying these remnants of sin and purging them by the renewal of the Spirit.

Augustine, Treatise 61 on John: "He does not say, 'let it not exist,' but, 'let it not reign.' For as long as you live, sin must necessarily exist in your members. Even so, it must not be given the power to reign, lest it happen that it give orders."

Theodoret in his commentary observes: "Paul attributes to sin, not tyranny, but the power to reign. For a tyrant rules over subjects who have been conquered, while a king rules over those who are willing to be ruled."

When he calls our body "mortal," (1) he shows that sin is not fully removed from us, since our body is still subject to death because of it. (2) He introduces an encouraging argument: We bear a mortal body. Therefore, let us not indulge in depraved desires that make us subject to eternal death if we indulge in them securely.

Ἐν ταῖς ἐπιθυμίαις αὐτοῦ [In its desires], namely, σώματος [of the body]. He attributes depraved desires to the body, not as if the soul were immune to them or free from them, but because they mainly exert themselves in the body and through the body.

v.13 μηδὲ παριστάνετε τὰ μέλη ἡμῶν ὅπλα ἀδικίας τῇ ἁμαρτίᾳ, ἀλλὰ παραστήσατε ἑαυτοὺς τῷ Θεῷ ὡς ἐκ νεκρῶν ζῶντας, καὶ τὰ μέλη ὑμῶν ὅπλα δικαιοσύνης τῷ Θεῷ.

v.13 *Neither yield ye your members as instruments of unrighteousness unto sin: but yield yourselves unto God, as those that are alive from the dead, and your members as instruments of righteousness unto God. (KJV)*

He explains what he wants to be understood with the βασιλείαν [reign] of sin in the preceding verse.

Just as Christ παρέστησεν ἑαυτὸν ζῶντα [presented Himself alive] after His resurrection from the dead (Acts 1:3), so also it is fitting that, if you rose spiritually with Christ, you παραστήσατε [present] yourselves as alive from the dead to God.

Τὰ ὅπλα [the weapons] is a Hebraism meaning "instruments." כֵּלִים are the "instruments, vessels, utensils, weapons" with which something is brought to completion and perfected. 1 Sam. 21:5: "The vessels of the young men," that is, metaphorically, the bodies. For the sense is that we should not enslave our members, which are the organs of the soul living in the body, to the servitude of sin. Meanwhile, not without emphasis does he call our members "weapons." For he implies that our entire life on this earth should be a continuous battle against the sin that still dwells in our members.

"Weapons of righteousness to God," for God's service. The Syriac translates "weapons of righteousness of God," that is, the righteousness that is approved by God.

v.14 Ἁμαρτία γὰρ ὑμῶν οὐ κυριεύσει, οὐ γάρ ἐστε ὑπὸ νόμον, ἀλλ᾽ ὑπὸ χάριν.

v.14 *For sin shall not have dominion over you: for ye are not under the law, but under grace.* (KJV)

The Apostle runs to meet the objection, for the godly could have asked: *In this weakness of the flesh that we still carry around with us, how are we able to consecrate and offer our members to God as weapons of righteousness?* The Apostle answers: You are not under the strict rigor of the law, demanding perfect and absolute obedience in each and every point. You are under the grace of the Gospel, which teaches that the obedience that has begun is pleasing to God through faith, if a person has been reconciled to Him. To the reborn he promises victory over sin from the fact that they have been given the gift of grace, which causes them to mortify the desires of the flesh and which brings it about that the weaknesses of sin that cling to them are remitted to them.

Pererius explains the phrase "to be under grace" in this way, that "the man who has been freed from sins and given the gift of the grace of God, and who remains under its shelter and protection, wants to—and is able to—fulfill the whole law, and so is able to guard against sins from now on." But if this is understood to refer to the perfect obedience of the law and the complete absence of sin, then it repudiates the analogy of faith and this very apostolic text.

Some understand "to be under grace" as a comparative statement concerning those who live during the time of the New Testament in a state of grace, which is much more plentiful and abundant in the New Testament than in the Old. The saints who lived during the time of the Old Testament, compared to the saints who live in the New Testament, were under the law that terrifies, while the New Testament saints are under the grace that raises up and vivifies.

It is most simply understood concerning the grace of regeneration and renewal, which is common to the saints living under each Testament, although the levels of grace in the Old Testament were reserved. Therefore, "to be under grace" means to be reconciled to God through faith in Christ, to be freed from the curse and constraint of the law, to be renewed by the Holy Spirit. Therefore, not only the grace of renewal is to be understood, but also the grace of the remission of sins. For that is when all the commandments of God are regarded as having been done, when anything that is not done is pardoned.

v.15 Τί οὖν; Ἁμαρτήσομεν, ὅτι οὐκ ἐσμὲν ὑπὸ νόμον, ἀλλ᾽ ὑπὸ χάριν; Μὴ γένοιτο.

v.15 What then? shall we sin, because we are not under the law, but under grace? God forbid. (KJV)

The Apostle had previously denied that the reborn are under the law, that is, under the curse, constraint and strict rigor of the law. Lest anyone should take him to mean that the reborn are also "not under the law" when it comes to obedience, the Apostle runs to meet the objection.

v.16 Οὐκ οἴδατε, ὅτι ᾧ παριστάνετε ἑαυτοὺς δούλους εἰς ὑπακοήν, δοῦλοί ἐστε ᾧ ὑπακούετε; ἤτοι ἁμαρτίας εἰς θάνατον, ἢ ὑπακοῆς εἰς δικαιοσύνην;

v.16 Know ye not, that to whom ye yield yourselves servants to obey, his servants ye are to whom ye obey; whether of sin unto death, or of obedience unto righteousness? (KJV)

The Apostle responds to the objection set forth in the preceding verse and concludes in this way: A person must present himself for service to the one to whom he has enslaved himself for service.

But the reborn have enslaved themselves for service to Christ, who has freed them from sin and death. Therefore...

He contrasts ἁμαρτίαν [sin] and ὑπακοὴν [obedience] with each other, since sin is properly "disobedience." Likewise he contrasts θάνατον [death] and δικαιοσύνην [righteousness], since sin leads to death, to which obedience and righteousness are opposed. But here it must be noted that the Apostle is not dealing with the righteousness of a person before God, but with the righteousness of a good conscience. The sense is that "you are slaves of obedience for righteousness," that is, you are obliged to Christ the Liberator, so that you serve and obey Him in righteousness and holiness, which He requires of His servants. The Syriac translates: "That is, of the obedience of righteousness."

v.17 Χάρις δὲ τῷ Θεῷ, ὅτι ἦτε δοῦλοι τῆς ἁμαρτίας, ὑπηκούσατε δὲ ἐκ καρδίας εἰς ὃν παρεδόθητε τύπον διδαχῆς.

v.17 But God be thanked, that ye were the servants of sin, but ye have obeyed from the heart that form of doctrine which was delivered you. (KJV)

He demonstrates the source of this benefit. They are no longer slaves of sin, but have been freed from the yoke of sin, namely, because they have received by faith the benefits of Christ offered to them in the Word of the Gospel.

Χάρις τῷ Θεῷ [Thanks to God]. The Apostle is not giving thanks to God that the Romans had once been slaves to sin, but that, after they had once served sin, they now have obeyed the heavenly doctrine. For there is a difference between saying, "I give thanks to God," or "Thanks be to God, that you were indeed slaves of sin! But you obeyed from the heart that form of doctrine," and saying, "Thanks be to God, that, although you were once slaves of sin, you now have obeyed from the heart."

Some refer the passage in Mat. 11:25 to this: "I praise You, Father, that You have hidden these things from the wise and revealed them to children." But in any case, Christ in that place is celebrating His heavenly Father, not only because He had, by grace, revealed the mysteries of the Gospel to children, but also because, by His righteous judgment, He had hidden them from the wise.

Observe: (1) We are, by nature, slaves of sin and free from righteousness. But by the grace of God, we are free from sin and slaves of righteousness.

(2) To be free from righteousness is a crime; to be a slave of righteousness is praiseworthy. Therefore, freedom is discovered to be blameworthy, while slavery is praiseworthy.

With τύπον διδαχῆς [form of teaching] he understands the doctrine of the Gospel, in which God has prescribed to us the form and norm of obedience, namely, that we embrace the Gospel by the obedience of faith and live worthily for the Gospel (Phi. 1:27).

Τύπος [pattern] means not only "form," but also "rule." An old glossary has, *Τύπος: formula, form, norm*. In Rom. 2:20, τύπος is explained with μόρφωσιν [form]. For as it says in this passage, "you have been delivered εἰς τῦπον διδαχής [to a pattern of teaching]," so it says there that "you have in the law μόρφωσιν τῆς γνώσεως καὶ τῆς ἀληθείας [a form of knowledge and of truth]," of the true doctrine and knowledge.' The Syriac translates τύπον [pattern] in this passage with רְמוּתָא, "likeness;" it translates μόρφωσιν [form] with רוּמְיָא, a related word.

Therefore the sense of the Apostle is that, since the Roman believers have been transferred out of that state in which they once used to serve sin, a certain rule and pattern of doctrine has been set forth to them which they should use from now on as the rule of faith and life. They should conform themselves to it and imitate it precisely in faith and life.

But it must be noted that he does not say that that norm has been handed down to believers. Rather, he says that believers have handed themselves over to this norm, so as better to express the force of the word ὑπακούειν [to obey]. He means that this norm of faith and life has been set forth to believers in the Word of the Gospel, not so that they might bend it to their will, to shape and reshape it, but so that they might conform themselves to it.

268

v.18 Ἐλευθερωθέντες δὲ ἀπὸ τῆς ἁμαρτίας ἐδουλώθητε τῇ δικαιοσύνῃ.

v.18 *Being then made free from sin, ye became the servants of righteousness. (KJV)*

Since sin and righteousness are contrasted with one another, liberation from sin brings with it an obligation to serve righteousness.

Ἐλευθερωθέντες [Having been set free]—not only through the remission of sin, but also through the giving of the Holy Spirit and through the mortification of sin that arises from it.

Ἐδουλώθητε τῇ δικαιοσύνῃ [You were enslaved to righteousness]. "To righteousness" is emphatic in the dative case. When someone says that he has become a slave "of" someone, he indicates that he has become his slave, not willingly, but by force. But when he says that he has become a slave "to" him, he expresses a deliberate and voluntary subjection to slavery.

v.19 Ἀνθρώπινον λέγω, διὰ τὴν ἀσθένειαν τῆς σαρκὸς ὑμῶν. Ὥσπερ γὰρ παρεστήσατε τὰ μέλη ὑμῶν δοῦλα τῇ ἀκαθαρσίᾳ, καὶ τῇ ἀνομίᾳ εἰς τὴν ἀνομίαν, οὕτω νῦν παραστήσατε τὰ μέλη ὑμῶν δοῦλα τῇ δικαιοσύνῃ εἰς ἁγιασμόν.

v.19 *I speak after the manner of men because of the infirmity of your flesh: for as ye have yielded your members servants to uncleanness and to iniquity unto iniquity; even so now yield your members servants to righteousness unto holiness. (KJV)*

He says that he wants to speak ἀνθρώπινον [in a human way], because he wants to provide his exhortation with a comparison taken from earthly affairs.

As for this protherapeia[59]: (1) Some ascribe it to the modesty and civility of the Apostle. For since a little earlier he had called the Romans "slaves of righteousness," he mitigates that word so as not to seem to be offending them, as if he were making slaves out of men who were free-born. So he demonstrates that he is not

59 Rhetorical device used to prepare one's audience for what one is about to say.

speaking about a disreputable, but about a noble servitude.

(2) Some ascribe it to the comparison that has been set forth between servitude and freedom which he had used to compare the avoidance of sin with the obedience of righteousness, namely, the heavenly and spiritual matter with the earthly and civil human custom, although that comparison does not exactly agree.

(3) Some ascribe it to the characteristic of the precept, as if the Apostle wished to say: I could demand from you a greater eagerness in the servitude of righteousness than you once exhibited in the servitude of sin. But since your weakness is known to me, it is sufficient for you, who are men, if you now employ the same kind of zeal in doing good as you once employed in doing evil.

(4) Some take this ἀνθρώπινον [in a human way] as "not impossibly," or even with much difficulty, as if he were to say that he requires nothing of the Romans that exceeds the powers of human nature.

With the phrase ἀσθένειαν τῆς σαρκὸς [weakness of the flesh], he understands their carnal and base intellect.

Δοῦλα τῇ ἀκαθαρσίᾳ, καὶ τῇ ἀνομίᾳ εἰς τὴν ἀνομίαν [Servants to impurity, and to iniquity unto iniquity]. He expresses emphatically the zeal for sinning, that they had gone from committing one iniquity to the next.

v.20 Ὅτε γὰρ δοῦλοι ἦτε τῆς ἁμαρτίας, ἐλεύθεροι ἦτε τῇ δικαιοσύνῃ.

v.20 *For when ye were the servants of sin, ye were free from righteousness. (KJV)*

"You were free of righteousness," not in a legal sense, but in a practical sense[60]. You behaved in such a way as if God's commandments did not restrain you at all.

v.21 Τίνα οὖν καρπὸν εἴχετε τότε, ἐφ᾽ οἷς νῦν ἐπαισχύνεσθε; Τὸ γὰρ τέλος ἐκείνων, θάνατος.

v.21 *What fruit had ye then in those things whereof ye are now*

---

60 Latin: *non de jure, sed de facto*

ashamed? for the end of those things is death. (KJV)

He concludes with an exhortation to hate sin and to be zealous for righteousness, setting forth a contrast of them both.

Ἐφ᾽ οἷς νῦν ἐπαισχύνεσθε [Of which you are now ashamed]. With those things of which the Romans "are now ashamed," he understands the disgraceful things committed by them when they were pagans. The sentence is elliptical. "What fruit did you have at that time from those things of which you are now ashamed?"

Τέλος ἐκείνων, θάνατος [The end of those things, death]. In one sense, the τέλος [end] of sins in this passage is said to be "eternal death;" in another sense, the τέλος [end] of faith is said to be "eternal life." In 1 Pet. 1:9, the τέλος [end] of sins is said to be "death" with regard to merit, namely, since the debt of sins is a wage given on the basis of merits. But the τέλος [end] of faith is eternal life with regard to the result, since eternal life follows the perseverance in faith, that is, the faith that perseveres.

Observe: Death is called "the end of sins," not that the one who sins aims at this end, but that the slavery of sin leads the one who sins to this end.

v.22 Νυνὶ δὲ ἐλευθερωθέντες ἀπὸ τῆς ἁμαρτίας, δουλωθέντες δὲ τῷ Θεῷ, ἔχετε τὸν καρπὸν ὑμῶν εἰς ἁγιασμόν, τὸ δὲ τέλος ζωὴν αἰώνιον.

v.22 But now being made free from sin, and become servants to God, ye have your fruit unto holiness, and the end everlasting life. (KJV)

This is the antithesis of the two preceding verses. Before, when you were not yet converted to Christ, you were slaves of sin, the end of which is death. And you were free of righteousness, only because you had the shameful fruits of your works. But now that you have been freed from sin (but sold to God), you have your fruit in holiness, while the end is eternal life.

v.23 Τὰ γὰρ ὀψώνια τῆς ἁμαρτίας, θάνατος, τὸ δὲ χάρισμα τοῦ Θεοῦ, ζωὴ αἰώνιος ἐν Χριστῷ Ἰησοῦ τῷ Κυρίῳ ἡμῶν.

v.23 For the wages of sin is death; but the gift of God is eternal life through Jesus Christ our Lord. (KJV)

Τὰ ὀψώνια [The wages] is not only money, but also the provisions and rations that are given to soldiers (1 Cor. 9:7, Luke 3:14). Polybius: "τῶν ὀψωνίων παρελκομένων καὶ καθυστερούντων. 'Since military provisions and grain were not distributed on a daily basis, but were delayed.'" The Apostle, therefore, has in view what he had said in v.19, παρεστήσατε τὰ μέλη ὑμῶν δοῦλα τῇ ἀκαθαρσίᾳ [you presented your members as slaves to impurity], and v.13, μηδὲ παριστάνετε τὰ μέλη ὑμῶν ὅπλα ἀδικίας [do not present your members as weapons of unrighteousness]. Secondly, he uses the plural τὰ ὀψόνια [the wages], because with the one word "death," he has many punishments in mind and various torments of the ungodly. Thirdly, since the reward of sin is called ὀψώνιον [a wage], he insinuates the filthiness of sin. For it was food—a certain kind of rations and sumptuousness—by which soldiers were enticed thus to expose their life to the influence of bribes for the sake of their appetite and belly. So also sinners are often led to commit sins for a trivial matter. And yet these sins have temporal and eternal death for a companion.

With τὸ χάρισμα [the free gift], Piscator understands, by metonymy, "the zeal for holiness that proceeds from the gift of God. This zeal," he says, "means eternal life, that is, it brings eternal life with it. But," he thinks that "the opinion of the rest of the interpreters, that eternal life is called a free gift of God, is foreign to the text (1) because τὸ χάρισμα [the free gift] is put in place of the subject; (2) because the article is added to this word; (3) because the antithesis of the text requires that one understand χάρισμα [free gift] as a zeal for holiness."

But these poorly conceived reasons are weaker than the commonly accepted opinion they pretend to debunk. For the explanation that eternal life is called "the free gift of God" agrees best with the context. For since the Apostle had said in v.22 that the Romans, before their conversion to Christ, had death as the τέλος [end] of their sins, he submits this antithesis lest someone should think that the reasoning of each member is equal.

In 1 Pet. 3:8, women are called συγκληρόνομοι χάριτος ζωῆς [co-heirs of the grace of life], "of the grace of life," that is, of the life that is given to believers in Christ out of free mercy. In 1 Tim. 6:2, believers are called τῆς εὐεργεσίας ἀντιλαμβανόμενοι [partakers of the benefit], where the free "benefit" clearly means the inheritance of eternal life.

Chrysostom, Sermon 10 on this Epistle: "Eternal life is given neither as a debt nor as compensation for work. Rather, it is given as a free gift of divine service."

Some object to this. Pererius, Disputation 4 on Romans ch. 6: "Eternal life is called by Paul a τέλος [end]—revenue or reward—in v.22." We reply: (1) τέλος [end] in that passage is not used politically or ethically, but physically, that is, not as a prize, reward or tribute, but as the final result of the matter. Just as the final end of sin is death and ruin, so the service of righteousness finally reaches its ultimate and desired goal, namely, eternal life. (2) And even if it were being used chiefly for "a reward," as Erasmus says, it still should not be taken in the stricter sense as "a reward of merit," where there is a proportionate relationship between reward and merit. Pererius concedes (Disputation 11 on Rom. ch. 6, n. 54) that there is no proportionate relationship between our works (considered by themselves) and eternal life. But it could be taken in the broader sense as a reward of grace, so that it signifies a gracious compensation, paid out from the promise of God. In this sense it is called "a reward of inheritance" (Col. 3:24).

Lyranus on John chapter 10: "Heavenly glory is not properly called a 'reward,' but only generally, inasmuch as everything that is given in return for labor is called a 'reward.' But the reason for this is that the inheritance is distinguished from a wage properly so called, just as a son, to whom the inheritance is owed, is distinguished from the hired hand to whom a wage is owed. But heavenly glory is rendered to the faithful as an inheritance to children. Because of this, it does not have the connotation of a wage."

Bellarmine, in Bk. 5, *On Justification*, ch. 5, also objects: "Eternal life is called 'grace,' not because it is not a wage of merit, but because we have those merits by grace."

We reply: (1) The apostolic text is sufficiently clear and perspicuous. For what is the reason why death is called "the wages of sin," while eternal life is not called "the wages of good works," but "the free gift of God," except that a different relationship is signified between death with respect to sins, and eternal life with respect to good works?

(2) The Apostle notably adds that "eternal life is the grace of God in Christ Jesus our Lord." He therefore most clearly demonstrates that this gift is given to us, not because of the merits of our works, but by faith that has laid hold of Christ (John 3:39; 1 John 5:11-12; Acts 4:12).

(3) Some of the ancients considered this emphasis of the apostolic saying. Origen on this passage: "It was not proper for God to give wages to His soldiers as some sort of debt; rather, He gives them a gift and grace, which is eternal life in Christ Jesus."

Chrysostom, Homily 12 on the Epistle to the Romans: "He did not observe the same word order in speaking of the good things as he did when he called it 'the wages of sin.' For he did not say that the reward is rightly for our deeds, but he called it 'the grace of God,' demonstrating that they were not freed by force of arms, nor was it done in payment of a debt, nor was it given to them as a payment or remuneration for work, but all things came about by grace, and He gave these things through the Son."

Augustine, *On Grace and Free Will*, ch. 9: "Although he could have said, and rightly so, that the wages of righteousness is eternal life, he preferred to say that the grace of God is eternal life, so that we might understand from this that God brings us to eternal life, not by our merits, but according to His mercy."

Theodoret on this passage: "When he speaks of eternal life, which is given in return for righteousness, he did not call it a 'reward,' but 'grace.' For the gift of God is eternal life. For even if someone were to furnish an exemplary or absolute righteousness, eternal things do not correspond equally to temporal labors."

Jerome, Vol. 1, Epistle 8: "If it is grace, then it is not repayment for works, but the generosity of the Giver."

Fulgentius, Bk. 1, *Ad Monim.*, p. 41: "Not only is a good life given by grace to the justified, but eternal life is also given to the glorified. Yet why is death called a wage, while eternal life is called grace, except that death is something that is paid, while grace is something that is given?"

(4) Among the adversaries, Cajetan himself makes the following comment on this passage: "He does not say that eternal life is given as the wages of righteousness, but that the gift of God is eternal life, so that we may understand that we gain eternal life in the end, not by the merits of works, but by the free gift of God. This is why he adds, 'in Christ our Lord.' Behold, here is the merit! Behold, here is the righteousness whose wage is eternal life! But to us, it is a gift given for the sake of Jesus Christ Himself."

To The Reader:

This gift and prize for labor, even eternal life—that unfading crown of glory—has at last been obtained by my most beloved father from God the supreme Judge, the Highest and the Greatest, after toiling day and night in so many and various important labors with which he was pleased to be of service to the Church Militant of Christ. He obtained these prizes even as he was commenting on this last verse of the sixth chapter of Romans.

Indeed, this is the only reason, dear reader, why these annotations are so concise, so brief, and, to be honest, incomplete. He certainly would have given you a fuller and more complete commentary on this Epistle that he used to call "the Key to Theology," if fate (as a certain learned man describes the intervention of death), that too-harsh Tribune, had not disturbed all these things by interrupting him while in the midst of this work. As a result, we are forced to place into your hands—maimed and mutilated and, in a word, unworthy of the name of Gerhard—not only these annotations that we now provide to you (in which we have chosen not to alter or add even a single word, although we might have done so—so sacrosanct it is and ever shall be to us—lest any labor except for that of my father of blessed memory should come to you under the cover of his name. You will, we hope, take note of this piety of ours in doing what is good and right.), but also others, which up till now, by the will of our patrons and by the counsel and request of our friends, we have sent to be published. In the future, if we discover that our zeal to please our patrons and to gratify our friends finds our critics not to be overly harsh, we will also bring to light his observations on various books of the Bible.

But you, dear reader, whoever you are—we beg of you, be kind. Beware, lest, with insults and mockery concerning the scholarship of my beloved father, you, too, are found among those who presume to pursue the dead with hostility. Even natural man—not to mention the Christian!—agrees with the whole of antiquity that there is nothing more indecent, nothing more disgraceful than that. Thus we bid you goodbye and farewell.

Scriptural Index